Conciliation
and arbitration procedures
in labour disputes

Conciliation and arbitration procedures in labour disputes

A comparative study

International Labour Office   Geneva

ISBN 92-2-102339-7 (limp cover)
ISBN 92-2-102338-9 (hard cover)

First published 1980

Photocomposed in India
Printed in Switzerland

Most systems of labour relations, in which employers and workers seek together to regulate their dealings with each other and particularly to determine terms and conditions of employment, presuppose the possibility of disagreement and dispute. As these systems of labour relations have developed, it has also been gradually recognised that procedures were needed to assist the parties to settle their disputes. The principal procedures developed to this end, apart from the determination of legal disputes by courts or tribunals, are conciliation (or mediation) and arbitration.

The present book is a comparative study of different national systems of conciliation and arbitration in labour disputes. It complements several comparative studies on collective bargaining systems published by the International Labour Office over the past few years[1] and provides a background to the practical guides which have been prepared by the ILO on two kinds of disputes settlement procedure: conciliation[2] and grievance arbitration.[3] Although disputes settlement procedures have frequently been reviewed as part of more general surveys of collective bargaining or labour-management relations matters, this is the first full-length comparative study by the ILO devoted specifically to this subject to have appeared since 1933.[4] While principally a comparative survey of national systems, it also seeks to provide guidance with regard to the development of various types of conciliation and arbitration procedure.

The study attempts to cover the principal disputes settlement systems existing throughout the world, as far as the information available permits. It consequently deals with both industrialised and developing countries. However, no attempt is made to cover disputes settlement procedures in socialist countries with centrally planned economic systems, since in those countries collective bargaining is viewed not as an adversary process but as a means of ensuring the full co-operation of management and workers in carrying out the economic and social plans and improving the management of undertakings.

The importance of an appropriate system of disputes settlement, adapted to the needs of each national labour relations system, is widely accepted today. In many countries which have reviewed their labour law and labour relations system in recent years, or are doing so now, considerable attention is devoted to this question. This is so because the absence of effective disputes settlement procedures can result in widespread industrial conflict, with adverse effects on the community as well as on the relationship between employers and workers and the collective bargaining process itself. On the other hand, it is also widely recognised that excessive third-party intervention in the settlement of labour disputes can undermine collective bargaining as an institution for the joint regulation of terms and conditions of employment and of relations between employers and trade unions. The need to strike a balance between effective disputes settlement and the freedom of the parties from outside intervention that is necessary for effective collective bargaining has been a central concern of labour policy in both industrialised and developing countries during the past three decades.

The basic draft of this study was prepared by Mr. Eladio Daya, formerly of the Labour Law and Labour Relations Branch of the International Labour Office.

Notes

[1] ILO: *Collective bargaining in industrialised market economies* (Geneva, 1973); ILO/Friedrich-Ebert-Stiftung: *Collective bargaining and labour arbitration in the ASEAN region* (Bangkok, 1977); ILO: *La negociación colectiva en América latina* (Geneva, 1978). A world-wide survey of systems of collective bargaining has been prepared for discussion by the International Labour Conference with a view to the possible adoption in 1981 of an international labour Convention or Recommendation on the subject. See ILO: *Promotion of collective bargaining*, Report V(1), 66th Session, International Labour Conference, Geneva, 1980.

[2] idem: *Conciliation in industrial disputes: A practical guide* (Geneva, 1973).

[3] idem: *Grievance arbitration: A practical guide* (Geneva, 1977).

[4] See idem: *Conciliation and arbitration in industrial disputes*, Studies and reports, Series A, No. 34 (Geneva, 1933).

CONTENTS

LABOUR DISPUTES AND THEIR SETTLEMENT

1

The problem of settling labour disputes cannot be viewed in isolation. It is a part of the problem of disputes settlement in general, and is a major element of the larger problem of labour relations policy. It may therefore be useful to begin this study by considering conciliation and arbitration in labour disputes in relation to these two major subjects. This chapter is concerned with disputes settlement in general, including the application of the various methods of settlement to labour disputes, while the question of labour relations policy and disputes settlement will be considered in the next chapter.

DISPUTES SETTLEMENT PROCEDURES IN GENERAL

Disputes are a characteristic of human society. They fall into various categories and occur at different levels of relationship. Three main methods have been evolved for their settlement through the intervention of third parties: *(a)* judicial settlement or adjudication by courts of law; *(b)* conciliation and mediation; and *(c)* arbitration.

The method of judicial settlement needs no elaboration here. Suffice it to say that every country in the world today has a judicial system within which its courts of law operate; that the cases that come up before these courts normally involve the application and interpretation of legally binding rules (such as those embodied in law or contract); and that the courts are generally empowered to enforce compliance with their decisions with the aid of the sovereign authority of the State.

Conciliation, mediation and arbitration may be used in disputes which may be amenable to judicial settlement, as well as in other categories of dispute arising from a wide variety of causes. Conciliation and arbitration have been devised in civil and commercial cases because of the parties' interest in avoiding the costs and delays normally associated with the judicial procedure. The two methods are frequently mentioned in civil codes as a voluntary alternative to judicial adjudication, and commercial arbitration is well developed in certain countries. However, it is in the fields of labour relations and international relations that the application of conciliation, mediation and arbitration in

1

disputes settlement has been of special significance. More recently, the usefulness of conciliation in the field of community relations has been increasingly recognised, particularly with respect to the application of laws for the protection of minorities and the removal of race discrimination in employment. In certain countries ombudsmen, or public mediators, have been appointed by governments to serve as a bridge between public authorities and private citizens, and conciliation is an inherent aspect of their functions. There are grounds for supposing that the experience of a particular method of settling disputes in one field would be relevant to the problems of the application of that method in other fields and would be useful in the approach to such problems.

Conciliation, mediation and arbitration were used in the settlement of disputes between nations before the world became acquainted with the type of labour dispute generated by the Industrial Revolution. However, since the last decade of the nineteenth century it is in the field of labour relations that these methods of settlement have been most widely, frequently and intensively applied. One notable aspect of this experience is the establishment of permanent conciliation and mediation services in many countries; this has led to suggestions that a similar permanent agency might be useful for international disputes. Students of race or community relations who pin their hopes on the use of conciliation in this field appear more and more to be seeking guidance from the experience gained with this method of settling labour disputes.

Those using conciliation and arbitration in labour disputes can also benefit from experience in the other fields. The techniques of conciliation and mediation in labour disputes and in international disputes will always be mutually relevant. One instance of experience in disputes settlement in international relations which appears to be applicable to the settlement of labour disputes may be found in the arrangements made for the acquisition of jurisdiction by the International Court of Justice. Under the Statute of the Court acceptance of its jurisdiction is essentially voluntary: for the Court to have jurisdiction, States parties to a dispute must agree to submit the dispute to the Court. However, provision is also made for acceptance by States of a sort of compulsory jurisdiction, by declaring (at any time) that they recognise as compulsory *ipso facto* and without special agreement, in relation to any other State accepting the same obligation, the jurisdiction of the Court in certain specified categories of dispute. An adaptation of this arrangement might be useful in a policy of promoting and encouraging voluntary arbitration in labour disputes, so that a permanent arbitration court established for that purpose could acquire jurisdiction over a dispute not only when agreed to by the parties after a dispute between them arises but also under a continuing agreement providing for such an arrangement.

In each field efforts are being made to improve methods of disputes settlement. Such efforts are likely to be more productive if as many options as possible are considered. Comparative studies of experiences in the various fields are a means of enlarging such options, and there probably remains plenty of scope for studies of this kind.

While such studies are still rare, comparative studies of national experience in the settlement of labour disputes are more common.[1] They show that the main developments in the application of settlement procedures to labour disputes have occurred during the late nineteenth and the twentieth centuries, with the recognition that industrial conflict was an important feature of modern society and that there was a need for its peaceful resolution. This has involved the establishment of ad hoc or permanent machinery for the settlement of labour disputes by the parties thereto or by government.

In setting up such machinery it has been found necessary to resolve certain basic issues of a general character, whether explicitly or implicitly. These include a determination of what is meant by a labour dispute for the purposes of the settlement procedures, of the objectives aimed at through the institution of settlement procedures, of the types of settlement procedure to be established and of the degree to which these procedures should be voluntary or compulsory in character. These matters will be discussed in the following sections.

CONCEPT OF LABOUR DISPUTE

Those legislation or collective agreements which make provision for settlement procedures generally indicate the disputes to which the procedures are to apply. In some countries the same procedures are applicable irrespective of the type of labour dispute, and a general definition is usually given of labour disputes. In other countries different procedures apply to different types of labour dispute (e.g. individual or collective disputes, legal or interests disputes), and consequently the legislation or collective agreements generally distinguish between these different types, although in some of these countries there are also general definitions of labour disputes for certain purposes.

General definitions

In some countries, including many following the British tradition of industrial relations, the relevant legislation gives a general definition of labour disputes, without distinguishing different types of dispute to which different procedures would apply. Generally, the provisions define a labour dispute by reference to the parties thereto (employers or their organisations and workers or their organisations) and the subject-matter of the dispute (terms and conditions of employment and sometimes trade union rights and the labour-management relationship itself). On some occasions the general definition covers disputes between workers or between parties which are not placed in an employer-employee relationship. Some comparative studies also tend to view labour disputes in a very general way without making substantive distinctions between different types. A recent OECD study, for instance, looks at disputes from the standpoint of their external or behavioural manifestations and regards them as "conflicts of view between employers and workers . . . which are manifested by departures from normal working".[2]

The early definition in the United Kingdom, which served as a model for the legislation in Ireland and in a number of former British territories, was contained in Section 5(3) of the Trade Disputes Act, 1906, and incorporated in the Industrial Courts Act, 1919: " 'trade dispute' means any dispute between employers and workmen, or between workmen and workmen, which is

3

connected with the employment or non-employment or the terms of employment, or with the conditions of labour, of any person".[3]

This early definition in British legislation has been substantially maintained in most of the former British territories, but new definitions are provided for in recent enactments in Jamaica, Trinidad and Tobago and Zambia. While those in Trinidad and Tobago and in Zambia are based on a distinction between interests disputes and rights disputes (see below), that provided for in the Labour Relations and Industrial Disputes Act, 1975, of Jamaica is, like the original British model, of a general character. Under that Act "industrial dispute" means a dispute between one or more employers or organisations representing employers and one or more workers or organisations representing workers which relates wholly or partly to terms and conditions of employment, or to the physical conditions in which workers are required to work; to engagement or non-engagement, or termination or suspension of employment; to allocation of work as between workers or groups of workers; or to any matter affecting the privileges, rights and duties of any employer or organisation representing employers or of any worker or organisation representing workers.[4]

In the United States (where, however, practice distinguishes between legal disputes and economic disputes) a general definition of "labour dispute" was given in the Norris-La Guardia Act, 1932,[5] a law which was intended to protect labour unions by regulating the power of the federal courts to issue injunctions in labour disputes; that definition was subsequently incorporated in the National Labour Relations Act, 1935[6] as well as in the Labour-Management Relations Act, 1947.[7] As provided in the last two Acts, "the term 'labour dispute' includes any controversy concerning terms, tenure or conditions of employment, or concerning the association or representation of persons in negotiating, fixing, maintaining, changing, or seeking to arrange terms or conditions of employment, regardless of whether the disputants stand in the proximate relation of employer and employee".

In Indonesia, where compulsory arbitration applies, "labour dispute" means any controversy between an employer or an association of employers and a trade union or a confederation of trade unions in connection with a disagreement in industrial relations, conditions of employment or conditions of work.[8]

The Labour Code of Jordan[9] defines "industrial dispute" as any dispute occurring between an employer (or employers) and workers which is connected with employment or non-employment, the terms or conditions of employment or the refusal of the employer to enter in good faith into negotiations with a registered trade union.

In Australia the law establishing the procedures of conciliation and arbitration in industrial disputes defines such disputes as those relating to all matters pertaining to the relations of employers and employees, and gives a lengthy but not limitative enumeration of matters so considered.[10]

In some countries it is the threat or occurrence of a strike or lockout which generally will give rise to a dispute, in which the conciliation and arbitration authority will be competent to intervene. This concept of labour dispute has been embodied in the Adjustment of Labour Relations Law, 1946, of Japan.[11] In Section 6 of that Law "labour dispute" means any conflict of claims arising

4

between parties concerned with labour relations in respect of their labour relations and resulting in a situation where acts in the furtherance of disputes occur or there is danger of their occurring.

Definitions based on a distinction between different types of labour dispute

In a number of countries national law or practice distinguishes between different types of labour dispute for the purpose of applying different procedures of settlement. Two main distinctions have been developed: the first is based on the number of persons involved in the dispute, which determines its individual or collective character, the second on differences in the nature of the issues involved, essentially the difference between issues regarding the application or interpretation of existing rights and those regarding the establishment of new rights (in which case the distinction is between rights and interests disputes). In some countries disputes regarding trade union rights constitute a separate category, dealt with by distinct procedures.

In general, under the first method, a dispute is individual if it involves a single worker or a number of workers in their individual capacities or in relation to their individual contracts of employment, while a dispute is collective if it involves a number of workers collectively. Under the second distinction, for the purpose of the settlement procedures, conflicts of rights (or "legal" disputes) are those arising from the application or interpretation of an existing law or collective agreement (in some countries of an existing contract of employment as well), while interests or economic disputes are those arising from the failure of collective bargaining, i.e. when the parties' negotiations for the conclusion, renewal, revision or extension of a collective agreement end in deadlock. It should be noted that all individual disputes under the first distinction are rights disputes, while collective disputes may be rights disputes (for example, if they involve the interpretation of the terms of a collective agreement) or interests disputes (when they arise in the course of negotiating new terms). It should also be noted that interests disputes under the second distinction are always collective disputes. Within any given country, while one distinction pre-dominates under disputes settlement procedures, the other may be used for certain purposes (for example, in some countries following the distinction between individual and collective disputes, where individual disputes go before special courts, there may be separate procedures for collective rights disputes and collective interests disputes).

The development of these distinctions in different countries seems to be essentially linked to the historical development of particular settlement procedures.

Individual and collective disputes

The first steps leading to the distinction between individual and collective disputes were taken in France under legislation establishing the "probiviral"[12] courts (conseils de prud'hommes) to settle differences in relation to a contract of employment. These courts were first established by an Act of 1806. At that time, however, trade unionism was still at an early stage of development and the concepts of collective bargaining and collective agreements were to wait for nearly a century before seeing the light of day. Disputes between employers and workers over the contract of employment were distinguished not from other types of labour dispute but rather from disputes arising from other types of contract which were brought before the ordinary courts. In relation to employment contracts, it was considered desirable to establish the probiviral courts, composed of persons from the various trades and industries, with special competence over disputes arising from individual contracts of employment; these courts were constituted on a different basis from that of ordinary courts and followed a different procedure.[13] This system was also adopted in Belgium and in several cantons of Switzerland.

The probiviral courts functioned in a quite satisfactory manner, and when later laws were passed providing for new procedures for the settlement of labour disputes, the probiviral courts with their limited jurisdiction over individual disputes were left intact; the new disputes settlement procedures were designed for disputes which were generally initiated by trade unions and necessarily collective in character. A similar system has been followed in a number of African and Middle Eastern countries (e.g. Benin, the United Republic of Cameroon, Chad, the Congo, Gabon, the Ivory Coast, Lebanon, Madagascar, Mali, Senegal and Zaire), where labour courts have been established for settling individual disputes and where separate machinery exists for conciliation and arbitration in collective disputes.

The French Labour Code (Overseas Territories), 1952,[14] introduced in many former French territories the distinction between individual and collective disputes and provided for the establishment of labour courts "to hear such individual disputes as may arise in connection with a contract of employment between workers and their employers". That Code did not contain a definition of "collective dispute", but it was clear that such a dispute was one involving a number of workers which did not arise in connection with a contract of employment. This distinction has been retained in the new labour codes adopted in many of these countries after they became independent.[15]

While the Labour Code of the United Republic of Cameroon[16] contains similar provisions regarding individual disputes, it also provides for a definition of "collective dispute". Under Section 169 any dispute which arises out of modification of the substantive rights of workers and which is characterised by (i) the intervention of a group of wage-earning workers, whether or not the said workers are organised in trade unions, and (ii) the collective nature of the interests at stake, is deemed to be a collective labour dispute.

A similar pattern is followed in the Labour Code of Zaire,[17] which defines a collective dispute to mean "any dispute arising between one or more employers, on the one hand, and a certain number of their staff, on the other hand, respecting conditions of work, where such dispute is liable to interfere with the smooth running of the undertaking or industrial peace and does not fall within the competence of the labour courts".

Rights and interests disputes

Among the first countries to adopt the second type of distinction (that between rights and interests disputes) were Austria, Denmark, the former Weimar Republic of Germany, Norway and Sweden. At the time that the relevant laws were enacted in those countries, trade unions were already well developed and collective bargaining was an accepted institution. The problems raised by the negotiation of a collective agreement and its application had become subjects of study. It was seen that, while they were closely related, they were distinct processes and posed different problems. In negotiating a collective agreement the parties were in effect deciding on the terms of a contract which was to be a law for them and for the individual workers and employers covered thereby. The jurists and legislators who studied the problems were undoubtedly aware of the situation in France, in relation particularly to the probiviral courts. The decision taken was that collective agreements created legal rights and that disputes over their existence, application, interpretation or enforcement were to be entrusted to labour courts and not to ordinary courts. In Denmark,[18] Norway[19] and Sweden[20] the competence of labour courts over rights disputes is limited to questions relating to collective agreements, while in the Federal Republic of Germany[21] it also includes disputes arising from the contract of employment and from certain legal provisions relating to employment. Disputes arising in the course of collective bargaining regarding the terms to be embodied in a collective agreement were considered to be of a different order; each party sought the best terms for itself, guided largely if not exclusively by its own interests, and as such disputes involved non-justiciable issues and were therefore considered to be outside the province of judicial settlement, conciliation and mediation became the principal methods for their peaceful settlement.

With the growth of trade unions and collective bargaining in Canada and the United States, substantially the same conclusions were reached as regards the distinction between interests disputes and rights disputes, which many writers in these two countries designate as economic disputes and legal disputes respectively. Conciliation and mediation were also accepted as the principal methods of peacefully settling economic or interests disputes, but for rights disputes under the collective agreement a system of private arbitration was evolved. Unlike the system of industry-wide bargaining between employers' associations and trade unions which prevailed in continental Europe, collective bargaining in Canada and the United States developed on the basis of plant-level or enterprise-level negotiations between a company and a trade union. Under this system of collective bargaining the contracting parties were immediately involved in the administration and application of the collective agreement. At an early stage in the development of collective bargaining in these two countries, the parties began to provide in their agreements for a procedure for adjusting workers' grievances arising from the application or interpretation of the agreement. Gradually it became the practice to include as a last stage in the grievance procedure the submission of grievances to private arbitration for final settlement; this practice became widespread during and after the Second World War.[22]

The Canada Labour Code distinguishes interests disputes from rights disputes. The first, under the term "dispute", is defined (Section 107) as "a dispute arising in connection with the entering into, renewing or revising of a collective agreement, in respect of which notice may be given to the Minister under Section 163" (regarding conciliation), while rights disputes are defined (Section 155) in a provision requiring every collective agreement to provide for "final settlement without stoppage of work, by arbitration or otherwise, of all differences between the parties to or employees bound by the collective agreement, concerning its interpretation, application, administration or alleged violation".

The practice of distinguishing between interests disputes and rights or legal disputes has been followed in Finland, Iceland and a number of Latin American countries (e.g. Argentina, Colombia, Costa Rica, the Dominican Republic, Ecuador, El Salvador, Guatemala, Panama, Peru and Venezuela), where labour courts exist for settling legal disputes; more recently, New Zealand and Pakistan have followed suit. In the Philippines the aim of public policy, as in Canada and the United States, is to use private arbitration for settling grievance disputes under collective agreements.

In New Zealand the distinction between rights and interests disputes was introduced in the Industrial Relations Act, 1973. Under that Act a "dispute of interest" means "a dispute created with intent to procure a collective agreement or award settling terms and conditions of employment of workers in any industry". A "dispute of rights" means a dispute concerning the interpretation, application or operation of a collective agreement or award; or a dispute concerning a matter of the interpretation, application or operation of an enactment or contract of employment, being a matter related to a collective agreement or award; or any dispute that is not a dispute of interest, including any dispute that arises during the currency of a collective agreement or award; or a personal grievance.

The 1972 Labour Code of El Salvador distinguishes, in Sections 468 and 469, between collective disputes of a legal nature and those of an economic nature: "A collective dispute of a legal nature is one arising out of non-compliance with or interpretation of a collective contract or agreement or one seeking the enforcement of the legislation or works rules, where a collectivity of workers is affected; a collective dispute of an economic nature is one arising out of a difference of collective economic interests of workers and employers or of the defence of the common occupational interests of workers."

It was previously indicated that in the United Kingdom and some countries following the British tradition no distinction has been made between different types of labour dispute such as rights and interests disputes. Various reasons have been given to explain this. In the first place, the parties to the collective agreement themselves rarely intend that their bargain shall be a legally enforceable contract, but rather that it shall be binding in honour only—a gentlemen's agreement. As mentioned in a British report, "the law goes out of its way to provide that such bargains between employers' associations and trade unions shall not be directly enforceable".[23] It is therefore not possible to speak of collective agreements establishing legal rights *per se*, or of legal disputes arising from their application. "Moreover, because of the prevalence of 'custom and practice' in British industrial relations, a sharp distinction between the two types of dispute is unrealistic. . . . Another impediment to distinguishing between the two types of dispute is the general practice in this country of allowing agreements to run for an indefinite period."[24] Collective bargaining "is in fact a continuous process in which differences concerning the interpretation of an agreement merge imperceptibly into differences concerning claims to change its effects".[25] It may, however, be noted that in the United Kingdom, and in other countries (e.g. India and Sri Lanka) where no general distinction between various types of dispute has been made, labour courts or arbitration tribunals have been established to deal with a specified class or classes of disputes which involve individual workers only or issues of a legal character.

Individual disputes or rights disputes have been distinguished from other types of dispute in many countries usually for the purpose of providing for their submission to special settlement procedures, before either a labour court or an arbitrator. One of the reasons for this is to obtain advantages over proceedings before the ordinary courts for enforcing the rights and obligations involved, particularly in the way of avoiding the delays, the formalities and the technicalities as well as the high costs of litigation proverbially associated with ordinary court procedure. No less important is the fact that judges of ordinary courts have often been found to lack knowledge of industrial conditions; in this respect labour courts and arbitrators in labour disputes acquire specialisation and expertise for their work. Furthermore, disputes which can be settled by labour courts or arbitrators are generally not brought before the government bodies responsible for the settlement of interests or collective disputes. These bodies are thus saved from having to deal with disputes involving only one or a few workers, which can be very numerous and can otherwise seriously clog their calendars. In turn, these organs also become specialised institutions for settling interests or collective disputes.

Disputes concerning trade union rights

The various types of dispute referred to above relate mainly to terms and conditions of employment. In a few countries special procedures have also been set up for settling disputes relating to the exercise of trade union rights. Two types of dispute are involved: *(a)* those arising from acts of anti-union discrimination in respect of employment; and *(b)* those arising over the recognition of a trade union for purposes of collective bargaining. The method used for settling these two types of dispute in the countries concerned (e.g. Argentina, Canada, Ghana, Japan, the Philippines and the United States) is often that of administrative determination. Although this method of settlement is not covered in this study, it may be useful to emphasise that a main purpose of the public policy underlying these procedures is to remove controversies over acts of anti-union discrimination and trade union recognition from the arena of industrial conflict.

Parties to labour disputes

Most definitions of labour dispute indicate the parties between whom a dispute can arise. That there must be parties to a dispute is indeed implicit in the very concept of a dispute. The question of who may be parties to labour disputes is therefore an inevitable issue of labour relations policy and has to be resolved one way or another. It is, however, of particular significance in connection with disputes involving the collective interests of employers or workers. The practical issue is the extent to which any group of employers or workers should have the capacity to raise and be parties to collective disputes.

When any group or organisation is recognised to have the capacity to be a party to labour disputes, that capacity normally carries with it certain rights and privileges as well as certain obligations. Such a party, when a dispute has in fact arisen, will be entitled to request the assistance of the state conciliation and arbitration service in settling the dispute. It will also have the right, unless prohibited by statute, and subject to any prescribed conditions, to take industrial action (strikes, lockouts, etc.) in relation to the dispute. Where the law provides for compulsory conciliation or arbitration, it will be subject to this method of settlement and will necessarily be bound by a compulsory arbitration award. Finally, legislative provisions regulate in other ways the conduct of parties to labour disputes, in connection either with acts in the furtherance of disputes or with their participation in settlement procedures. However, the question of subjecting a party to certain obligations is only one side of the picture; the other side is the question of its capacity to comply with any such obligation.

In view of such rights, privileges and obligations, not any group of employers or workers will be recognised to have the capacity under any circumstances whatsoever to raise and become parties to labour disputes; provisions on this question may therefore be seen to form part of the general arrangements to promote orderliness in the raising and furtherance of labour disputes and in their settlement. The question may be settled by definite legislative provisions or by implication, combined with conventional or traditional practices. The main problems concern the capacity of organisations and of unorganised and underorganised workers.

In many countries employers' associations and trade unions have to be registered before they can become parties to labour disputes and participate in conciliation or arbitration procedures under government auspices. Registration may be compulsory or optional; it may be a simple formality, involving nothing more than the filing of certain documents, or it may involve the exercise of some discretionary power by the registering authority. Apart from those cases where registration is a condition for legal existence, the problem of capacity in connection with this requirement arises in two main forms.

In the first place, registration is a method of acquiring legal personality. This may be the reason for the requirement of registration, as in the case of labour unions in various Latin American countries, where they must be incorporated. Under another approach, especially where registration is optional, the acquisition of legal personality is only one of the consequences of registration. However, the question of whether or not trade unions or employers' associations should have legal personality is more a problem of labour relations policy in general than one concerning labour disputes only. It appears that the problem is considered mainly when collective agreements (including those concluded with the assistance of third parties) are made legally binding and it is intended that such organisations should be able to assume responsibility and to perform acts with legal effects as juridical persons in the fullest sense.

Second, registration confers legal standing for certain purposes only. In Australia (and similarly in New Zealand) only those organisations which have been registered under the Conciliation and Arbitration Act can participate in the system of conciliation and arbitration established by the Act. In Japan "certificated" unions only can take advantage of the formal procedures and avail themselves of the remedies under the Trade Union Law, 1949, and the Adjustment of Labour Relations Law, 1946. In the United States no labour organisation can raise a question of employee representation or file a complaint for unfair labour practice unless it has been registered with the Secretary of Labour. In the Philippines a labour organisation acquires by registration the right to act or be certified as the exclusive bargaining representative of all the employees in an appropriate collective bargaining unit. And in the United Kingdom, under the Employment Protection Act, 1975, a trade union must obtain a "certificate of independence" in order to be able to refer a recognition issue to the Advisory, Conciliation and Arbitration Service.

Since the parties to the negotiation of a collective agreement will be the same parties to the dispute which will arise if the negotiations reach a deadlock, the capacity of trade unions and employers' associations to become parties to such disputes is often determined by provisions concerning their capacity to enter into collective agreements. In certain countries the main provisions are found in the legislative definition of "collective agreement", which generally includes the parties between whom it may be concluded. In the Federal Republic of Germany it is provided that a party to a collective agreement must be a trade union, an individual employer or an employers' association.[26] In several other countries the capacity to bargain collectively is governed by more detailed provisions or practices or by decisions of the courts.

In Austria, under the Act of 14 December 1973 respecting collective labour relations,[27] the capacity to conclude collective agreements is enjoyed by employers' and workers' organisations which fulfil certain conditions as regards their objects, territorial and occupational scope, economic importance and independence of the other party; but any such organisation has to apply to the Central Conciliation Office to have its capacity to conclude collective agreements formally recognised.

The problem of the capacity of trade unions to bargain collectively is bound up with the question of their recognition by employers and employers' associations. In a good number of countries a system of voluntary trade union recognition has been evolved, based on a union being sufficiently representative of the class or group of workers it seeks to represent and on certain other criteria. In addition to, or in the absence of, a system of voluntary recognition, a statutory procedure exists in some countries for resolving the issue of recognition, under which a trade union may be granted "trade union status", be certified as a collective bargaining representative or obtain a declaration that it is entitled to recognition.

The system of recognition, whether voluntary or statutory, has two important effects. On the one hand, it entitles the recognised or "certified" union to bargain collectively with the employer concerned. On the other hand, it restricts the right to bargain collectively (and thus to become party to disputes arising from deadlocks in negotiations) to trade unions which are recognised; non-recognised unions do not have this right.

There may, however, be no recognised or certified union for a group of workers. The question then arises whether such workers should have the capacity to raise collective disputes. This appears to be more particularly a problem in plant-level or enterprise-level bargaining than in industry-wide bargaining, and arises in two different situations. In one situation no union has been able to establish itself in the undertaking, a situation which is not rare in countries where the trade union movement is still young. The other situation is one where there may be one or more unions in the undertaking, but no union has enough members or workers' support to qualify for recognition or certification; this situation is by no means exclusive to developing countries and may also be found in certain industries and areas in various industrialised countries.

It can be argued that, as a matter of principle, these workers should not be denied the possibility of obtaining wage increases, better working conditions or the modification of proposed management decisions which they consider inimical to their interests by being able to negotiate and raise disputes with their employers over their demands for such purposes. The question, however, involves certain practical considerations which will differ in character, urgency and importance from country to country according to local factors. Among these considerations are the possible adverse effects on trade union development of widespread employers' negotiations with unorganised or underorganised workers. An employer may purposely make use of such negotiations in order to "neutralise" any desire on the part of his workers to form or join a trade union. There is also the danger that a negotiating workers' group may come into being under the employer's inspiration and be under his control.

The need for endowing those workers with the capacity to raise disputes has been recognised in several countries. In the United Republic of Cameroon and in Israel[28] the legislation expressly refers to disputes in which the workers are not organised or represented by a trade union. In Jamaica and the United Kingdom the definitions of "trade dispute" or "industrial dispute" quoted above would cover disputes to which a group of workers was a party. The capacity of unorganised or underorganised workers to become parties to labour disputes may also be derived from their capacity to enter into collective agreements. At least five Latin American countries (Colombia, Costa Rica, Ecuador, Peru and Venezuela) have long recognised the right of unorganised groups of workers (sometimes called "coalitions") to become parties to collective agreements, subject to certain conditions.[29] In Sri Lanka, under a 1957 amendment to the Industrial Disputes Act, 1950,[30] a collective agreement may be concluded by "any workmen or any trade union or trade unions consisting of workmen". It would also appear that in other countries where the law does not expressly limit the capacity on the workers' side to negotiate and raise disputes to trade unions, and is silent on the question of the capacity of unorganised or underorganised workers, it may be possible for such workers to raise disputes with their employers.

Legislative provisions dealing with the question generally contemplate a situation where the workers are not represented by a trade union. It is often provided that the party (on the workers' side) to collective bargaining or a dispute shall be the representative elected by a prescribed proportion (the majority, as in Ethiopia, Israel and Peru, or at least 75 per cent, as in Venezuela) of the group or category of workers concerned. In the United States an employer has to bargain collectively with the representative chosen by the majority of the employees concerned, but the law leaves open the possibility that such a representative may be an entity other than a trade union, subject to the condition that it is not under the employers' domination and control.

OBJECTIVES OF LABOUR DISPUTES SETTLEMENT PROCEDURES

The choice of policy regarding the extent of state intervention in the settlement of labour disputes is affected by the objectives which the settlement procedures should be intended to serve. In this respect it is commonly accepted that the settlement procedures should aim at the peaceful and orderly settlement of disputes so as to make it unnecessary to resort to strikes and lockouts. However, the question is whether this should be the only objective of the system of conciliation and arbitration or whether it should have any other objective. In effect, there have been developments in the latter direction, but it may be useful before referring to them to consider the objective which has been universally recognised.

This objective was often simply described and emphasised as "industrial peace". Its classical expression was "the prevention and settlement of disputes". Originally, the idea of prevention, in this statement of the objective, was tied up with the conception of disputes in the form of actual or threatened strikes and lockouts. In other words, what was actually meant, besides the settlement of disputes, was the prevention of strikes and lockouts, where the procedures of settlement were themselves intended as a means of prevention.

For many years the settlement of disputes without or with a minimum of strikes and lockouts was the first and only recognised objective of conciliation and arbitration, and this still seems to be largely the position in certain countries. In an increasing number of countries, however, especially where voluntary procedures are the only recognised or the prevailing methods of settlement, it is also the aim of conciliation and arbitration to foster the growth of collective bargaining. The use of conciliation and arbitration for this purpose will no doubt be thought of particularly under a labour relations policy specially directed to the promotion of collective bargaining and will be only one of the measures which can be taken to implement that policy.[31]

As may be supposed, the need for using conciliation and arbitration to advance collective bargaining came to be recognised only after some experience of collective bargaining had been acquired and after the thinking about it and its role in the system of labour relations had become clearer and more crystallised. But it is difficult to specify any one moment when it could be said that the first steps were taken to give conciliation and arbitration a supporting role to collective bargaining. This policy has been largely developed by administrative action, which may be given legislative sanction by budgetary or other provisions.

There are indeed only a few instances of specific legislative statements of policy on the matter. Perhaps the first instance was the Conciliation Order of 30 October 1923 in the former Weimar Republic of Germany.[32] Section 3 of that Order provided as follows: "Conciliation committees and conciliators shall assist in the conclusion of collective agreements (collective contracts and works agreements) where there is no conciliation authority set up by agreement or where such conciliation authority fails to bring about the conclusion of a collective agreement."

In Sweden the Act respecting the right of association and of collective bargaining of 11 September 1936[33] provided for state conciliation facilities to be made available to parties possessing the right of negotiation in connection with the exercise of this right. For this purpose the Act established special arrangements for cases of central organisations of employees which had been registered with the Department of Social Affairs for the purposes of the exercise of the right of negotiation. In other cases, any party could call upon a state conciliator to intervene under the provisions of the Act respecting conciliation in trade disputes.[34]

In the United States the Labour-Management Relations Act, 1947,[35] declares it to be the policy of that country that "the settlement of issues between employers and employees through collective bargaining may be advanced by making available full and adequate government facilities for conciliation, mediation, and voluntary arbitration to aid and encourage employers and the representatives of their employees to reach and maintain agreements concerning rates of pay, hours, and working conditions, and to make all reasonable efforts to settle their differences by mutual agreement reached through conferences and collective bargaining . . ." (Section 201).

In more recent times an effort to reconcile the promotion of collective bargaining in the public sector in the United States with the protection of the public interest has given rise to experiments with new forms of arbitration which aim at inducing the parties to come as near as they can, through negotiation, to a reasonable agreement before having recourse to arbitration (thereby increasing the chances of reaching an agreement without arbitration). These systems require the arbitrator to consider the final offers of the parties and to choose the offer that seems most reasonable. Two systems of this type have been developed: the final offer selection system and the last-offer-by-issue system (see below, p. 179, footnote 20).

Finally, a more recent trend in industrial relations sees conciliation and arbitration procedures as contributing to the important objective of economic and social development, on the one hand by promoting an atmosphere of industrial peace conducive to development efforts and on the other hand by promoting the settlement of conflicting interests in accordance with the requirements of economic and social development. The need for the industrial relations system in general to take into account the requirements of development has been emphasised in the legislation of a number of countries, including Jamaica,[36] Kenya,[37] Tanzania,[38] Trinidad and Tobago[39] and Zambia.[40]

PROCEDURES FOR LABOUR DISPUTES SETTLEMENT

Types of procedure

As previously indicated, the same types of disputes settlement procedure as have been used in international conflicts have been applied to labour disputes.

These include adjudication, conciliation and mediation and arbitration. Two further procedures—fact-finding and administrative determination—have been developed in some countries in recent times.

Adjudication

Adjudication, as understood in the present study, is a procedure whereby ordinary courts or special labour courts settle finally any disputes over rights and obligations. This procedure will not be discussed in the present study, which is devoted to the non-judicial settlement procedures.

Conciliation and mediation

These are procedures whereby a third party provides assistance to the parties in the course of negotiations, or when negotiations have reached an impasse, with a view to helping them to reach an agreement. While in many countries these terms are interchangeable, in some countries a distinction is made between them according to the degree of initiative taken by the third party. Such distinction reflects the etymological origins of these terms: "conciliation" is derived from the Latin *conciliare*, meaning "to bring together" or "to unite in thought", while "mediation" is derived from the Late Latin *mediare*, meaning "to occupy a middle position". Thus, some systems of disputes settlement distinguish between conciliation as a procedure whereby the third party brings the parties together, encourages them to discuss their differences and assists them in developing their own proposed solutions, and mediation as a procedure in which the third party is more active in assisting the parties to find an acceptable solution, going so far as to submit his own proposals for settlement to the parties. For the purpose of the present study, such distinctions are considered to be differences of degree, not differences in kind, since in both cases settlement of the dispute depends upon the agreement of the parties. For this reason, and also because such distinctions between the two methods of settlement have tended to disappear in industrial relations practice, with conciliators and mediators intervening in the discussions more or less actively according to the particular circumstances of the dispute, conciliation and mediation are here discussed together as one type of procedure.

Arbitration

Arbitration, as understood in the present study, is a procedure whereby a third party (whether an individual arbitrator, a board of arbitrators or an arbitration court), not acting as a court of law, is empowered to take a decision which disposes of the dispute. If the decision concerns a legal dispute and involves deciding the rights and obligations of the parties, it is similar in function to adjudication. If it concerns an interests or economic dispute, it involves replacing negotiations by an award considered by the third party to be appropriate. In both cases, even if the arbitral award is obligatory under the law, it is usually not executory (as is a judgement of a court of law) but is similar in legal nature to a legally binding collective agreement, and a party will have to seek its enforcement before the courts of law.

15

Fact-finding

This is a process whereby a third party establishes the facts relevant to the solution of a dispute. This, of course, is an essential aspect of judicial settlement, and conciliation and arbitration also involve a certain amount of fact-finding by a third party. However, in a number of countries fact-finding has developed as a distinct procedure for the settlement of labour disputes. This procedure is generally a more active form of intervention in labour disputes than conciliation and mediation, but like the latter it aims at an amicable or voluntary settlement by the parties.

Administrative determination

This procedure was not specifically devised for the settlement of disputes but rather as a means of enabling administrative authorities to carry out public policies to safeguard the public interest through the investigation and determination of specific questions on the application of interested parties. These questions, however, may include those which involve the conflicting claims or interests of the applicant and other parties who eventually take part in the proceedings. This method has grown in importance because of the increasing complexity of government affairs in industrial society. In the labour field it has come to be used in some countries particularly in connection with the enforcement of certain trade union rights.

The present study focuses on conciliation and mediation, fact-finding and arbitration as methods of settlement of labour disputes. Since it is concerned with the non-judicial procedures, it does not cover adjudication as a settlement procedure. Nor does it investigate administrative determination, mentioned in Chapter 2 in connection with disputes regarding trade union rights, which are beyond the scope of this study.

Establishment of procedures by the parties or by the government

Conciliation, mediation, fact-finding and arbitration are disputes settlement procedures which may be established either by agreement of the parties or by the State. Today, most countries have established official machinery for disputes settlement, whether as part of the labour administration or as separate agencies. However, a number of countries have in addition adopted a policy of favouring prior recourse to procedures which may be set up by the parties themselves in their agreements. Such jointly established procedures will be reviewed in Chapter 4, while official machinery will be discussed in Chapters 5, 6 and 7.

Voluntary or compulsory nature of procedures

The voluntary and compulsory elements in the various procedures will depend upon public policy concerning disputes settlement. Where the greatest emphasis is placed on the freedom of the parties and on the importance of disputes settlement by a compromise that has been freely arrived at, the voluntary elements will predominate. Where the greatest emphasis is placed on the avoidance of work stoppages, the compulsory elements tend to increase.

With respect to machinery jointly established by the parties, the establishment of such procedures is usually left to the free decision of the parties. However, in a number of countries legislation obliges the parties to include certain types of disputes settlement procedure in their collective agreements. These matters will be discussed in Chapter 4.

As regards state intervention in the settlement of disputes through official machinery, a distinction can be made between disputes regarding rights and obligations under collective agreements, individual contracts of employment and legislation (including disputes regarding trade union rights), on the one hand, and interests disputes, on the other. In most countries it appears that most rights or legal disputes may be brought by one of the parties to some body (whether an ordinary court, a labour court, a private arbitrator or some other body) for binding decision. However, as previously indicated, this situation is not universal, since in some countries, particularly those following traditional British practice, disputes arising under collective agreements are dealt with by negotiation, not by binding third-party decision. On the other hand, interests disputes arising out of the revision or conclusion of a collective agreement are generally dealt with by other procedures, including conciliation, fact-finding and arbitration, and it has been mainly with respect to these procedures in interests disputes that the issue of the extent to which they should be voluntary or compulsory in nature has been raised.

In fact, the application of these methods of settlement to interests disputes has been frequently characterised by a combination of voluntary and compulsory features. In practically every country, some form or degree of compulsion is used, either as a permanent feature of the national conciliation and arbitration system or on an ad hoc basis.

The compulsory features may relate to the initiation of the procedure, the conduct of proceedings or the manner in which settlement is effected. Because of these features, it has become usual to speak of "voluntary conciliation" and "compulsory conciliation" and of "voluntary arbitration" and "compulsory arbitration". However, the words "voluntary" and "compulsory", when used to characterise conciliation, do not have the same meanings as when applied to "arbitration".

Conciliation is deemed to be voluntary when the parties are free to make use of it as they wish. It is compulsory when they are required to participate in or to make use of the procedure. There are various ways by which conciliation can be made compulsory in this sense, but "compulsory conciliation" does not mean that the parties have to accept the terms of settlement proposed by the conciliator (or mediator).

Behind the expressions "voluntary arbitration" and "compulsory arbitration" is a more complicated situation. The initiation of the procedure is voluntary if it depends on the consent of both parties and compulsory otherwise. As regards the manner of effecting the settlement, it is voluntary if the consent of both parties is essential for giving effect to the arbitration award and compulsory if the award is legally binding, irrespective of whether both parties accept it or not.

In one situation there is voluntary initiation of the procedure, i.e. on the basis of agreement by the parties, and acceptance of the award is voluntary. In a second situation there is voluntary initiation of the procedure, but the award is legally binding. In a third situation there is compulsory initiation of the procedure, i.e. without the consent of both parties, with voluntary acceptance of the award. And, finally, in a fourth situation, both the initiation of the procedure and the award are obligatory. For the purposes of this study, the expression "voluntary arbitration" includes the first three situations and "compulsory arbitration" is limited to the fourth situation.

The form of arbitration in labour disputes indicated in the second situation is the traditional and most prevalent form of voluntary arbitration. And it is the form of voluntary arbitration which is generally used in contradistinction to compulsory arbitration, in the sense indicated in the fourth situation. In India, however, the legislation simply uses the term "arbitration" for voluntary arbitration, while compulsory arbitration is referred to as "adjudication".

Most national systems of conciliation, mediation, fact-finding and arbitration in interests disputes fall into three main categories so far as their voluntary or compulsory character is concerned.

In the first category, only voluntary settlement procedures are employed, although they may be characterised by certain specific compulsory features. The national system may comprise one or more of the following procedures: conciliation, mediation, fact-finding or investigation, and any of the three forms of voluntary arbitration (i.e. voluntary submission with voluntary award, voluntary submission with binding award and compulsory submission with voluntary award). Among the national systems in this category are those of Austria, Belgium, Canada (at the federal level), Denmark, Finland, France, the Federal Republic of Germany, Israel, Italy, Luxembourg, the Netherlands, Norway, Sweden, Switzerland, the United Kingdom and the United States (at the federal level).

In the second category, the national system includes, in addition to voluntary settlement procedures, a limited application of compulsory arbitration to a specified class of disputes or cases, usually disputes in essential services or those affecting the national interest (see below, pp. 164–165).

Finally, in a third group of national systems, compulsory arbitration is of more or less general application and may be resorted to in any case, irrespective of whether or not the dispute affects essential services or the national interest, when there is failure of settlement by conciliation or any other available procedure (see below, pp. 165–166).

Notes

[1] See most recently Jean de Givry: "Prevention and settlement of labour disputes, other than conflicts of rights" (Tübingen, J. C. B. Mohr (Paul Siebeck); Alphen a/d Rijn, Sijthoff & Noordhoff, 1978), Ch. 14 of Otto Kahn-Freund (ed.): Labour law, Vol. XV of International Association of Legal Science: International encyclopedia of comparative law; and Roger Blanpain: "Prevention and settlement of collective labour disputes in the EEC countries", in Industrial Law Journal (London), June 1972, pp. 74–83, and Sep. 1972, pp. 143–158.

[2] OECD: Labour disputes: A perspective (Paris, 1979), p. 6.

[3] Royal Commission on Trade Unions and Employers' Associations, 1965–1968: Report (London, HMSO, 1968), para. 816.

[4] ILO: Legislative Series (LS), 1975—Jam. 1.

[5] ibid., 1932—USA 2.

[6] ibid., 1935—USA 1.

[7] ibid., 1947—USA 2.

[8] Act respecting the settlement of labour disputes (ibid., 1957—Indo. 1), Section 1(1).

[9] ibid., 1960—Jor. 1, Section 90; 1965—Jor. 1, Section 37.

[10] Conciliation and Arbitration Act, 1904–1976 (ibid., 1956—Aust. 1), Section 4.

[11] ibid., 1946—Jap. 1.

[12] An expression of Latin origin meaning "men of probity".

[13] The probiviral courts did not consist of magistrates. At first they were composed of employers and foremen, but following the reform of 1848 they were made up of employers (to whom foremen and supervisors were assimilated) on the one hand and workers on the other, chosen respectively by employers' and workers' electoral colleges. They were to settle a dispute by conciliation or, if this failed, by judgement. See A. Brun and H. Galland: *Droit du travail*, Vol. I (Paris, Sirey, 2nd ed., 1978), pp. 219 ff.

[14] ILO: *LS*, 1952—Fr. 5.

[15] For example, in the Labour Codes of Benin (ibid., 1967—Dah. 1), Gabon (ibid., 1962—Gab. 1), Ivory Coast (ibid., 1964—IC 1), Mali (ibid., 1962—Mali 1) and Mauritania (ibid., 1963—Mau. 1).

[16] ibid., 1967—Cam. 1.

[17] ibid., 1967—Congo (Kin.) 1.

[18] ibid., 1929—Den. 2. The court was first set up in 1910.

[19] ibid., 1927—Nor. 1.

[20] ibid., 1928—Swe. 2.

[21] ibid., 1953—Ger. FR 2. The labour courts were first established by the Labour Courts Act, 1926.

[22] See idem: *Grievance arbitration: A practical guide*, op. cit., pp. 13–14.

[23] Royal Commission on Trade Unions and Employers' Associations, 1965–1968, op. cit., para. 39.

[24] ibid., para. 60.

[25] ibid., para. 471.

[26] Collective Agreements Act, 1949, as amended (ILO: *LS*, 1969—Ger. FR 4).

[27] ibid., 1973—Aus. 2.

[28] Settlement of Labour Disputes Law (ibid., 1957—Isr. 1).

[29] See idem: *La negociación colectiva en América latina*, op. cit., pp. 22–23.

[30] idem: *LS*, 1957—Cey. 1B.

[31] See idem: *Collective bargaining in industrialised countries: Recent trends and problems*, Labour-management relations series, No. 56 (Geneva, 1978), pp. 36–37.

[32] idem: *LS*, 1923—Ger. 6.

[33] ibid., 1936—Swe. 8.

[34] ibid., 1920—Swe. 6. The 1920 and 1936 Acts have now been superseded by the Act respecting co-determination at work of 10 June 1976 (ibid., 1976—Swe. 1).

[35] ibid., 1947—USA 2.

[36] Jamaica, Labour Relations Code, 1976, para. 16(i) (in collective bargaining "due regard should always be paid to the interest of the community").

[37] Kenya, Guidelines issued under Section 9(10) of the Trade Disputes Act, 1965 (which require the Industrial Court to ensure that collective agreements and its decisions do not adversely affect the regular growth of employment opportunities, in line with the Development Plan).

[38] Tanzania, Permanent Labour Tribunal Act, 1967 (ILO: *LS*, 1967—Tan. 1), Sections 6, 22–23 (the Tribunal in deciding whether to register a negotiated agreement must consider various questions related to economic and social development).

[39] Trinidad and Tobago, Industrial Relations Act, 1972 (ibid., 1972—Trin. 1), Section 20(2) (requiring the Industrial Court, upon intervention of the Attorney-General, to consider various questions related to economic and social development).

[40] Zambia, Industrial Relations Act, 1971 (ibid., 1971—Zam. 2), Sections 94, 100 (the Tribunal in deciding whether to approve a negotiated agreement and make an award in terms thereof, must take into account public policy and the Government's declared policy on prices and incomes).

LABOUR RELATIONS POLICY AND DISPUTES SETTLEMENT

2

Conciliation and arbitration in labour disputes are but one of the aspects of public policy concerning the relations between employers and workers. Labour relations systems combine elements of both collaboration and conflict, and include aspects of personnel management, individual and collective dealings and statutory regulations. All these elements are closely inter-related. It is important that this complexity be recognised, because it provides the basis for the development of an integrated labour (or industrial) relations policy.

NEED FOR AN INTEGRATED LABOUR RELATIONS POLICY

From this viewpoint the government approach to conciliation and arbitration in labour disputes would be inadequate unless it were conceived within the framework of labour relations policy as a whole and in relation to the other main aspects of that policy. As is now also generally recognised, these other aspects include those relating to the direct participants in the system of labour relations (i.e. the employers and workers and their organisations), collective bargaining, grievance procedures within the undertaking, consultation and co-operation between employers and workers and the broad area of human relations at the place of work.

This approach reflects the current, widely held concept of labour relations policy. It is, however, a dynamic concept, which evolves with experience and increasing understanding of the problems. The general understanding today of labour relations policy is based on the experience and knowledge so far acquired; but for many decades after the onset of the Industrial Revolution, labour relations policy was much more narrowly conceived. In various countries the laws dealing with labour relations were (apart from statutory provisions relating to trade unions) almost exclusively concerned with labour disputes, their prevention and their settlement.

During the earlier part of this period, collective bargaining was, as indicated earlier, largely unknown. As a process of collective relations, it did not begin to develop until the second half of the nineteenth century, when trade union movements became more stable. In the United Kingdom it probably constituted the first stage of the agreed machinery for the avoidance of disputes which was set up at that time by employers' associations and trade unions in certain industries. In fact, during this period there appeared to be some confusion between collective bargaining and conciliation in the minds of many people, and the distinction between the two processes was not well established.

It was not until after the First World War that collective bargaining became an object of positive government policy and that legislation concerning the relations between employers and workers began to cover such matters as the protection of the right to organise, collective bargaining, consultation and co-operation. Nevertheless, during the inter-war period the countries in which these developments took place were few. Only after the Second World War did the broader concept of labour relations policy described earlier begin to be more widely recognised. It is, however, often necessary to go beyond the statute book in order to discover the complete picture of the labour relations policy of a country. While in many countries this mainly takes the form of legislation, it also includes administrative decisions. In former times in many countries the means for achieving the objectives of policy were largely confined to legislative commandments and prohibitions; in recent years increasing reliance has been placed on promotional work by the government, including the establishment of guidelines, the provision of information and advice, and educational and training activities.

As indicated above, the development of an integrated labour relations policy requires that the problem of disputes settlement be considered in relation to the other main aspects of that policy, in particular those aspects relating to the direct participants in the system of labour relations (management, workers, trade unions and employers' associations), to collective bargaining and to grievance adjustment. The promotional work referred to in the preceding paragraph is largely concerned with the participants in labour relations, much of it being aimed at improving their capacity to fulfil their respective roles in the system.

Underlying this promotional work is the realisation that the development of positive attitudes and the acquisition of the understanding and social skills required for effective collective bargaining and fruitful participation in conciliation and arbitration procedures cannot be brought about by legislative injunctions but are more essentially a product of experience and training. It is of course true that legislative provisions frequently deal with the participants' behaviour in the furtherance of labour disputes and in the conduct of conciliation and arbitration proceedings under government auspices. However, national practices vary greatly regarding the appropriateness of regulating by legislation other aspects of labour-management relations affecting the major participants therein.

DISPUTES SETTLEMENT AND TRADE UNION RIGHTS

Among those aspects, surely none is of more fundamental importance than the exercise by workers of their right to organise or to form or join trade unions independent of the employers' control. It was noted earlier that among the types of labour dispute for which special provisions have been made in a number of countries are those arising from acts of anti-union discrimination in respect of employment which may be committed by employers or their agents. This problem arises in varying degrees of seriousness in different countries, and within a given country at different stages of its economic and social development. Generally, however, it has been a much more serious problem in countries where collective bargaining is carried out mainly at the level of the undertaking than in countries where industry-wide bargaining prevails.

During the early days of the trade union movement in the United Kingdom and continental Europe the trade unions sought to deal with individual employers, whose initial reaction was often hostile; but in most of those countries this attitude changed and the employers eventually decided to form organisations of their own to defend their interests vis-à-vis the trade unions (as well as the government). A system of labour relations developed on the basis of collective bargaining between employers' organisations and trade unions in the industries in which they operated. In accepting this system of collective bargaining, the employers also implicitly accepted that the trade unions had a particular role to play within the system. The collective agreement thus concluded established labour standards which the individual employer members of the contracting employers' organisations were bound to observe. However, apart from this responsibility, and in the absence of other arrangements, the individual employer had no direct dealings with any trade union which was a party to the collective agreement. Furthermore, the trade union officials responsible for initiating and directing trade union work were not generally employed in individual establishments. They could therefore not become victims of anti-union discrimination in respect of employment.

On the other hand, in plant-level bargaining the trade union poses a direct challenge to the authority of the individual employer in making decisions concerning the workers employed by him, and collective bargaining operates as a more pervasive constraint on what have been considered traditional management prerogatives than in the case of industry-wide bargaining. If an employer did not like this prospect and felt strongly about it, he would actively resist the establishment or operation of a trade union in his plant, even going as far as to dismiss workers who had actively engaged in a union organisational drive or a union-organised strike. Among the countries where the system of plant-level bargaining first developed were Canada and the United States.

Trade unions naturally feel bitter when acts of anti-union victimisation occur. They regard these as nothing less than a direct attack on their existence, on trade unionism as an institution, and on fundamental human rights. Past experiences in controversies over victimisation have shown that the participants are likely to be much more emotionally involved than in other types of dispute. Such controversies can poison the climate of labour relations as no other cause or shortcoming of employers is capable of doing. In such a climate the process of settling disputes becomes more difficult.

The question of anti-union discrimination presents two sets of problems. One is how to deal with disputes over acts of victimisation. Under the practice in many countries these disputes are amenable to the normal conciliation, arbitration or adjudication procedures. As indicated earlier, in some countries they are referred to a special procedure of administrative determination, in which the resolution of the controversy is similar to that usually demanded by a trade union in the process of conciliation or arbitration (e.g. reinstatement of and/or other relief to a dismissed worker).

The other set of problems is of a more long-term and substantive character, rather than merely a question of providing relief for a past wrongdoing: it involves a decision whether there is a need for appropriate legislative measures to deter and prevent the commission of acts of victimisation. In a number of countries the need for such measures has been found to exist, and one of the measures resorted to is the penalisation of acts of victimisation as a criminal offence. The extent to which such a measure operates as an effective deterrent to victimisation, in the experience of countries in which it has been applied, may be an interesting subject of study. However, apart from the question of deterrence, the legislative provisions in question can be a useful tool in the hands of a conciliator dealing with this type of dispute.

In certain countries the same procedure of administrative determination for resolving disputes over acts of anti-union victimisation is also used for their prevention. Under this procedure, in addition to providing relief to the worker concerned, the order of the administrative authority may contain provisions which operate as a continuing restraint on the employer against the commission of acts of which he has been found guilty.

DISPUTES SETTLEMENT AND COLLECTIVE BARGAINING

What should be the relationship, in the labour relations policy of a country, between collective bargaining and disputes settlement? More particularly, should collective bargaining be considered and dealt with as a method of settling labour disputes or as a procedure of an entirely different type?

National practices do not give uniform answers to these questions. To explain the differences, it is perhaps necessary to go back to the earlier experiences of collective bargaining. These demonstrate that collective bargaining is an evolving social institution, subject to a continuing process of change and growth. As practised today in many countries, it is far different from the process of negotiation which trade unions sought to carry on with employers until late in the nineteenth century.

At that time it was often necessary for trade unions to threaten a strike or actually to declare a strike before employers would negotiate with them over their demands. The trade unions resorted to the strike weapon not only to enforce their demands but also to obtain recognition or at least to get the employers to deal with them. The conception of "labour dispute" thus came to be equated with the use of the strike, either imminent or actually started. The real negotiations between the parties could begin only when a dispute, in this sense, had arisen. On this basis, collective bargaining came to be viewed as a method of settling disputes. This view is still accepted in a number of countries.

In an increasing number of countries, however, collective bargaining has assumed the form of an institutionalised procedure (whether by law or by practice) of joint determination of the rules to govern the terms and conditions of employment of the workers concerned and the labour-management relationship itself. This development has proceeded on the basis of the recognition of trade unions by employers or employers' associations for the purpose of collective bargaining. Collective bargaining is usually initiated by the recognised union's presentation of its proposal to the other side; the negotiations are begun without waiting for the union to threaten a strike. In principle a dispute will arise, for purposes of third party intervention, when the negotiations between the parties become deadlocked; but there is no dispute as long as the two sides entertain the hope of reaching agreement and are willing to continue amicable discussions between themselves.

The question of whether collective bargaining is to be considered as only one of the methods of settling disputes or as a distinct process of a fundamentally different character is one of paramount importance in the development of an integrated labour relations policy. If it is to be considered only as a method of settling disputes, it will be dealt with as a procedure on the same level as conciliation and arbitration; but if the intention is to foster and promote collective bargaining as an institution for rule-making and policy-making which has its own *raison d'être*, a different approach will be necessary. This will be much more so if the purpose is to make it the central feature of labour relations policy.

In 1944 the International Labour Conference adopted the Declaration of Philadelphia, which redefined the aims and purposes of the ILO. It may be noted that under the Declaration of Philadelphia the ILO has a solemn obligation to further among the nations of the world programmes which will achieve, inter alia, "the effective recognition of the right of collective bargaining". This principle, subsequently defined in the ILO Right to Organise and Collective Bargaining Convention, 1949 (No. 98), attests to the importance to be accorded to collective bargaining as one of the major aspects of labour relations policy as well as in relation to conciliation and arbitration.

A policy of promoting collective bargaining as an institution for joint decision-making will require the consideration of specific measures which are not likely to be considered necessary if collective bargaining is dealt with only as another method of settling disputes. National experiences show various types of measures which can be taken to promote collective bargaining as such an institution.

Among the most important of these measures is that directed at resolving the problem of trade union recognition for the purpose of collective bargaining. In certain countries it may suffice to leave the question of recognition for free agreement (or disagreement) between the parties concerned, and this appears to be generally the position in industry-wide bargaining. In many countries where plant-level bargaining is the norm, the question of recognition has been a frequent and serious cause of conflict; and the development of collective bargaining can be seriously handicapped unless effective measures are taken to deal with it. This raises the question whether disputes over recognition should be referred, like other types of dispute, to the same procedure of conciliation and arbitration or whether they should be dealt with in some other way (for example, through a special procedure of administrative determination or certification based on given criteria of representativity), as occurs in a number of countries.

Other types of measure for promoting collective bargaining include the imposition on employers of a duty to bargain collectively with trade unions recognised as fulfilling certain conditions as regards representativeness; the prohibition of unfair labour practices; the establishment of appropriate negotiating machinery; the provision by the public authorities and the employers of the information required for meaningful negotiations; an emphasis on the use of conciliation and mediation to further and support collective bargaining as an institution and not only for disputes settlement; legislative provisions defining the legal effects to be given to collective agreements, including those reached with the aid of conciliation and mediation; and the provision of various services to employers and trade unions in regard to collective bargaining, including the undertaking of studies and surveys concerning collective bargaining procedures and problems.

Various methods have been devised in the functioning of conciliation and arbitration with a view to fostering collective bargaining. One relates to the timing of government intervention when disputes occur. It is the practice in many countries that the conciliation and arbitration authority will not intervene ex officio in a dispute if the parties have not exhausted every possibility of a settlement by direct negotiations. If this appears to be the situation in a case where a request for government intervention has been made, the parties may be asked to continue the negotiations by themselves or under an impartial chairman whose main role will be to preside over the joint discussions rather than to act formally as a conciliator.

Under another method conciliation proceedings are conducted under conditions that are as close as possible to those that characterise the direct, unassisted negotiations between the parties. This requires, inter alia, that the proceedings be carried out, as far as possible, in the same informal atmosphere and with the same degree of flexibility as in collective bargaining sessions. In such cases conciliators have to be made aware that in trying to resolve interests disputes their real function is to assist the parties to negotiate a collective agreement. In general, however, the understanding of this function is promoted by administrative policies as to the nature and objectives of conciliation, by administrative instructions and guidelines for conciliators and by formal training programmes.

Other methods of ensuring that conciliation or arbitration foster collective bargaining relate to the nature and form of the settlements. It is considered essential that collective agreements should not be considered as of a lower order than settlements reached by conciliation or arbitration. While this appears to be the position in most countries, it is well to emphasise that, where conciliation settlements and arbitration awards are apparently given a higher legal status than collective agreements (for example, where only the former are given legislative recognition), there may be a tendency for the parties in labour relations to consider conciliation and arbitration as more important than collective bargaining.

Collective bargaining is also advanced by the practice of embodying settlements reached by voluntary procedures (such as conciliation, mediation, fact-finding and advisory arbitration in interests disputes) in the form of collective agreements. This is almost universal practice with regard to conciliation settlements, although in some countries it appears that they take the form of instruments signed and issued by the government conciliator who has assisted in settling the dispute. The practice of embodying voluntary settlements in the form of a collective agreement emphasises the fact that, although the settlement was obtained with the assistance of a third party, it was essentially a product of the parties' being able to reach agreement, and this can have a favourable psychological value in the minds of the parties concerned for future negotiations.

Where the objectives of disputes settlement policy are to foster collective bargaining as an institution as well as to settle disputes and avoid work stoppages, the tendency appears to be to emphasise the procedures for voluntary settlement and to limit recourse to compulsory procedures.

While compulsory arbitration has often been opposed on the grounds that it adversely affects the collective bargaining process, it should be noted that it has occasionally been instituted as a method of promoting collective bargaining. This is the case in the United Kingdom under the Employment Protection Act, 1975, which grants trade unions the right unilaterally to invoke compulsory arbitration, first, where an employer has not complied with a recommendation of the Advisory, Conciliation and Arbitration Service to recognise that trade union for negotiation purposes, if conciliation has failed to settle the matter; and second, where an employer has failed to disclose to the representatives of the trade union information which he is required to disclose by the Act for purposes of collective bargaining and has continued to fail to disclose such information after being required to do so by the Central Arbitration Committee. In such cases the Committee is authorised to make an award specifying the terms and conditions of employment that it considers to be appropriate for the employees concerned. Those terms and conditions have effect as part of the contracts of employment of such employees.[1]

DISPUTES SETTLEMENT AND ADJUSTMENT OF GRIEVANCES

Workers' grievances, fancied or real, are inevitable in the day-to-day relations between the management and workers within undertakings. When an undertaking is covered by a collective agreement, grievances of individual workers may be expected to arise from the way it is being implemented. Grievances may also arise from any measure or situation which the worker or workers concerned consider to be contrary to their contract of employment, to work rules, laws or regulations or to relevant custom and usage.

As indicated in the ILO Examination of Grievances Recommendation, 1967 (No. 130), it is highly desirable that "As far as possible, grievances should be settled within the undertaking itself according to effective procedures which are adapted to the conditions of the . . . undertaking concerned and which give the parties concerned every assurance of objectivity." In practice, grievance procedures often include a number of steps, and the last step within the undertaking will generally involve discussion between the top management and the workers' representative or the union concerned. This process is essentially

27

one of joint discussion between the parties for resolving an issue by agreement on both sides, and in this sense is essentially similar to the process of negotiating a collective agreement. While the two processes (grievance procedures and collective bargaining) differ over the nature of the issues involved, the resolution of an issue in both processes depends on a joint decision and agreement by the parties. If no agreement is reached in settling a grievance within the undertaking and the worker or trade union insists on pursuing the claim further, a dispute may be said to have arisen for purposes of outside intervention.

Grievance disputes belong to the category of rights or individual disputes to which reference was made earlier. Where no other method has been provided for by legislation or agreement for their final settlement, they will be referred to the normal conciliation and arbitration machinery maintained by the government for settling labour disputes or to the ordinary courts of law. In certain countries these disputes are settled, under industry-wide collective agreements, by a procedure of joint examination between the employers' and workers' organisations concerned. Where these organisations fail to reach agreement and in the absence of other agreed arrangements, the state conciliation and arbitration machinery will be available for settling the disputes. However, as previously indicated, labour courts have been set up in a good number of countries for settling rights or individual disputes, while in some other countries private arbitration has been provided for by collective agreements for their final settlement. In these countries grievance disputes which come within the competence of labour courts or private arbitrators will not normally be brought before the state conciliation and arbitration machinery.

If, within an undertaking, for want of an effective grievance procedure, an excessive number of grievances become open disputes, a situation is created the adverse effects of which can go beyond the undertaking. As far as the undertaking itself is concerned, an accumulation of unsettled grievances is bad for employees' morale and for the climate of labour-management relations within it. Among other consequences, it can heighten the workers' feeling that injustice is being done to them, thus increasing the danger that any minor dispute will flare up into a major conflict. If too many grievances remain unsettled within the undertaking, this can also cause difficulties for the external machinery of disputes settlement to which they will eventually be referred. The machinery's case load may become too heavy because of such disputes, leading to inevitable delays and perhaps inefficiency in the processing of cases; additional expenses have to be incurred and additional efforts expended.

DISPUTES SETTLEMENT AND STRIKES AND LOCKOUTS

As previously indicated, one of the main objectives of conciliation and arbitration is the avoidance and prevention of strikes and lockouts. For this purpose a particular settlement procedure may be intended either as an obligatory substitute for industrial action or as a voluntary alternative to industrial action.

Settlement procedures as an obligatory
substitute for industrial action

Where a procedure involves empowering a third party to make a legally
binding decision on the terms on which a dispute is to be settled, and where it can
be initiated at the instance of only one of the parties to the dispute or of the
competent authority, the procedure may be said to be intended as a substitute
for the right to strike or to lock out.

There has been practically no controversy over the use of certain settlement
procedures (e.g. special labour courts or compulsory arbitration) as a substitute
for industrial action in legal or rights disputes, which are decided on the basis of
existing provisions of law, contract or agreement. The established procedure for
these cases may thus be considered to have rendered the strike or lockout a
needless instrument for obtaining justice. In some countries the mere availability of the procedure may be enough to ensure resort to it in such disputes in
place of strikes (e.g. under the labour court systems in Belgium, France and
Switzerland). In certain other countries, where the established procedure was
conceived against the background of collective bargaining and trade union
action, the legislative intention to make it a substitute for industrial action has
been reinforced by prohibitions against strikes and lockouts. Such prohibitions
exist in connection with the labour court systems in, for example, Austria, the
Federal Republic of Germany, Sweden and Trinidad and Tobago; and a
substantially similar situation obtains with respect to the labour court systems in
Argentina, the Dominican Republic, Uruguay and other Latin American
countries, where the right to strike or to lock out is permitted only in relation to
collective labour disputes. In Canada (federal jurisdiction), where arbitration of
rights disputes is compulsory, no strike or lockout may be declared except in
connection with a "dispute". However, the legislative definition of the term
"dispute" is limited to a dispute arising in connection with the negotiation of a
collective agreement. This definition does not include a difference over the
interpretation or application of a collective agreement, and as a result strikes and
lockouts are not permitted in connection with this category of dispute.[2]

The special administrative procedures established in a number of countries
for the prevention of acts of anti-union discrimination in employment (unfair
labour or industrial practices) and for the settlement of disputes over the
recognition of trade unions for purposes of collective bargaining may be said to
be also intended as substitutes for industrial action. In these cases the
administrative authority exercises its jurisdiction and powers according to
certain principles or criteria established by legislation, and its decisions are thus
really intended to give effect to these principles and criteria in appropriate cases
after investigation and hearing.

The main purpose of public policy underlying those procedures is evidently
to remove controversies over acts of anti-union discrimination and over trade
union recognition from the arena of industrial warfare. In most countries where
this system is followed the legislation does not expressly prohibit strikes over
unfair labour practices; these can often provoke strikes as a form of spontaneous
protest by the workers, and it would be difficult to penalise strike activity in such
circumstances. Therefore, while there may be no express prohibition against

resorting to strike action in retaliation against an act of anti-union discrimination by the employer or his agents, the expectation is that if a special and effective procedure for obtaining relief is available, the workers and trade unions concerned will be encouraged to make use of it instead of striking.

In view of the procedure for dealing with trade union recognition, a strike to compel recognition will be illegal under federal law in Canada; this type of controversy also is not covered by the legislative definition of "dispute". Under this approach a trade union may request an employer to accord it voluntary recognition; but if the employer refuses its request and the union insists in prosecuting its claims, it cannot resort to strike action but must have recourse to the procedure specially provided for the purpose, by which it will have every opportunity to prove that it possesses all the required conditions for recognition. Under another approach, such as that followed in the United States, there is no general interdiction against striking to compel recognition; but it will be an unfair practice for a union to engage in a strike with a view to forcing an employer to grant recognition in derogation of an existing certification of another union as bargaining representative. A strike in such a case is not a protected concerted activity within the guarantee of the workers' right to organise, and workers who participate in it do so at the risk of legitimate reprisal by the employer.[3]

In interests disputes compulsory arbitration (whether limited to essential services or of general application) operates as a substitute for and as a deterrent to industrial action. The dispute will be settled according to the terms decided upon by the arbitration authority, and a strike or lockout will not normally affect that result. In many countries with systems of compulsory arbitration, strikes and lockouts respecting disputes subject to arbitration have been expressly prohibited, either by legislative provisions or by clauses in arbitration awards. As previously indicated, the question of compulsory arbitration and its role in the prevention of strikes and lockouts is a highly controversial issue in many countries.

Settlement procedures may be established as a substitute for industrial action not only by legislation but also on a voluntary basis by the parties concerned, by means of a collective agreement. In quite a number of countries collective agreements have been concluded that set up joint machinery for settling disputes that may arise during the period of the validity of the agreement between the parties. Since national practices in this connection will be discussed in Chapter 4, the only important point that may be emphasised at this stage is that such collective agreements also usually provide that the parties shall not resort to strikes or lockouts in connection with disputes within the purview of the agreed settlement machinery.

Settlement procedures as a voluntary alternative to industrial action

Where, in connection with a settlement procedure, the parties to a dispute retain the right to declare a strike or lockout at any time or after a certain period, that procedure may be said to be intended as a voluntary alternative to industrial action. The procedures that come into this category include conciliation, mediation, fact-finding and voluntary arbitration, all of which aim at the settlement of a dispute on an amicable, or voluntary, basis. When a government provides for these procedures, it in effect offers to employers and workers the choice of seeking a settlement of disputes between them through such procedures or by a trial of strength.

Voluntary settlement procedures may be intended as an alternative to industrial action in disputes over rights, over acts of anti-union discrimination and over trade union recognition when such disputes are not subjected to compulsory settlement by special labour courts or by arbitration or administrative tribunals. However, the use of settlement procedures as a voluntary alternative to strikes and lockouts is of especial importance in connection mainly with interests disputes, in relation to which the settlement procedures may be regarded as being essentially an extension of collective bargaining.

Where the parties are not denied the freedom to engage in industrial action, it is still desirable that strikes and lockouts should be avoided as far as possible. For this reason, in actual disputes, it is generally the aim of public policy to obtain a postponement of the commencement of a strike or lockout. By such postponement the settlement procedures are given an opportunity to perform their beneficial role. When a strike or lockout takes place, the process of settlement generally becomes more difficult.

The postponement of strike or lockout action may be effected on a voluntary basis or by temporary legislative restrictions. Voluntary postponement may be provided for in connection with an agreed disputes settlement machinery or in a collective agreement, or may be obtained on an ad hoc basis.

The agreed disputes settlement machinery may consist only of conciliation or arbitration with a non-binding award. In such a case the collective agreement setting up the machinery may provide that neither party shall engage in a work stoppage without previous recourse to the agreed procedure and while it is in progress. For example, in the Model Conciliation Agreement agreed to by the German Confederation of Trade Unions and the German Confederation of Employers' Associations,[4] it is provided in Section 7 that "the parties shall refrain from direct action contrary to the objective of Section 1 during the conciliation procedure (peace obligation)" and that "such action may be resorted to only when the conciliation procedure has failed".

In some countries basic agreements between central organisations of employers and workers contain provisions for postponing strikes and lockouts. The first notable example is the September Agreement (1899) between the Danish Employers' Confederation and the National Confederation of Danish Trade Unions, which provided that no stoppage of work could be effected unless notice had been served upon the executive committee of the other central organisation.[5]

Provisions to postpone strikes and lockouts were also embodied in the Basic Agreement of 1962[6] between the Cyprus Employers Consultative Association and the four central workers' organisations in Cyprus (prohibition of strike or lockout during mediation by the Ministry of Labour and in case of voluntary arbitration), in the General Agreement of 1946 between the Finnish Employers' Confederation and the Confederation of Finnish Trade Unions (notice of intended work stoppage),[7] in the General Collective Agreement on the

Regulation of Labour Relations of 1967 between the Manufacturers' Association of Israel and the Trade Union Department of the Histadrut (notice of proposed strike or lockout),[8] and in the Basic Agreement of 1938 between the Swedish Employers' Confederation and the Confederation of Swedish Trade Unions (notice of contemplated action).[9]

Voluntary postponement of industrial action may also take place on an ad hoc basis, mainly by the use of persuasion upon the parties, if not by their own volition. It may be noted in this connection that under the ILO Voluntary Conciliation and Arbitration Recommendation, 1951 (No. 92), if a dispute has been submitted to a conciliation procedure or to arbitration with the consent of all the parties concerned, the latter should be encouraged to abstain from strikes and lockouts while conciliation or arbitration is in progress.

In a number of countries public policy relies exclusively on voluntary restraints (over the country as a whole or in large sectors of the economy) to postpone strikes and lockouts. One of the important questions of labour relations policy is whether such an approach should be considered sufficient or whether some kind of legislative restraint would be necessary, what form it should take and to what industries it should apply.

Various types of legislative provision have been devised for postponing the commencement of a strike or lockout.[10] Under one type of provision a condition for the legality of a strike or lockout is that the dispute should have been reported to the competent authority. As may be evident, the object of such a requirement is to afford the authority in question an opportunity of examining the dispute with a view to assisting in its solution. The same object is attained by the legal requirement that no stoppage of work shall begin within a stated period after notice has been given to the other party or the competent authority, or after some other specified period of time, commonly referred to as a "cooling-off period".

The commencement of a strike or lockout is also postponed under systems which provide for a compulsory conciliation procedure. A usual legislative requirement in these cases is that there shall be no stoppage of work before the conciliation procedure is exhausted or while it is in progress. Under another arrangement the law may authorise a conciliator to urge the parties, pending a settlement, not to strike or lock out. The prohibition against strikes or lockouts may be extended to the pendency of voluntary arbitration proceedings.

In principle, after the period of postponement, the parties recover their full freedom of action. One of the main problems in this connection is the length of such a period, which is more serious if the violation of the prohibition against strikes or lockouts is punishable. That it is of essential importance that it should be a reasonable period seems to be indisputable, although views may differ on what is to be considered a reasonable period. The effectiveness of an intended strike or lockout which depends on timing may be nullified by an excessively long period of postponement.

When legislation is adopted or a collective agreement is concluded, the reasonableness of a proposed period of postponement can be debated in advance, in connection with defining a period of advance notice of the intention to declare a strike or lockout or a cooling-off period; but when the period of postponement is linked to the pendency of conciliation or arbitration proceedings, the problem of reasonableness of the period becomes more complicated and other problems also arise. It becomes important, for example, to establish rules for fixing the dates on which the proceedings will be considered to have been commenced and to have been terminated.

With regard to conciliation, the period of postponement will vary according to the duration of the proceedings. A conciliator will require more time to settle a dispute involving more complicated issues or harder attitudes on the part of the parties than in other cases. There is thus a potential conflict between the need to fix a reasonable period of postponement and the need of a conciliator for sufficient time to work out a settlement. Probably partly with a view to overcoming this problem (but mainly to avoid unnecessary delays), the legislation in some countries fixes a period for concluding conciliation proceedings with the possibility of extension where necessary.

One further problem may be noted concerning settlement procedures intended as a voluntary alternative to strikes and lockouts. Under such procedures the parties retain the right sooner or later to have recourse to work stoppages. Therefore, for the procedures to be effective, they must be seen by employers and workers to be a real alternative to strikes and lockouts.

It is thus clear that any system of conciliation, mediation, fact-finding or voluntary arbitration must be so fashioned that it will be able effectively to perform its intended role as an alternative to strikes and lockouts.

DISPUTES SETTLEMENT AND WORKERS' PARTICIPATION

During recent years in many countries throughout the world there has been a growing interest in different forms of workers' participation in decision-making within the undertaking, other than collective bargaining. Such schemes include self-management, most extensively developed in Yugoslavia; workers' representation on management organs, practised in particular in a number of European countries such as Austria, Denmark, the Federal Republic of Germany, Luxembourg, Norway and Sweden, but also occasionally elsewhere (notably in some public enterprises); participation in decision-making through works councils (the most widely spread system of participation, now found in many countries in different regions of the world); and shop-floor level participation.[11]

Each method of workers' participation has a bearing on disputes, both as a potential means of reducing disputes and as a potential occasion for them to arise.

Clearly, one of the principal objectives of many of the workers' participation schemes is to reduce conflict between employer and worker through the "institutionalisation" of channels of communication and influence on decision-making on matters of concern to the workers. To the extent that such participation schemes are effective, they can be expected to eliminate a certain number of causes for dispute.

On the other hand, the various workers' participation schemes provide the opportunity for new types of disputes to arise. Thus, for instance, in the case of self-management systems (such as those in Yugoslavia, where collective bargaining in the traditional sense does not exist since no distinction is made between employer and worker), differences may arise, for example, in connection with the conclusion of self-management agreements between units regarding such matters as distribution of income and labour. Similarly, conflicts may arise within the "basic organisation of associated labour" regarding decisions of the management organs; such conflicts may be referred for decision to the workers' council (the collective organ of self-management) or the workers' assembly (the highest self-management organ); in some cases unsettled disputes may be referred to associated labour courts.

In the case of systems of workers' representation on management organs, differences between the representatives of the workers and of shareholders will be resolved by compromise or by the appropriate voting procedure. Usually the workers' representatives are in the minority on such boards; even in the Federal Republic of Germany, where there is equal representation on the supervisory boards of large undertakings, in practice it is the chairman (who is usually a representative of the shareholders) who has the casting vote (in the coal and steel industry the chairman is a neutral person).

In the case of works councils, the need for disputes settlement procedures arises principally in respect of the co-determination powers accorded on some questions in several countries, notably Austria[12] and the Federal Republic of Germany.[13] In these countries works councils are empowered to conclude agreements with the management of the undertaking on certain specified questions (or are granted a power of veto over certain management decisions), and differences are subject to a conciliation or arbitration procedure. In the Federal Republic of Germany the legislation expressly prohibits the employer and works council from engaging in acts of industrial warfare (strikes and lockouts).

DISPUTES SETTLEMENT AND HUMAN RELATIONS IN WORK

Under national practices regarding the development of labour relations policy, the main concerns have almost exclusively been with the institutional or formal aspects of labour relations: the formation, development and role of trade unions and employers' associations, collective bargaining, grievance adjustment, disputes settlement and joint consultation. Rarely has public policy been directed to that broad, largely undefined area where labour relations are not of an "institutional" character, to that type of labour relations which managers and workers carry on as they perform their appointed tasks in the undertakings, and which, for want of a better term, may be referred to as human relations in work. The problems are those relating to the behaviour of workers as individuals and as members of a group, to motivation deriving from biological, economic as well as socio-psychological needs, to the informal organisation as opposed to the formal organisation, to the relations between a worker and his immediate superior and fellow-workers in his work unit, to management styles, personnel policies and management-employee communication.

However, it is difficult to pinpoint any specific aspect of human relations for consideration in relation to disputes settlement. This is perhaps unnecessary in connection with the development of national labour relations policy, although different aspects may require special attention at different times. An example may be the phenomenon of the informal group constituted by workers, any number of which may exist in an undertaking where a good number of workers are employed. Usually a spontaneous growth, an informal group will have its own common values and goals and its own leaders; it can support or promote allegiance to the management or trade union, but it can also be an element of opposition to either or both. Informal groups may not be total strangers to many cases of unofficial, "wildcat" or lightning strikes or to other dem-onstrations of workers not authorised by, or initiated even against the advice of, their unions; the problem becomes serious enough where eventually the unions have to give their support to the workers, where the unofficial or wildcat strike may thus easily develop into a vast stoppage.

Such instances will not occur often. It is rather the whole process of day-to-day relations, of day-to-day living and working in the undertaking that requires consideration. Reference was made earlier to the general climate of labour-management relations in individual undertakings, and it may be no exag-geration to say that this climate is mainly the result or reflection of the whole process of day-to-day living and working in the undertaking. The general climate of labour-management relations can be such that it easily breeds differences between the management and the workers, and these differences may easily be distorted, adulterated, exaggerated or magnified; it can be an inauspicious climate for adjusting differences and disputes.

Such a climate will generally have various causes. The workers' feelings of frustration can contribute to it. So can an autocratic type of management or supervision, and a lack of effective communication between the management and the workers. The personnel policies in the undertaking may induce in the workers a belief that the management has no concern for them as people; there may be workers' distrust of and even hostility to the management for a variety of reasons.

These are only illustrations and there is no need to prolong the list, its purpose being only to show a possible relationship between human relations in work and disputes settlement that may usefully be considered in the develop-ment of national labour relations policy. However, it may be useful to point out that many recent developments have led to improvements as regards attitudes in general or some specific aspects of human relations. As an example, the development regarding "participative" management may be cited, an aspect of which is the participation of workers in decision-making at the shop-floor level itself.

Undoubtedly, among the most significant of these developments are those relating to communications between management and workers. It is worthy of note that the ILO Communications within the Undertaking Recommendation, 1967 (No. 129), refers to "the importance of a climate of mutual understanding and confidence within undertakings that is favourable both to the efficiency of the undertaking and to the aspirations of the workers". There can be no doubt but that such a climate can also be favourable to the prevention and adjustment of differences between the management and the workers in the undertaking.

Notes

[1] ILO: *Legislative Series (LS)*, 1975—UK 2, Sections 15–16 and 19–21.

[2] Canada Labour Code, Part V (Industrial Relations), Sections 107(1) and 180.

[3] ILO: *LS*, 1947—USA 2, Section 8.

[4] See idem: *Basic agreements and joint statements on labour-management relations*, Labour-management relations series, No. 38 (Geneva, 1971), pp. 63–65.

[5] The September Agreement, which was for more than 60 years the "constitutional basis" of Danish labour relations, was replaced by the Main Agreement of 11 May 1960 between the same organisations (ibid., pp. 28–32) which was in turn replaced by the General Agreement of 31 October 1973.

[6] ibid., pp. 25–27. The Agreement has now been replaced by the Industrial Relations Code of 25 April 1977, signed by the employers' and workers' federations and the Government.

[7] ibid., pp. 42–45.

[8] ibid., pp. 75–83.

[9] ibid., pp. 168–186.

[10] See "Report of the Committee on Freedom of Employers' and Workers' Organisations", paras. 324–326, in idem: *Official Bulletin* (Geneva), 1956, No. 9, pp. 575–577.

[11] See with regard to these various systems of workers' participation, idem: *Workers' participation in decisions within undertakings: Oslo Symposium*, Labour-management relations series, No. 48 (Geneva, 1976); and idem: *Participation of workers in decisions within undertakings* (Geneva, forthcoming; provisional title).

[12] Collective Labour Relations Act, 1973. idem: *LS*, 1973—Aus. 2.

[13] Works Constitution Act, 1972. ibid., 1972—Ger. FR 1.

FORMULATION AND IMPLEMENTATION OF NATIONAL POLICY REGARDING DISPUTES SETTLEMENT

3

The issues discussed in the preceding chapters relate to the content of public policy with regard to conciliation and arbitration in labour disputes. The question of how to formulate and implement policy involves issues of a different character; although not generally as controversial or complicated as the substantive issues, they also require careful study and consideration. The following sections deal with several of those issues, namely: *(a)* the association of employers' and workers' organisations in policy-making and implementation; *(b)* the study of experience in policy implementation and the use of statistics on labour disputes for that purpose; and *(c)* the structure of the national system of disputes settlement.

ASSOCIATION OF EMPLOYERS' AND WORKERS' ORGANISATIONS IN POLICY-MAKING AND POLICY IMPLEMENTATION

Legislation is the highest and most authoritative expression of public policy. However, public policy also includes policies developed by a government through executive or administrative decisions. Administrative policies may be designed mainly to implement the objectives of legislative policy, including regulations which the administrative authority is empowered to make; but they may also deal with matters not expressly dealt with by legislation, within the scope of the powers of the administrative authority concerned, to which the legislature has not interposed its objection. In a good number of countries administrative policies now constitute a large part of the public policy concerning labour relations or the prevention and settlement of labour disputes.

In recent years there have been increasing instances of a government's adopting as its own policy a decision or recommendation of a national bipartite or tripartite consultative or advisory body, either by securing the enactment of legislation for the purpose or, more simply, by making such a decision or recommendation the basis of administrative policy. This development is itself partly a reflection of the growth of consultation and co-operation between the public authorities and employers' and workers' organisations at the national level, which has been especially significant during the past 10 or 15 years.[1]

The need to associate employers' and workers' organisations in one form or another in the formulation and implementation of labour policy in general rests on the broad principle of democratic decision-making as well as on practical considerations. While these considerations are well known, it may be advisable to emphasise that they apply with particular force and cogency to public policy relating to conciliation and arbitration in labour disputes. In the first place, in designing these procedures the public authority can benefit from the experience and practical knowledge of trade unions and employers' associations; what may appear as ideal in theory may be found to be inadequate or unworkable when seen through the eyes of those to whom it is to be applied. Second, and still more important, no system of conciliation and arbitration can succeed in the long run unless it is acceptable to the people who will make use of it, and this means in the first place that the system must be so conceived as to be truly responsive to their felt needs and requirements. National experiences are indeed replete with instances where legislation providing for specific settlement procedures has virtually become a dead letter. While the reasons for this may vary from country to country, it is almost certain that one of them is the fact that parties in labour disputes had not found such procedures to be useful.

Employers' and workers' organisations may be associated in policy-making and policy implementation with regard to conciliation and arbitration in labour disputes through bipartite or tripartite consultation. National practices reveal a wide variety of arrangements regarding the manner in which these two main forms of consultation may be utilised; and the issue that generally arises in a country is what specific arrangements would best suit its purposes.

Bipartite consultation

Bipartite consultation consists of the "joint consideration by employers' and workers' organisations of matters of mutual concern with a view to arriving . . . at agreed solutions".[2] While the question of the development of a national system of conciliation and arbitration in labour disputes is essentially a problem of public policy for the government, there is nothing to prevent employers' and workers' organisations from considering any aspect of the question as a matter that is of mutual concern to them and from taking the initiative in forwarding their joint views on it to the government. This has occurred in, for example, New Zealand in 1972 and Sierra Leone in 1970, when the respective employers' and workers' federations of those countries jointly agreed on proposals for new legislation on industrial relations.

In some countries the central employers' and workers' organisations have formally set up joint consultative bodies with comprehensive terms of reference empowering them to deal with all matters of mutual concern (e.g. the General Joint Council in Belgium, subsequently made an official body in 1952 as the National Labour Council; the Liaison Committee in Denmark; the Labour Foundation in the Netherlands; and the Labour Market Board in Sweden);[3] a similar body (the National Joint Consultative Council of Kenya) was set up in 1961 by the Federation of Kenya Employers and the Kenya Federation of Labour.[4] Bipartite consultations may also take place on an ad hoc or more informal basis, and may result in the adoption of an agreement on a joint recommendation by the organisations concerned.

Tripartite consultation

More widespread than bipartite consultation for the purpose of making policy recommendations to the government is tripartite consultation, by which the competent public authorities seek the views, advice and assistance of employers' and workers' organisations in respect of such matters as: (a) the preparation and implementation of laws and regulations affecting their interests; (b) the establishment and functioning of national bodies dealing with labour questions; and (c) the elaboration and implementation of plans of economic and social development.[5]

Tripartite consultation on the formulation of social policy and, in particular, the preparation of labour legislation is now practised in most countries, very often through national consultative/advisory bodies set up for the purpose, either by legislation or by administrative decision. In some countries these bodies have wide-ranging terms of reference extending beyond labour questions (such as, for example, the economic and social councils in Western Europe); in many countries their advisory role is primarily concerned with labour matters or measures,[6] including proposed legislation concerning labour relations or conciliation and arbitration.

In India and Malaysia permanent tripartite consultative machinery has been instrumental in the adoption of certain principles concerning labour relations which, by reason of the Government's participation in the machinery, have become part of official labour relations policy. In India a number of such principles are embodied in the Code of Discipline in Industry adopted by the Indian Labour Conference in 1958.[7] In Malaysia the main principles now being applied were adopted in 1962 by the National Joint Labour Advisory Council[8] and in 1975 by an ad hoc committee composed of employers' and workers' representatives and headed by the Minister of Labour; this committee adopted a code of conduct for industrial relations.

While the National Labour Council in Belgium continues to be an organ for bipartite consultation, it has been given an important advisory role vis-à-vis the Government in the field of labour policy, especially with respect to labour relations. In Ghana the Industrial Relations Act, 1965, authorises the Minister responsible for labour to establish a tripartite committee to be known as the National Advisory Committee on Labour, to advise him on matters of policy and proposals for legislation relating to labour and labour relations.[9] The arrangements for the various national tripartite consultative bodies mentioned above probably include in many cases the establishment within the boards or councils of standing committees to deal with certain specific questions, including that of labour relations. In certain countries (e.g. Canada, New Zealand and the United States) special consultative machinery has been set up for labour relations and the settlement of labour disputes.

The Canada Labour Relations Council, of which the Minister of Labour is Chairman, is composed of government, management and labour representatives. Established by administrative decision in 1975, its function is to consider ways and means to promote industrial peace by exploring methods and developing procedures by which labour and management may better reconcile their differences through collective bargaining.[10]

The Industrial Relations Council established by the Industrial Relations Act, 1973, of New Zealand is composed of the Minister of Labour (as Chairman), ten employers' members, ten workers' members and the Secretary of Labour, with the responsibility of advising the Government on industrial relations matters, manpower policies, industrial organisation and welfare, and of formulating industrial relations codes of practice.[11]

In the United States separate consultative bodies have been established to advise the President and the Director of the Federal Mediation and Conciliation Service. The Presidential Executive Order No. 10918 of 16 February 1961 created a body known as the President's Advisory Committee on Labour-Management Policy. This was replaced by the National Commission for Industrial Peace, set up by Executive Order No. 11710 of 10 April 1973 and consisting of members representing labour, management and the public, with an independent chairman. The Labour-Management Relations Act, 1947, provides for the creation of a National Labour-Management Panel consisting of six management members and six labour members. The Panel is to advise, at the request of the Director of the Federal Mediation and Conciliation Service, "in the avoidance of industrial controversies and the manner in which mediation and voluntary adjustment shall be administered, particularly with reference to controversies affecting the general welfare of the country".[12]

Direct contact, ad hoc bodies and meetings

The public authorities may also seek the views, advice and assistance of employers' and workers' organisations in the formulation of policy concerning labour relations or conciliation and arbitration in labour disputes through direct contact, ad hoc bodies and meetings. Recourse to these methods is generally made when the government has not set up permanent consultative machinery; but the existence of such machinery does not necessarily preclude recourse being occasionally had to such methods, as the importance of the question involved or the circumstances may require. For example, consultation through direct contact and ad hoc bodies may take place in connection with studies, inquiries and investigations preceding the actual drafting of specific proposals for legislation or policy, especially when important changes to or a major revision of existing legislation or policy are envisaged. Furthermore, consultation may be carried out through informal arrangements, including ad hoc conferences and meetings between public officials and officers of employers' and workers' organisations. Such meetings may be held to sound out the views of such organisations, or to arrive at a consensus or reach agreement on certain questions.

The need for consultation may also arise in connection with the implementation of legislation or policy, once this has been adopted. The administrative authority may be given the function of promoting the objectives of legislative policy, especially as regards the avoidance of disputes and the promotion of industrial peace, and of devising appropriate ways and means of accomplishing those purposes. Experience in the administration and application of the legislation or policy may show that serious difficulties are being encountered. In the field of labour relations generally it is essentially administrative implementation which gives real life and meaning to legislation and policy. This is the case particularly with regard to the development and functioning of state conciliation and arbitration services. How should employers' and workers' organisations be consulted on these problems of administrative implementation?

There seems to be no doubt that all the methods of consultation previously mentioned in relation with the formulation of policy or the preparation of legislation can also be applied to consultation on administrative implementation, if so desired by the government or the public authority concerned. In particular, the use of direct contacts or other ad hoc arrangements would be simply a matter of discretion and decision on the part of the public authority responsible for administering the legislation or policy in question.

As regards permanent consultative bodies, a distinction may be made between those concerned with labour matters in general and those more especially concerned with labour relations. With respect to bodies of the first type, it would be a question of whether their terms of reference include matters relating to administrative implementation; but even where the original terms of reference do not cover these matters, there would be no difficulty in having them amended so as to bring such matters within the scope of such bodies. On the other hand, bodies of the second type are invariably instituted for consultation not only on policy-making but also on policy implementation, as in the case of the Canada Labour Relations Council, the Industrial Relations Council in New Zealand and the National Labour-Management Panel in the United States.

Employers' and workers' organisations may be more directly involved in policy implementation through bodies responsible for the administration of the state conciliation and arbitration service. For example, in the United Kingdom the Advisory, Conciliation and Arbitration Service created by the Employment Protection Act, 1975, is directed by a council which includes members appointed after consultation with employers' and workers' organisations. This body lays down administrative policies for the Service, a function which was exercised by the Minister of Labour before it was established as an autonomous body, when the administration of conciliation and arbitration services was under his direct responsibility.

Another form of involvement of employers' and workers' organisations in the administration of disputes settlement procedures is provided by the Tripartite Committee in the Ministry of Labour in Kenya. When a dispute is reported to the Minister he may take any one or more of certain steps to promote a settlement of the dispute. He normally takes such a decision only after consultation with the Committee.

STUDY OF EXPERIENCE AND STATISTICS OF LABOUR DISPUTES

Governments do not normally wait for complaints to be made regarding the implementation of labour relations policy to inform themselves of the practical results of the policy as it is being implemented. It is widespread practice for experience acquired in the implementation of policy to be the subject of continuing study, to determine whether any specific difficulties or unforeseen problems are being met and whether changes in policy or in the methods of implementing it should be considered.

In most countries the practical issue in this regard is how much attention and resources should be devoted by the government to such a study and how it should be carried out. However, it is evident that the problem relates not merely to experience in the operation of the established procedures for settling disputes but rather to experience in the implementation of the labour relations policy as a whole. Nor is it only a question of the establishment of a study or research unit, its staffing and its organisational set-up; the possibility of utilising the resources and expertise of employers' and workers' organisations and of academic and research institutions needs also to be considered.

For such studies, statistics of labour disputes are essential. This subject was considered in 1926 by the Third International Conference of Labour Statisticians, which adopted a Resolution laying down detailed principles for compiling statistics of industrial disputes and for determining the importance of a dispute (number of establishments and workers involved, duration of the dispute, number of man-days lost) and for their classification (according to the matter under dispute, the result of the dispute, the method of settlement of the dispute, the industries affected, the importance of the dispute and the amount of wages lost).[13] These principles are still being applied today.

It is important to note that the 1926 Resolution deals only with disputes involving work stoppages. Under the Resolution, the basic unit (the case of dispute) is defined, in paragraph 1, as "a temporary stoppage of work wilfully effected by a group of workers or by one or more employers with a view to enforcing a demand".

It may also be noted that this concept of the case of dispute was primarily designed for international comparison. For this reason it was important to minimise, as far as possible, differences in the methods of compilation of the statistics published in various countries. It was thus considered that standards should be established to secure some degree of international comparability. The social fact which was to form the subject of statistics—the thing which was to be counted, measured and classified—must be one which presented certain uniform characteristics and could thus be brought under a uniform statistical definition[14] (such as that established in the Resolution).

On the basis of this Resolution and with the help of experts, the OECD Secretariat has recently developed a set of recommendations regarding definitions and methods of data collection to facilitate international comparability of disputes statistics. These also define the labour dispute in terms of work stoppage.[15]

The type of statistics envisaged in the Resolution has some value for studies of national experiences. Within a country they provide a basis (with due regard to changing economic conditions) for comparisons of strike and lockout experiences from year to year. They may also give some indication of trends regarding strikes and lockouts under existing labour relations policy and of the adequacy of that policy in preventing work stoppages. However, statistics on strikes and lockouts are not a sufficient basis for studying national experience in the implementation of the policy for the prevention and settlement of disputes and particularly in the operation of conciliation and arbitration. Since it is the purpose of state policy, in providing assistance in the settlement of disputes, to prevent dispute situations from developing into open conflicts by the parties' resort to industrial action, it is important to develop information as a basis for determining how far that objective is being attained and how policy may need to be altered where that objective is not being attained. For this purpose a different concept of dispute from that embodied in the 1926 Resolution would be necessary. That concept would be one which conforms to the concept of dispute envisaged in local legislation, for the settlement of which the state conciliation and arbitration service may intervene.

The decisive factor would be the submission of a dispute to an available settlement procedure, whether or not it has been accompanied by a work stoppage. Statistics and other information on disputes handled by state conciliation and arbitration services are actually being collected in various countries, and they invariably show that in fact only a small proportion of such disputes involve work stoppages, although threats of strike or lockout are often made. However, because of differences in national practices regarding the concept of labour dispute and the specific arrangements for conciliation and arbitration, these statistics do not easily lend themselves to international comparison.

In general, the statistics collected are included in the annual reports on activities of the government departments, offices or organs responsible for administering or conducting settlement procedures, which are thus intended to show, by means of the statistics on labour disputes, the volume of work accomplished by the department, office or board concerned during the reporting year and the results.

STRUCTURE OF THE NATIONAL SYSTEM OF DISPUTES SETTLEMENT

Problems concerning the structure of the national system of conciliation and arbitration are of the highest practical importance because they are concerned with the basic problem of ensuring the effective operation of the system as a whole and of its component parts.

For the system of conciliation and arbitration to be effective in accomplishing the purposes for which it has been designed, certain conditions must be taken into account in planning the structure and specific arrangements for the system (or any changes in such structure and arrangements) as well as in its actual operation. At least four conditions may be noted.

In the first place, the process of settlement must be *inexpensive*. The parties to a dispute should not incur heavy expenses in participating in a settlement procedure. Recourse to voluntary conciliation machinery under state auspices should be free of charge.[16]

A second condition is that the process of settlement must be *expeditious*. A dispute should be settled or the proceedings in connection therewith terminated as early as possible. The main problem is to keep the duration of the proceedings from being unreasonably long and to avoid undue and excessive delays, which may amount to a denial of justice and cause dissatisfaction and discontent among the workers and employers concerned.

Problems of costs and delays may arise from structural problems (discussed below) or in connection with procedural aspects (i.e. representation by counsel, observance of formalities, postponement of hearings, filing of appeals, etc.). The attitudes of conciliation and arbitration authorities, as well as their case load, will be decisive factors in determining whether the proceedings are expeditious and whether unnecessary expenses and delays are avoided.

Experience in many countries also makes it clear that two further conditions are essential for an effective system of conciliation and arbitration: first, it must be seen by employers and workers to be *fairly and justly administered*; and second, the persons entrusted with the responsibility of discharging on behalf of the State the duties and functions of a conciliator or arbitrator must be *independent and impartial* persons possessing the *necessary qualifications* (independence refers to freedom from undue outside pressures and influences as well as the ability to withstand them; impartiality refers to the attitude towards the parties in dispute). These conditions are important in order that employers and workers may consider that the settlement procedures provided for are an acceptable alternative to strikes and lockouts. Some of the most serious problems met with in providing appropriate administrative arrangements for the system of conciliation and arbitration relate to these conditions.

When speaking of a "national system of conciliation and arbitration" in labour disputes, many people tend to think only of the official machinery operated and maintained by the government. However, the important role played in a number of countries by the disputes settlement machinery set up by agreement between employers' and workers' organisations or by the parties concerned should not be overlooked. In many other countries instances may also be found of similar agreed machinery of varying scope, importance and effectiveness, which have not, however, attracted much attention.

Organisation by sector or branch of activity

The structure of the state-sponsored machinery may be considered from various angles. From the point of view of the private or public character of the activities involved, it is generally divided into two main segments: a general system covering the private sector, and a separate system for the public service. The latter system is designed mainly for officials and employees of the government engaged in public administration, whose terms of service are often laid down in laws and regulations and whose remuneration is provided for in state budgets.

In most countries today the government is also the ultimate employer of a large number of workers employed in public enterprises, and has to decide how the disputes involving these enterprises and their workers are to be dealt with. There have been three main approaches to this question.

Under the earliest of these approaches the status of workers in public enterprises is assimilated to that of public or civil servants; they are thus also covered by the public service system. This approach appears to have evolved from the time when the activities involved were managed by government departments, and it may still subsist where this method of management has been continued. In certain countries it may be followed only partially: for example, in the Federal Republic of Germany only about one-half of the employees of the federal railways have the status of civil servants—the rest of the railway workers (i.e. those engaged under a contract of employment) are subject to the system covering the private sector.[17]

In a large number of countries public enterprises and their workers have been brought within the ambit of the general system. This seems to be the trend especially in cases where the enterprises are organised as companies or corporations possessing a distinct legal personality, with the management enjoying a considerable measure of autonomy from ministerial control not only in the conduct of day-to-day business but also in matters of policy and finance. In these cases, including those in which the government is only a minority partner, the status of public enterprises is assimilated (at least for purposes of collective bargaining and disputes settlement) to that of private undertakings.

Under a third approach, a separate system has been devised for the public enterprises. This approach has been followed in, for example, Japan, under the Public Corporation and National Enterprise Labour Relations Law.[18] In France also, in accordance with an Act of July 1957,[19] certain specified public undertakings have been excluded from the general system and placed under a special system; and in Argentina an Act of 1967 lays down special arrangements for state and semi-public enterprises (as well as concessionaires of public electricity and telephone services).[20]

In a number of countries separate arrangements have also been established for certain branches of economic activity, either because they involve distinctive problems and have traditionally been the subject of special regulations or because of their special position in the national economy. Such arrangements have been set up, for example, for agriculture in Argentina[21] and France,[22] for the merchant marine or for mariners in France[23] and Japan;[24] and for the railways and airlines in the United States.[25]

Organisation according to type of procedure employed

Another way of looking at the structure of the state-sponsored machinery is from the viewpoint of the type of settlement procedure being utilised and the stages of state intervention. The question of what procedure or combination of procedures should comprise the machinery depends on a basic decision of policy: what is to be the extent and manner of state intervention in the settlement of disputes? This, in turn, may depend on another basic policy decision: should a distinction be made between different types of dispute with a view to establishing a separate procedure of settlement for each type? (See above, pp. 5–9.)

As regards the settlement of interests disputes under the general system, the state-sponsored machinery invariably includes conciliation or mediation; and in a few countries (e.g. Austria, Belgium, Denmark, Finland, France, Italy, Sweden and Switzerland) this is the only procedure that is used under normal conditions. In many other countries provision is made for some other procedure if conciliation fails; but in many of these countries that procedure may be applied only to limited categories of dispute (disputes in essential services and disputes affecting major national interests), with conciliation or mediation being the only available method of settlement in all other cases.

Where more than one settlement procedure is provided for, state intervention in the process of settlement will often consist of at least two stages. In this connection, under national practice in a number of countries the procedure of conciliation may itself involve two levels of intervention: by an individual conciliator, and by a conciliation committee, council or board. Experience shows that the more stages there are, the greater the likelihood is that the whole settlement process will last longer. It is probably to shorten the duration and to avoid the possibility of delays that in many countries state intervention has generally been limited to two main stages and that the procedure at each stage has to be concluded within a prescribed period (generally subject to the possibility of its being prolonged). (In a few countries three or more stages of state intervention may be possible, especially where appeals may be made from arbitration awards.)

From national practices it appears that the second stage is generally reserved for a stronger form of third-party intervention, with regard either to procedural matters, to the form of the proposals for settlement, or to both. Essentially the question involves a choice of policy among the following procedures: fact-finding (with or without power to make recommendations); voluntary arbitration (in any of its forms); or compulsory arbitration. However, where the initial procedure consists of intervention by an individual conciliator, the choices for the second stage may also include a conciliation council or board. Under one approach the procedure to be used in the first or second stage may be specified in the legislation; under another approach the legislation may provide for a number of available procedures, the competent authority being authorised to select on an ad hoc basis which one of these is to be used for a particular dispute.

In some cases the competent public authority is provided by law with a choice of procedures, which can be invoked as that authority deems appropriate, either alternatively or successively. This was the case, for example, in Massachusetts (United States), where the Governor was authorised, if he found that a dispute in certain essential services threatened public health or safety, to submit the dispute to a moderator-mediator, to request the parties to submit the dispute voluntarily to a tripartite emergency board empowered to recommend terms of settlement or to declare an emergency and arrange for continued production or seize and operate the plant or facilities.

Geographical placement of disputes settlement bodies

One of the principal problems in seeking to ensure an effective national system of disputes settlement is that of assuring that the government facilities for conciliation and arbitration are available equally to all parties who may be involved in labour disputes, wherever these may occur. The problem arises because of the practice of establishing the headquarters of a government department in the city which is the seat of the government, whereas enterprises are also located and disputes may arise in outlying parts of the country. Parties to these disputes should not be disadvantaged, compared with parties residing in or near the area of the capital city, in availing themselves of the conciliation and arbitration facilities; and they should be able to do so without substantial additional expenses or delays. Three main systems have been devised for meeting this problem.

Under one system a national office, which is responsible for conciliation and/or arbitration throughout the country, carries out its functions through a number of regional offices, each of which is responsible for dealing with disputes arising within its assigned territorial jurisdiction. This system, under which the regional offices are constituted as administrative units of the national office, is followed in a good number of countries, particularly with regard to conciliation and mediation.

Under a second system there is also a national office, the responsibility of which also extends throughout the country, but it does not have regional offices. Instead, its officials are peripatetic and can go to any part of the country where a dispute may arise or their services are needed. The Australian Conciliation and Arbitration Commission, for example, operates under this system.

The third system is similar to the first in that the country is also divided into districts (which may correspond to the pre-existing political subdivisions), to each of which an official is assigned or an office is set up to be responsible for dealing with disputes occurring within its borders. However, the district officials or offices are statutory authorities in their own right and are not subordinate to or simply parts of a higher administrative body. The local labour relations commissions in Japan, for example, function under this system.

Of course, in those federal States in which the competence for labour matters is divided between the federal government and the federated political units, the above-mentioned federal administrative structures would parallel the administrative structures established by each federated unit.

Locus of administrative responsibility in the government

It was noted earlier that, among the conditions for the effective operation of a system of conciliation and arbitration, the system would need to be seen by employers and workers as being fairly and justly administered, and the persons appointed to act as conciliators and arbitrators would need to be qualified for their work. These two conditions are inter-related and both are concerned with the fact that, apart from any other qualifications which they need to possess, state conciliators and arbitrators must be completely independent and impartial in performing their functions. However, independence and impartiality are not only qualities that should characterise the persons entrusted with these functions; they should also pervade that branch of the government service or institution of which they form a part. A conciliator or arbitrator can be independent and impartial only to the extent that he is permitted to be so by the policies and conditions under which he works.

One aspect of the independence and impartiality of the government office or organ which is to have responsibility for conciliation and arbitration is the question of its location within the government for purposes of administrative responsibility and supervision. More specifically, the question is whether such an office or organ should be placed under the ministry or department responsible for labour affairs (hereinafter simply referred to as the labour ministry) or whether it should function more or less as an autonomous body.

47

It appears that where an organ is vested with quasi-judicial functions, such as those of compulsory arbitration and administrative determination, the general tendency is to set it up as an autonomous body, either completely separated from the labour ministry or linked to it for certain administrative or budgetary purposes only. In the case, for example, of compulsory arbitration tribunals, in order to emphasise their independence and impartiality they are often accorded a legal status similar to that of courts of law. While such tribunals may also be given the function of conciliation, it is the arbitration function which appears to be the main reason for their autonomous status.

National practices are less uniform as regards the location of the office or agency which is to be responsible for maintaining and administering the government conciliation and voluntary arbitration service, including the constitution of ad hoc bodies (for conciliation, fact-finding or arbitration) or the making of ad hoc appointments of conciliators and arbitrators. The traditional approach, which is followed in a large number of countries, has been to place it under the labour ministry, on the principle that disputes settlement is just one of those labour questions logically within the province of that ministry, like the question of employment or that of labour law enforcement or labour inspection. Experience has indeed shown that in many countries this approach has been satisfactory, and that the independence and impartiality of the service are not necessarily impaired by its being under the labour ministry.

In some countries (e.g. Denmark, Finland, New Zealand, Norway and Sweden) government conciliators are appointed as independent, statutory authorities, while in certain other countries the bodies responsible for administering the government conciliation and voluntary arbitration service are constituted as autonomous organs. Among such bodies are the Labour Court in Ireland, the labour relations commissions in Japan,[26] the Federal Mediation and Conciliation Service in the United States, and the recently established Advisory, Conciliation and Arbitration Service in the United Kingdom. In most cases, however, the minister of labour retains certain administrative responsibilities in regard to them. It should, however, be noted that the trend towards establishing more or less autonomous bodies to carry out certain functions in the labour field, at least in the more developed countries, extends to other functions as well as conciliation and arbitration.

Among the reasons for deciding to give autonomous status to the government conciliation and voluntary arbitration service may be to give the service a higher official status in order to enhance its prestige and moral authority for its work, to permit a wider choice in the selection of conciliators and arbitrators beyond the normal limitations of civil service regulations, to insulate the service more completely from influences and considerations of partisan politics and to emphasise more clearly its independence and impartiality.

A further reason occasionally advanced relates to the role of the labour ministry as perceived in certain countries. In these countries the ministry is sometimes seen as an agency the principal function of which is to protect the workers. Where such is the view, the trade unions might come to expect the ministry to favour them in conciliation or arbitration proceedings and the employers might suspect the impartiality of these procedures. If this were the case, it might become impossible for the service to carry out its mission successfully. One solution to this problem has been to give the conciliation and arbitration service a separate administrative existence within the ministry, coupled with directives emphasising its independence and impartiality. Another has been to establish the service as an autonomous body.

Another factor which may lead to the conclusion that it is desirable to give an autonomous status to the conciliation and arbitration service is the involvement of the labour ministry in policies and programmes which affect the terms of collective agreements and agreed settlements. The government, for example, may inaugurate a policy of wage stabilisation or limitation of wage increases, in the implementation of which the labour ministry has the primary or at least a substantial responsibility. What, then, should be the role of the conciliation and arbitration service in that situation?

Views differ on this question. One school of thought holds that it will be entirely proper for the service to be positively involved in the implementation of the policy and for the conciliators and arbitrators of the service to aim at terms of settlement within the limitations established by the policy. Under this view no difficulty will arise from the fact that the conciliation and arbitration service is under the labour ministry and is performing its share of the ministry's responsibility in the implementation of the policy.

Another school of thought maintains that such an involvement of the conciliation and arbitration service would not be consistent with its own independence and with that of its conciliators, fact-finders and arbitrators, since their essential role is to assist in bringing about agreed settlements and to serve as the servants of the parties for that purpose; they should therefore be less concerned about the contents of the agreement than about the achievement of an agreement as such. The acceptance of this view could lead to a decision to separate the conciliation and arbitration service from the labour ministry and convert it into an autonomous body.

Size of competent services

As a practical matter, the conciliation and arbitration service will not be established as an autonomous body, even if there are convincing reasons of policy for doing so, unless it is sufficiently large. This, however, depends not only on the number and magnitude of the disputes it has to deal with but also on the fact that, in addition to disputes settlement, it may be given other functions (such as functions concerning trade unions, collective bargaining, grievance procedure, joint consultation, etc.) within the framework of the country's labour relations policy.

However, the question of the size of the staff of the conciliation and arbitration service is a more general one and does not arise only in connection with a proposal to set it up as an autonomous agency. Whether the service is a purely administrative unit of the labour ministry or is a more or less autonomous body, it should be able to respond promptly and speedily to all situations calling for its assistance. Inadequate staffing will inevitably result in an accumulation of pending cases and consequent delays in acting upon them, whilst at the same time augmenting the danger of hasty and ill considered action. The need for adequate staff is becoming particularly urgent as a result of the increase in the number of disputes submitted to conciliation and arbitration proceedings in some countries.[27]

Technical support for conciliation and arbitration

Finally, state conciliators and arbitrators need technical support to increase their effectiveness in their work. In considering this requirement it may be useful to compare their functions with those of the judges of law courts. The latter perform their functions in what are commonly described as "adversary" proceedings, in which the burden of presenting evidence rests exclusively on the litigants. In practice, a conciliator or arbitrator may seek to act like an honourable judge of a court of law and to invest the proceedings before him with the aura of judicial proceedings, limiting himself in the course of the proceedings to hearing what the parties have to say and making his pronouncement on how the dispute should be settled after hearing.

However, to do this would be contrary to the accepted view of the role of a conciliator or arbitrator. He is rather expected to be an active participant in the search for facts and information that would provide enlightenment and contribute to a satisfactory resolution of the dispute. Part of the information that he can contribute in any particular case would be included in the technical knowledge that he should possess as a qualification for his original appointment; but he would need to keep himself up to date and to supplement his technical knowledge with information on changed conditions and new developments, and in any particular case in which he were currently involved he would have to seek as much relevant information as possible.

National practices indicate that this requirement is best met by a separate technical staff which can collect, assemble and analyse facts, data and statistics and undertake other research in connection with labour disputes. While this work will be done for the benefit generally of employers and workers as well as conciliators and arbitrators, such a staff can also supply relevant information to a conciliator or arbitrator in connection with a pending case.

Where the conciliation and arbitration service is under the labour ministry, the technical support can be provided by the ministry's statistical and research branch. This is one of the advantages of locating the service within the ministry, as it is easier to arrange working relationships with the other administrative units of the ministry whose work has some bearing on labour disputes. In this case, however, there may still be a need for some specialised staff within the service to co-ordinate its working relationships with the other units and to expedite and facilitate the relaying of information to the conciliators and arbitrators. The question of technical support is one of the questions to be considered in connection with a proposal to establish the conciliation and arbitration service as an autonomous body, and much depends on the degree of autonomy it will actually enjoy and what type of administrative links it will have with the labour ministry; while the establishment of working relationships with the ministry's statistical and research branch cannot be ruled out, other arrangements for ensuring timely and adequate technical support may be necessary.

Notes

[1] See in this connection the ILO Consultation (Industrial and National Levels) Recommendation, 1960 (No. 113), and the Resolution concerning freedom of association for workers' and employers' organisations and their role in social and economic development, adopted by the ILO Seventh Asian Regional Conference (Teheran, 1971), which calls on each Asian country to associate workers' and employers' organisations in the elaboration of national labour relations policy through appropriate arrangements or machinery for consultation and co-operation between the government and such organisations (ILO: *Record of proceedings*, Seventh Asian Regional Conference, Teheran, 1971, pp. 219–220).

[2] idem: Consultation (Industrial and National Levels) Recommendation, 1960 (No. 113), Paragraph 5*(a)*.

[3] See idem: *General survey of the reports relating to the Consultation (Industrial and National Levels) Recommendation, 1960 (No. 113)*, Report III (Part 4B), International Labour Conference, 61st Session, 1976, para. 65.

[4] See the Memorandum of Agreement between the two organisations setting up the Council, in ILO: *Basic agreements and joint statements . . .*, op. cit., pp. 104–109.

[5] Recommendation No. 113, Paragraph 5*(b)*.

[6] See ILO: *General survey of the reports . . .*, op. cit., pp. 29–31.

[7] For the text of the Code, see idem: *Basic agreements and joint statements . . .*, op. cit., pp. 66–68.

[8] ibid., pp. 116–118.

[9] idem: *Legislative series (LS)*, 1965—Ghana 2, Section 35.

[10] Canada Department of Labour: *The Labour Gazette* (Ottawa), Anniversary issue 1975, p. 617.

[11] ILO: *LS*, 1973—NZ 1, Part II.

[12] ibid., 1947—USA 2, Section 205*(b)*.

[13] For the text of the Resolution, see idem: *International recommendations on labour statistics* (Geneva, 1976), pp. 121–124.

[14] idem: *Methods of compiling statistics of industrial disputes*, Studies and reports, Series N (Statistics), No. 10 (Geneva, 1926), pp. 6 and 12.

[15] OECD, Working Party on Industrial Relations: *Labour dispute statistics* (Paris, doc. SME/IR/75.7, 24 Mar. 1975; mimeographed). See also Malcolm Fisher: *Measurement of labour disputes and their economic effects* (Paris, OECD, 1973); and OECD: *Labour disputes: A perspective*, op. cit.

[16] ILO: Voluntary Conciliation and Arbitration Recommendation, 1951 (No. 92), Paragraph 3.

[17] idem: *Methods of collective bargaining and settlement of disputes in rail transport*, Labour-management relations series, No. 29 (Geneva, 1967; mimeographed), p. 37.

[18] Law No. 257 of 20 December 1948. Ministry of Labour: *Japan Labour Laws 1968* (Tokyo, 1968).

[19] ILO: *LS*, 1957—Fr. 2A.

[20] Act No. 17494. See "The settlement of labour disputes in Argentina", in *International Labour Review* (Geneva), July–Aug. 1971, p. 90.

[21] Act No. 13020 of 27 September 1947 (ILO: *LS*, 1947—Arg. 1). See "The settlement of labour disputes in Argentina", op. cit., p. 89.

[22] Ch. II, Section 7(II), Act No. 57–833 to promote the settlement of collective labour disputes (ILO: *LS*, 1957—Fr. 2A).

[23] Decree No. 50–391 establishing regulations concerning collective agreements and settlement of collective disputes in the mercantile marine (ibid., 1950—Fr. 4); and Decree No. 61–124 (amendment) (ibid., 1961—Fr. 1).

[24] Article 19(21), Trade Union Law, Law No. 174 of 1 June 1949 (ibid., 1949—Jap. 3).

[25] Arbitration and Conciliation (Railways) Act (ibid., 1926—USA 1, and its amendment, ibid., 1934—USA 1).

[26] As tripartite organs these commissions are vested with conciliation and arbitration functions; through their members representing the public interest, they are also responsible for the certification of trade unions and the investigation of unfair labour practices.

[27] In Mexico, for example, the number of complaints pending before the Federal Conciliation and Arbitration Board in December 1976 was 32,902, and another 17,452 were pending before the newly created regional boards during 1977 (Secretaría del Trabajo y Previsión Social: *Informe de labores: Diciembre de 1976–noviembre de 1977* (Mexico City, 1978), p. 45).

BIPARTITE ARRANGEMENTS FOR PREVENTING AND SETTLING DISPUTES

4

It was noted earlier that for certain countries the national system of conciliation and arbitration may be considered to consist of two parts: *(a)* the private system embracing the settlement procedures established by the parties themselves; and *(b)* the official system which is maintained and operated by the government. In a few countries the legislation has played a part in the establishment of agreed procedures; while these have thereby been given a sort of semi-official status, they are nevertheless operated by the parties themselves. This chapter will be concerned with these private and semi-official arrangements for conciliation and arbitration. First, however, it is necessary briefly to discuss collective bargaining itself as a method of settling disputes.

COLLECTIVE BARGAINING AS A METHOD OF SETTLING DISPUTES

Collective bargaining has been used as a method of settling disputes in at least two ways. In the first place, it has functioned thus when undertaken after a strike (or lockout) has occurred, with a view to settling the claims which had given rise to the strike. As previously indicated, the earliest use of collective bargaining was of this type, giving rise to a conception of the labour dispute as equivalent to a strike.

In the second place, collective bargaining has frequently been resorted to in many countries with a view to settling differences before a strike occurs. This is traditional practice in many countries (such as Belgium, Sweden and the United Kingdom), where efforts are frequently made to negotiate a settlement of disputes between the parties before recourse is had to conciliation machinery. In some countries, particularly in Latin America, provision is made in the national legislation for collective bargaining within the framework of settlement procedures, and negotiation and other procedures of settlement are consequently closely intertwined.[1] In Sweden the Basic Agreement (1938) between the Swedish Employers' Confederation and the Confederation of Swedish Trade Unions[2] provides in its Chapter II that "should a dispute arise regarding working conditions or other relations between the two parties, action may not

53

be taken as referred to under articles 7 and 8 [concerning strikes, lockouts, etc.] below, before either party has sought, through negotiations with the other party . . . , to bring about a settlement of the issue under dispute. It is incumbent upon either party to enter into such negotiations upon the request of the other party."

AGREED CONCILIATION AND ARBITRATION PROCEDURES

Instead of relying on the facilities for conciliation and arbitration provided by the State, the parties to a collective bargaining relationship may establish their own arrangements for settling future disputes between them. Under such arrangements the agreed procedures of conciliation and/or arbitration will be operated by the parties solely on the basis of their responsibility, as in the case of collective bargaining. As part of that responsibility, the parties will also bear the costs of operating the procedures.

So far there are still only a few countries where agreed procedures of conciliation and arbitration play an important role in the national system of disputes settlement. It seems, however, that this is an area of labour relations which is especially rich in potential for future development; there is possibly no country which may not hope to achieve a larger measure of industrial peace and national well-being through agreed procedures for preventing and settling labour disputes.

Advantages of agreed procedures

Of the various reasons motivating the parties in deciding to establish such procedures, perhaps the most important in purely voluntary systems is their desire to avoid strikes or lockouts (and the losses which such action usually entails) when they are unable to settle issues in disputes. Accordingly, collective agreements establishing procedures for settling unresolved disputes often make provision for what is known as the peace obligation, under which the parties undertake not to resort to a strike or lockout during the period and under the conditions specified in the agreement.

By establishing their own arrangements for conciliation and arbitration, the parties can also develop a procedure to suit their particular circumstances and needs. While the initial procedure agreed upon will be the result of their considered judgement, they retain the freedom and flexibility to adjust it. They may do so in order to make it work more satisfactorily or to reduce delays and expenses in its operation, as experience or changed circumstances may warrant. As the agreed procedure is the parties' own creation, they will normally have an interest in making it succeed.

In comparison with parties who depend on the state conciliation and arbitration service for third-party assistance in settling their disputes, the parties to an agreed procedure enjoy the advantage of being able to select the person or persons they wish to perform the third-party role. They will jointly select a person for his known qualifications and experience, for his reputation for integrity and fairness, for his independence of mind and impartiality. The person they choose will thus be one who has their trust and confidence, and who is considered by both of them to be fully capable of helping them. This does not ensure that he will always succeed in arranging a settlement, but it is a favourable condition for his effectiveness in performing his third-party role.

When the conciliator or arbitrator is appointed on a permanent (and not an ad hoc) basis, he is likely to gain a better knowledge of the parties, of their relationship and of the conditions of the industry, which can increase his capability and effectiveness. He is also likely to develop a personal interest in the long-term development of the parties' relationship and to be guided in his recommendations or decisions by that consideration. Where the parties so desire, his usefulness may extend beyond that of simply helping them to resolve disputed issues. He can become an important source of friendly and constructive advice and suggestions.

Agreed procedures also have advantages for the State. Perhaps the most important is their contribution to public policy aiming at the prevention of strikes and lockouts. It is probably true that voluntarily imposed restraints, in the form of the peace obligation in collective agreements, constitute the most effective means of avoiding resort to industrial strife. At least, voluntary restraints appear to work more satisfactorily in achieving the objective of public policy than legislative injunctions against strikes and lockouts, and they are generally free from the kind of bitter controversy usually engendered by attempts to prohibit strikes and lockouts by legislation.

Another advantage of agreed procedures for the State is one of economy. A dispute which is settled and terminated through an agreed procedure is a dispute with which the state conciliation and arbitration service does not have to be concerned. Agreed procedures can substantially reduce the number of disputes in which that service has to intervene, or in respect of which the State has to provide facilities for conciliation or arbitration; a smaller staff and lower financial resources would be required than would otherwise be the case.

When one considers the advantages of agreed procedures for the parties concerned and for the State, it may seem strange that they are not more prevalent and up to now are important in only a few countries. It may indeed be asked why more employers and trade unions have not agreed to set up their own arrangements for preventing and settling disputes. The various factors involved in the development and growth of agreed procedures are discussed in the following pages.

DEVELOPMENTS IN VARIOUS COUNTRIES

The countries in which an important proportion of labour disputes are settled through agreed procedures of conciliation and arbitration include Belgium, Canada, Denmark, the Federal Republic of Germany, Sweden, Switzerland, the United Kingdom and the United States. In Canada, Denmark, the Philippines and the United States the agreed procedures have assumed importance in connection mainly with grievance disputes. Significant developments concerning agreed procedures have also taken place in certain other countries, including India, Italy and Kenya. Grievance procedures are also

55

commonly included in an increasing number of collective agreements concluded in large undertakings in Mexico, Venezuela and other Latin American countries.

United Kingdom

The earliest known instances of agreed procedures for preventing and settling labour disputes appear to have occurred in the United Kingdom. Almost from the beginning they have developed as an essential feature of the British system of industry-wide collective bargaining. In effect, under this system of bargaining "the resulting agreements can be classified into substantive agreements, which deal with matters such as rates of pay, hours of work, overtime rates and holiday arrangements, and procedural agreements dealing with the procedures for reaching substantive agreements and for dealing with disputes which may arise in the establishments within the industry".[3]

At an early stage in the development of collective bargaining in the United Kingdom, the parties were faced with a question concerning the form of permanent machinery for collective bargaining. It was A. J. Mundella, from the inspiration, it is said, of the French *conseils des prud'hommes* (see above, pp. 5–6), who was instrumental in the establishment of the first joint board of any lasting importance, the one set up in 1860[4] for the hosiery trade in Nottingham. In 1864, in seeking the settlement of a threatened strike in the building trade in Wolverhampton, Rupert Kettle was able to persuade the parties to set up a permanent arbitration board to deal with future disputes. The Nottingham and Wolverhampton boards served as models for similar bodies in the same, as well as in other, trades in other localities.[5]

As well as being confined to local areas, these early boards did not involve the formal participation of trade unions, which at that time were largely organised at the local level, although trade unionists could be chosen as workers' representatives on the boards. When the legal position of trade unions was made more secure by the Trade Union Act, 1871, and the Conspiracy and Protection of Property Act, 1875, they were able to take a more active part in the formation of joint bodies. The structure and scope of these bodies expanded with the development of district/regional federations of trade unions and employers' associations, which began at the turn of the century, and finally of national organisations. The establishment of national joint bodies did not mean the disappearance of the earlier local and district boards; in most cases they were fitted into the new structure and made competent to deal with local or district questions.

Although these bodies were originally called "joint boards of arbitration and conciliation"[6] (or more simply "joint boards of arbitration" or joint committees), their primary function was really neither conciliation nor arbitration but negotiation or the process now known as collective bargaining. They were constituted either mainly as a joint negotiating machinery consisting only of representatives of the two sides, or as a joint negotiating machinery combined with third-party conciliation and/or arbitration. Of the latter kind of machinery, at least three types may be noted: *(a)* a joint body with an independent chairman, without a casting vote; *(b)* a joint body with an independent chairman, with power of a casting vote; and *(c)* a joint body without an independent chairman or constituted as in *(a)*, with provision for the reference of any unsettled issue to an umpire or arbitrator.

The joint boards or committees were intended by the parties mainly to prevent strikes and lockouts. It would seem that the willingness of trade unions to establish agreed procedures with employers and to refrain from striking without prior resort to such procedures had been a very important factor in the whittling down of the employers' opposition to trade unions and in the development of collective bargaining in the United Kingdom. It is significant that the period following the passage of the Trade Union Act, 1871, and the Conspiracy and Protection of Property Act, 1875, was characterised by the rapid expansion not only of trade unions but also of joint machinery for negotiation and for the prevention and settlement of disputes.

The Royal Commission appointed in 1891 to inquire into the relations between employer and employed took note of these developments and expressed the hope "that the present rapid extension of voluntary boards will continue until they cover a much larger part of the whole field of industry than they do at present".[7] The recommendations of the Commission marked the beginning of a legislative policy to encourage and promote the development of joint voluntary machinery for disputes settlement, which first found expression in the Conciliation Act, 1896.

This Act provided for the registration with the Board of Trade[8] of any joint board established before or after the passing of the Act. Registration was purely voluntary and did not confer any added legality to a board or to its decisions, but it was hoped that a board might thereby gain added status and weight.[9] Under the Act the Board of Trade might appoint, on application of the employers or workmen concerned, a person or persons to act as a conciliator or as a board of conciliation; but this decision was to be adopted "after taking into consideration the existence and adequacy of means available for conciliation in the district or trade and the circumstances of the case".

The recommendations of the Whitley Committee, which was set up in 1916 and whose final report was issued in 1918, led to a more active policy in favour of voluntary machinery for negotiation and disputes settlement. The Committee took pains "to emphasise the advisability of a continuance as far as possible of the present system whereby industries make their own agreements and settle their differences between themselves". The Whitley proposals which were accepted by the Government included the development of a new type of machinery—the joint industrial council, whose terms of reference were wider than those of the customary boards and in particular placed a special emphasis on consultation. However, it was not intended that joint councils should supersede the existing boards unless the parties concerned decided to reorganise them on the model of the new machinery.

The Ministry of Labour immediately took steps to encourage the establishment of joint industrial councils, including the preparation and distribution of pamphlets explaining the Committee's recommendations and suggestions on how joint councils might be formed. In 1918 the Joint Industrial Council Division was set up in the Ministry to take over the responsibility for the development of joint councils; among other measures it arranged conferences between interested parties, assisted in drawing up the constitution of a proposed joint council, sought to reconcile differences between trade unions as regards workers' representation and assisted in convening the first meeting of a new council.[10]

The recommendations of the Whitley Committee also resulted in the passing of the Industrial Courts Act, 1919. This Act empowered the Minister of Labour to refer a dispute to the Industrial Court (set up by the Act) under two conditions, the first of which was the agreement to the reference by the parties to the dispute. The second condition related to the arrangements for conciliation or arbitration which might exist in the trade or industry in which the dispute arose, pursuant to an agreement between representative organisations of employers and workers in that trade or industry; where such arrangements existed, they must be resorted to before a dispute could be referred to the Industrial Court.

The formation and operation in the private sector of joint industrial councils and of joint boards of conciliation and arbitration continue to be on a non-statutory basis. As regards the nationalised industries, specific provisions have been included in the relevant statutes, the pattern of which was first laid down in the Coal Industry Nationalisation Act, 1946. Under Section 46 of this Act it is the duty of the National Coal Board "to enter into consultation with organisations appearing to them to represent substantial proportions of the persons in the employment of the Board . . . , as to the Board's concluding with those organisations agreements providing for the establishment and maintenance of joint machinery for: *(a)* the settlement by negotiation of terms and conditions of employment, with provision for reference to arbitration, in default of such settlement . . .".

Most of the nationalised industries (e.g. coalmining, iron and steel, railway transport) were already operating under joint machinery of relatively long duration, being among the first or most important industries where joint boards were fairly well developed. In general, the main pattern of the arrangements which existed in the various industries at the time of nationalisation was continued, with the necessary substitution on the joint machinery of members of the statutory boards or corporations charged with their management, in place of the former private employers' representatives.

Belgium

As in the United Kingdom, agreed procedures developed in Belgium on the basis of joint bodies of employers and workers which also functioned as a form of negotiating machinery. However, in Belgium administrative action and legislation have played an important part in their development. In the wake of the great social unrest which swept over much of Europe after the end of the First World War, the Belgian Government sought to find effective means for the peaceful settlement of disputes on a voluntary basis. Showing especial concern for the basic industries, in March 1919 it set up a joint committee for the iron and steel industry; later in the same year and in 1920 similar committees were established for coalmining, mechanical engineering and several other industries.

Although these committees were established by the Government, the Government did not act by virtue of a specific power conferred by legislation; no party could be compelled to participate in a committee against its will; and the establishment of a committee was often the result of laborious negotiations. At first many employers had misgivings about them; in coalmining the employers agreed to participate only on the understanding that the committee should be nothing more than a research organ of a purely consultative character which would die out with the solution of the problem for which it was created.[11]

Those early committees were in fact called "study committees", with precise and limited terms of reference. However, with favourable experience of their working, the earlier doubts were largely dissipated. They were given a larger role; their permanent character was recognised; and they came to be known simply as "national joint committees" (without the "study" appellation). While their creation was mainly inspired by the need for the peaceful settlement of strikes and lockouts, their effectiveness was more evident in the prevention of disputes, through the peaceful negotiation of collective agreements.

Requests for the institution of joint committees came generally from the workers. However, until 1936 only very few more committees were established. In some cases the workers' request for the establishment of a committee encountered insurmountable opposition from the employers. On the other hand, some unions were indifferent to joint committees, preferring to deal directly with the employers or their association. In certain industries the workers were not sufficiently organised to think of negotiating with the employers.[12] A series of strikes in 1936 brought a revival of interest in joint committees and they rapidly grew in number; by the eve of the Second World War there were joint committees covering nearly every industrial activity in the country.[13]

After the end of the war it was decided to place the joint committees on a more stable statutory basis. This was done in 1945 through a Legislative Order respecting joint committees,[14] supplemented by a Royal Order of the same year laying down regulations concerning their operation and internal procedure. Their legal status is now governed by an Act of 5 December 1968 regarding collective industrial agreements and joint committees.[15] Under this Act it is the duty of a joint committee or subcommittee, inter alia, to: *(a)* collaborate in the drafting of collective agreements by the organisations represented; and *(b)* prevent or bring about the conciliation of disputes between employers and workers. Under the Act joint committees may be established by the Crown, at its own initiative or at the request of one or more employers' or workers' organisations. At the request of a joint committee, the Crown may also establish one or more joint subcommittees.

A joint committee (or subcommittee) is composed of an equal number of representatives of employers and workers, together with a chairman and a vice-chairman and two or more secretaries. The employers' and workers' members are appointed by the Crown from candidates nominated by representative employers' and workers' organisations. The chairman and vice-chairman are also appointed by the Crown, from among persons competent in social affairs. In practice they are chosen from the Ministry of Labour or are high administrative officials of the central Government. The secretaries are provided by the Ministry of Labour.

Only the employers' and workers' members are entitled to vote, and all decisions are normally taken by a unanimous vote of all the members present. Each joint committee or subcommittee draws up its own standing orders.

Two types of organ were evolved by which the joint committees performed their conciliation function: one was a smaller committee composed of some of the members of the joint committee; the other was a permanent conciliation office which included, in addition to employers' and workers' members, the chairman of the joint committee and a secretary. Generally, such arrangements were established by collective agreement or under the standing orders of the joint committee concerned.

Switzerland

In Switzerland too there was an early recognition in public policy of agreed disputes settlement procedures. Under the federal Factory Act, 1914, a cantonal conciliation office may not intervene in a dispute where the parties have set up their own joint machinery for conciliation.[16] A similar principle is embodied in the Act of 12 February 1949 respecting industrial disputes,[17] under which the federal administration may undertake conciliation in the case envisaged in the Act; it may do so "only . . . if attempts to bring about conciliation between the parties by direct negotiation have failed, and only if no joint contractual conciliation or arbitration board exists".

As a matter of practice, the present system of agreed procedures in Switzerland had its origins in a collective agreement on "labour peace", concluded in July 1937 between the employers' and workers' organisations in the machine and metallurgical industries. It is interesting to note that this seminal agreement had as its background the world-wide economic crisis of the 1930s and that the immediate occasion for the agreement was an attempt by the Government to institute a system of compulsory arbitration. Because of the crisis the Swiss franc had been devalued and it was feared that price increases would follow, which in turn would generate demands for wage increases. Faced with this possibility, in November 1936 the Federal Council issued an Order providing for final arbitration by the administrative authority in collective wage disputes.

As neither the employers' nor the workers' organisations in the machine and metallurgical industries desired such intervention by the Government, they agreed to avoid the effects of the Order by establishing their own machinery for conciliation and arbitration, combined with a mutual undertaking on the maintenance of industrial peace. A collective agreement for these purposes was signed on 19 July 1937, originally with a period of validity fixed at two years.[18] Since then it has been renewed a number of times, with some modifications and with a longer period of validity (five years).[19] It has served as a model for similar agreements in various other industries. These "labour peace" agreements—now frequently included in agreements covering conditions of employment as well—have been an important factor in the development of labour relations in Switzerland.

Federal Republic of Germany

In the Federal Republic of Germany also there is a legislative framework for the development of agreed procedures. Under Law No. 35 concerning conciliation and arbitration, dated 20 April 1946,[20] the interested parties may establish by collective agreement a procedure to be followed in the prevention and settlement of labour disputes. Further, it imposes on the labour administration in each Land (territorial unit) the function of promoting the establishment of agreed machinery for the negotiation of collective agreements and for the settlement of labour disputes.[21]

As regards interests disputes, the present system of agreed procedures is practically an outgrowth of the conciliation agreement concluded in 1954[22] between the German Confederation of Trade Unions and the German Confederation of Employers' Associations. By this agreement the two confederations expressed their conviction "that any disputes relative to the conclusion of collective agreements should be settled not by the decision of state-appointed bodies but exclusively through agreed conciliation machinery". Recognising the necessity for the parties to collective agreements to establish the requisite machinery for the purpose, the two confederations agreed upon certain proposals concerning a model conciliation agreement, the speedy implementation of which they recommended to their affiliated organisations, without prejudice to modifications in particular cases.

This model conciliation agreement provides that "the parties hereby agree on a conciliation procedure which shall come into operation when previous free collective bargaining between the parties has not led to an agreement". It then provides that conciliation boards shall be set up to implement the conciliation procedure, which boards shall have priority over any statutory conciliation machinery. Other suggested provisions deal with the composition of the boards, the initiation of the conciliation procedure and various details concerning the proceedings before the boards. The parties may agree to adopt, a priori, a conciliation proposal of the board.

In the most important branches of the economy, the respective employers' associations and trade unions at the national level have concluded special conciliation agreements. While these agreements largely follow the suggestions contained in the model agreement, they often differ in detail and sometimes even as regards important procedural matters. One of the earliest of these agreements was that concluded in 1955 in the metal industry. Because of a difficulty which arose over an alleged violation of the agreement, it was denounced by the union in 1959. However, the parties were able to negotiate a new conciliation agreement in 1964. Another important agreement was that concluded in the chemical industry in 1965.

There have also been notable developments concerning agreed procedures for the settlement of disputes arising out of the application or interpretation of collective agreements. However, the question is affected by the existence of labour courts which have been made specially competent for adjudicating legal disputes between employers and workers. In connection with the effects of an agreed arbitration procedure on the jurisdiction of labour courts, a distinction has been made in the law between individual and collective legal disputes.

As regards individual disputes arising out of contracts of employment (i.e. between an individual worker and his employer) governed by collective agreements, the Labour Court Act, 1953, does not permit an arbitration procedure to be provided for in the agreement which would exclude the jurisdiction of labour courts, except with regard to a few categories of workers whose employment is governed by special conditions, i.e. stage, screen or variety artists or members of a ship's crew. There is no similar limitation on agreed procedures to be followed by the parties to collective agreements for settling collective disputes arising out of the agreement (i.e. between a trade union and employer or employers' association) or as to the existence or non-existence of a collective agreement.

Collective agreements providing for the arbitration of individual disputes have been concluded between employers and workers in the theatre, merchant marine and deep-sea fishing industries. Arbitration agreements with respect to collective legal disputes are mostly a part of the collective agreement, belonging to the contractual or procedural (as distinct from the normative or substantive) part of the agreement.[23]

It may be noted that, besides collective agreements involving trade unions, the system of labour relations in the Federal Republic of Germany includes works agreements between individual employers and works councils. Under the Works Constitution Act, 1972, a standing conciliation committee may be established by works agreement, for the purpose of settling differences of opinion between the employer and the works council.[24] The committee is composed of assessors appointed in equal numbers by the two sides and an independent chairman accepted by both. The Act provides that the works council shall have the power of co-decision with the employer in regard to certain specified matters. If no agreement can be reached on these matters, the award of the conciliation committee takes the place of an agreement between the employer and the works council.

Denmark

In Denmark also agreed machinery plays an important part in the settlement of disputes arising out of collective agreements. A start was made in the printing trades in 1875, when unions agreed with employers to establish arbitration boards, and by 1900 such boards existed in most of the important skilled trades. However, it was an agreement concluded in the metal industry in 1902, specifying in considerable detail the rules for settling industrial disputes, that gave the system of agreed machinery in Denmark its modern shape. These rules provided the basis for the Standard Rules for dealing with industrial disputes, drawn up by a joint committee in 1908 and approved by the two principal central employers' and workers' organisations in 1910.[25] In 1934 a Law was passed which made these Standard Rules mandatory in those cases in which the collective agreements did not contain provisions for settling disputes under such agreements.[26] At present, the matter is governed by Section 22 of the Labour Court Act, 1973;[27] where appropriate rules for the settlement of disputes have not been drawn up between the parties to an agreement, the rules for the time being agreed to between the Danish Employers' Confederation and the National Confederation of Danish Trade Unions are to apply. These rules generally provide for conciliation and arbitration.

The role of agreed machinery in Denmark has been affected and delimited by the operation of the Labour Court, which was first established in 1910. In theory, the Labour Court's competence extends to breaches of collective agreements (including questions about the legality of collective action, as well as questions on whether a collective agreement exists or not), while the agreed machinery is concerned with the interpretation of industry-wide and plant-level agreements.[28] There is, however, no clear demarcation line between the jurisdiction of the Labour Court and that of the agreed machinery, since questions of breaches of collective agreements may involve issues of interpretation; but the purpose of the legislation is to prevent the Labour Court from becoming involved in a myriad of detailed problems, especially those relating to questions of fact or requiring special technical competence. It is considered that these problems can be better dealt with through the agreed machinery set up by the parties themselves; a much greater volume of work arising from the application of collective agreements is thus handled through the agreed machinery, while the importance of the Labour Court lies in its decisions as a source of basic labour law.[29]

The Basic Agreement between the Danish Employers' Confederation and the National Confederation of Danish Trade Unions concluded in 1973[30] also makes special provision for the settlement of disputes over dismissals. If a dispute is settled neither at the local level nor through negotiations between the workers' and employers' organisations concerned, it may be considered by a permanent tribunal set up by the two central organisations.

Sweden

Probably the best known example of agreed machinery in Sweden is that provided for in Chapter V of the Basic Agreement concluded in 1938 between the Swedish Employers' Confederation and the Confederation of Swedish Trade Unions for the handling of conflicts threatening essential public services. Under the Agreement the two confederations must jointly take up for consideration any conflict situation involving essential public services, where the protection of the public interest is called for by either of the two organisations or by a public authority or another similar body. Questions of preventing, limiting or settling labour conflicts are to be considered by the Labour Market Council, a joint body set up by the two organisations which oversees the application of the Basic Agreement. If a majority of the Council decides in favour of preventing or settling a dispute, each of the two confederations is to take corresponding measures to bring about a settlement between the parties concerned.

Agreed machinery is also relatively well developed in the Swedish printing industry. It is provided for in agreements between the Swedish Newspaper Employers' Association and the unions of the technical staff and the journalists. The collective agreement covering the technical staff was first concluded in 1939, and that with the journalists' union in 1969. These peace agreements are usually for a long-term period (the most recent peace agreement with the three technical unions was concluded in 1969 for the years 1970–79), while substantive agreements are concluded for shorter periods. The agreed machinery is based on the distinction, in the Swedish system of labour relations, between interests disputes and rights or justiciable disputes. For interests disputes the agreed procedure involves both mediation and arbitration; for justiciable disputes, after negotiation, only arbitration is employed.[31] Rights disputes occurring in the printing industry are thus referred for final determination to the agreed arbitration procedure instead of being brought before the Labour Court. The jurisdiction of this Court, which was first established in 1928, extends to all disputes relating to collective agreements, including cases involving the validity, contents or interpretation of any such agreement. Under the original Act by which it was created,[32] a dispute that would otherwise be heard in the Labour Court might by agreement be referred to arbitrators for decision in lieu thereof. This provision has been maintained in the new Law, passed in 1974, which now governs the jurisdiction and procedure of the Labour Court.

Under this provision a great number of arbitration boards have been established for various purposes. The normal pattern is for these boards to be concerned with the adjudication of special cases, and for possible disputes on other matters to be submitted to the Labour Court.[33] Perhaps the most notable example is that provided for in the 1938 Basic Agreement, under which the Labour Market Council is empowered to act as an arbitration board in disputes over dismissals. Its decisions regarding dismissals on personal grounds are binding, but in the case of layoffs for economic reasons they have the effect of a recommendation only. The Swedish Employers' Confederation has also concluded agreements with the Union of Salaried Employees and the Union of Supervisors providing for arbitration in disputes over dismissal and a good number of other situations. Arbitration is similarly used for resolving disputes over dismissals in many other industries. For instance, the building industry has an arbitration board for disputes over piece rates.

United States

Across the Atlantic some early instances of the use of agreed machinery for settling labour disputes occurred in the United States. Local joint arbitration boards, often patterned on the British model, were reported in at least three industries during the 1870s. In general, arbitration was thought of, during this period and until the early 1900s, essentially as a substitute for the strike in settling basic issues such as wages.

These early developments did not prove of lasting significance, and the system of private labour arbitration which was subsequently to evolve acquired a different form, aimed principally at the settlement of grievances or disputes arising out of the interpretation and application of collective agreements. A landmark in this development was reached in 1902 when the President of the United States put pressure on the parties in the anthracite mining industry to accept arbitration to settle a five-month-old strike. The arbitration award called for the establishment of machinery to resolve disputes which in any way arose from the relations between employers and workers; but the employers rejected from the outset the idea that the machinery should serve as an industry-wide agency for the negotiation of new agreements. The machinery's role was thus restricted to the interpretation of existing industry-wide as well as local agreements.[34]

It was, however, the apparel industries (clothing, millinery, hosiery, etc.) which served as the great testing ground for the system of private grievance arbitration. When, in 1910, 50,000 workers in the New York cloak and suit industry went on strike, Louis D. Brandeis was brought in by the two sides to help in settling the dispute. Brandeis was then a fairly well known personality, having acquired a reputation as an outstanding lawyer, social investigator and legal reformer (he eventually became better known as a justice of the United States Supreme Court). To settle the dispute he put forward a protocol of peace, providing for the establishment of permanent bodies for conciliation and arbitration; the machinery would be concerned with disputes over rates as well as over grievances.

The protocol collapsed in 1916 when a massive lockout/strike hit the industry. In the meantime, however, the protocol idea was copied in various branches of the industry in other areas, although there too in most cases the machinery broke down after a few years. Although short-lived, the protocol had a long-term result: it fixed arbitration in the minds of workers as a substitute for strikes over grievances, and thus formed the groundwork for the present vast system of private arbitration in all the needle trades.[35]

Until 1935 the growth of private arbitration was limited by the relatively small size of the labour movement. However, as a result of the passage in that year of the National Labour Relations Act[36] union membership increased rapidly. Many unions were able to obtain recognition as collective bargaining agents and to conclude collective agreements. The problem of how to deal with questions of the interpretation and application of collective agreements naturally arose, and the parties often turned to voluntary arbitration.

Grievance arbitration became more widespread during the Second World War, largely owing to the President's Executive Order No. 9017 of 1942, creating the National War Labour Board, and to the policy of the Board. The Executive Order empowered the Board to settle labour disputes which could disrupt production; but it did not apply to "disputes for which procedures for adjustment or settlement are otherwise provided until those procedures have been exhausted". The Board gave vigorous support to the utilisation of existing arbitration procedures, promoted the inclusion of arbitration in those agreements which did not provide for it, and ordered the parties to include the relevant provisions in appropriate cases. While wartime controls and compulsion did not survive the war, the habit of arbitration in grievance disputes had already become prevalent. Today it is estimated that about 95 per cent of existing collective agreements in the United States contain arbitration clauses, under which the submission to arbitration is usually the final step of the grievance procedure.

In peace-time, public policy concerning grievance arbitration has taken various forms. The Railway Labour Act, 1926,[37] is notable in this regard, being the first federal enactment to distinguish between interests disputes and grievance disputes. In effect, the Act provided for different settlement procedures for "disputes concerning changes in rates of pay, rules, or working conditions" and "disputes arising out of grievances or out of the interpretation or application of agreements" concerning such matters. For the latter type of dispute it originally provided for adjustment boards created by agreement of the parties; but in 1934 this system was modified by amendments establishing a National Railroad Adjustment Board on a statutory basis.[38]

The Railway Labour Act was extended to air transport by amendments introduced in 1936 but with different provisions for grievance adjustment. These amendments, like the original 1926 Act, provided for the establishment of adjustment boards by agreement of the parties. In addition, they empower the competent authority to establish a National Air Transport Adjustment Board if it should find it necessary to have a permanent board for an air carrier or group of air carriers and their employees.[39]

For private sector industries other than rail and air transport, public policy has mainly followed the lines recommended by the Labour-Management Conference convened by President Truman in October 1945. The unanimous report of the bipartite committee of the Conference which considered the matter suggested that collective agreements "should contain provisions that grievances and disputes involving the interpretation or application of the terms of the agreement are to be settled without resort to strikes, lockouts or other interruptions to normal operations by an effective grievance procedure with arbitration as its final step".[40] This was echoed in a provision of the Labour-Management Relations Act, 1947,[41] to the effect that "final adjustment by a method agreed upon by the parties is hereby declared to be the desirable method for settlement of grievance disputes" (Section 203(d)). Under Section 301(a) of this Act agreements on grievance arbitration are enforceable in the federal courts.

The Labour-Management Relations Act, 1947, also makes it a function of the Federal Mediation and Conciliation Service to provide assistance to employers and trade unions in formulating provisions on an agreed method for the final adjustment of grievances. The Service is directed to make available its conciliation and mediation services for this type of dispute "only as a last resort and in exceptional cases" (Section 203(d)); it also assists in the recruitment and selection of arbitrators for interested parties.

Although private labour arbitration in the United States is thought of mainly in connection with disputes over grievances, there have also been some interesting developments concerning the use of voluntary arbitration in interests disputes. In at least two industries (local transportation and printing) experience of arbitration in interests disputes goes back to the beginning of the century. In recent times the most significant development in this area has undoubtedly been in the steel industry since 1973.

Local transportation in the United States is now mostly municipally owned, but interests arbitration developed in the industry when it was largely under private ownership. The use of private arbitration to determine the terms of new collective agreements continues to flourish in this industry.[42] In the printing industry an agreement reached in 1901 between the publishers' association and the typographical union provided for arbitration to settle deadlocks in negotiations; for this purpose it established permanent machinery consisting of local boards and a national appellate board. The arrangement worked satisfactorily; more newspapers came under the agreement; and similar agreements were made with other unions. Although the national agreement with the typographical union was not renewed in 1922, the practice of settling disputes by arbitration was continued.[43] However, the industry has been subjected to certain tensions in recent years and arbitration has failed to command the support of all parties concerned.[44]

In the steel industry arbitration was included in the new bargaining procedure established in what the parties have officially designated as the Experimental Negotiating Agreement, concluded in April 1973. It was "experimental" in the sense that the agreement was to apply only to the negotiation of a national collective agreement, upon the expiry of the existing agreements, scheduled for 1974. Under this procedure, if bargaining on national issues did not result in agreement by a specified date either party could submit unresolved issues to arbitration; there would be no recourse to a strike or lockout. As it turned out, the parties' negotiations in 1974 proved to be successful and there was no occasion for referring any unsettled issue to arbitration. The parties then agreed to extend their Experimental Negotiating Agreement to the negotiations in 1977,[45] when the agreement was again renewed without the need to have recourse to the arbitration procedures.[46]

Canada

In Canada the settlement of disputes arising from the interpretation and application of collective agreements is subject to what amounts to a system of compulsory private arbitration. This policy was first enunciated in the Wartime Labour Relations Regulations, 1944.[47] It was carried forward, with some slight modifications, in the Industrial Relations and Disputes Investigation Act, 1948.[48] On this question, Part V of the Canada Labour Code (applicable to workers covered by the federal jurisdiction) now requires every collective agreement to contain a provision for the final settlement without stoppage of work, by arbitration or otherwise, of all differences "concerning its interpretation, application, administration or alleged violation". Where a collective agreement does not contain such a provision, the Canada Labour Relations Board is empowered, on application by either party to the agreement, to furnish a provision for final settlement; and a provision so furnished is deemed to be a term of the agreement (Section 155).

Philippines

In the Philippines, where plant-level or single-employer bargaining also prevails, grievance arbitration began to develop after the passage of the Industrial Peace Act, 1953.[49] This Act introduced a radical change in Philippine labour relations policy, which had been characterised under previous legislation by the dominant role of compulsory arbitration. The 1953 Act aimed at the development of collective bargaining and drastically curtailed the application of compulsory arbitration, restricting it to only a few situations affecting national safety.[50] As an essential element of the new policy the Act provided in Section 16 that parties to collective bargaining should "endeavour to include in their agreement provisions to ensure mutual observance of the terms and stipulations of the agreement and to establish machinery for the adjustment of grievances, including any question that may arise from the application or interpretation of the agreement or from day-to-day relationships in the establishment".

This provision led to the inclusion in many collective agreements of a grievance procedure, with arbitration as the final step and operating under a "no-strike, no-lockout" clause. However, the practice was not so widespread as the legislative policy had envisaged; there were not a few cases when strikes in grievance disputes occurred, or in which the government conciliation service had to intervene. The Labour Code promulgated in 1974[51] introduced an important modification in the policy concerning grievance adjustment; it makes it obligatory for the parties to include in collective agreements provisions establishing machinery for the adjustment of grievances. All grievance disputes not settled through the agreed grievance procedure shall be settled through "the prescribed voluntary arbitration procedure" in the collective agreement. For this purpose every collective agreement must designate in advance an arbitrator or panel of arbitrators or include a provision on his (or her) or their selection. Grievance disputes are not to be entertained by the government conciliation and arbitration machinery (Sections 260 and 262).

India

The textile industry in Ahmedabad has had a relatively long experience of agreed machinery for settling labour disputes. First instituted in 1920 by agreement between the Ahmedabad Millowners' Association and the Ahmedabad Textile Labour Association, it was a main factor in bringing about the fairly high degree of stable relations and industrial peace that prevailed in the industry over a period of years.[52] The machinery was established following a lockout and strike in February-March 1918, which also resulted in the formation of a trade union by the textile mill workers. The workers were led in that dispute by Mahatma Gandhi, by whose efforts the dispute was submitted to voluntary arbitration for final settlement. Gandhi was not then India's national leader, but he was already a well known personality and had taken an active interest in the social problems of the region. It was mainly through his influence that the Millowners' Association agreed in 1920 to the establishment of an arbitration board to settle future disputes. The board, established as a permanent body, consisted of a member representing the employers and a member representing the union. If the two arbitrators could not agree on an award, they were to appoint an umpire who would decide on the disputed issues. Disputes which could be submitted to the board included those concerning general terms of employment as well as workers' grievances.

In 1937 the parties decided to introduce changes in the machinery in order to meet certain deficiencies which had been experienced in its operation. As reconstituted, the machinery consisted of a two-member arbitration board for general questions, and a one-member subarbitration board for disputes arising out of agreements and awards. This system of private settlement was abandoned in 1939, but the parties decided to revive it in 1952 under a different form. Under the new arrangements disputes were to be dealt with first by a conciliation board; any unsettled dispute could then be referred to an arbitration board. Experience under these arrangements showed that the utilisation of the conciliation board could be dispensed with, and an agreement adopted in 1955 provided only for arbitration.

Kenya

In 1961 the Federation of Kenya Employers and the Kenya Federation of

Labour concluded an agreement on the setting up of a National Joint Consultative Council. Under this agreement the Council is empowered to deal with all differences and disputes referred to it, in accordance with the procedure set out in another agreement, the National Emergency Disputes Agreement.[53] Under the latter agreement ad hoc joint disputes commissions are appointed as required. The work of these commissions is conciliatory; when a commission fails, the National Joint Consultative Council considers the matter. Failing voluntary settlement, it has to refer the dispute to arbitration. The method of arbitration is decided in each case by majority vote.

PUBLIC POLICY CONCERNING AGREED PROCEDURES

As was indicated earlier, agreed procedures have beneficial effects for the public and the community. They contribute towards attaining public policy objectives to reduce industrial strife and promote better relations between employers and workers. Although in most cases the purpose of the parties is primarily or exclusively to serve their own interests, the fact that benefits do accrue to the public, if only as a by-product of the parties' agreement, makes the development of agreed procedures an object of public concern, and it becomes important to consider how far and in what ways such concern may be translated into public policy.

The question of agreed procedures in the settlement of labour disputes did not become an objective of public policy in any country until late in the nineteenth century, when as already mentioned (see above, p. 57), a Royal Commission was appointed in the United Kingdom in 1891 to inquire into the questions affecting the relations between employer and employed, the recommendations of which led to the passage of the Conciliation Act, 1896. Since then, and especially after the First World War, public policy on this matter in the United Kingdom has advanced beyond the purview of that Act. Agreed procedures have become an objective of public policy in an increasing number of other countries also. National practices reveal a wide variety of governmental measures which have been taken in regard to agreed procedures. In some countries public policy includes not merely one but a number of such measures.

Absence of policy

Before discussing the influence of public policy in establishing agreed procedures, it may be useful to consider the situation in countries where there is no legislative provision on the matter and where it has not become a subject of administrative policy-making. The right of interested parties to establish agreed procedures in the absence of specific legal provision on the question may be subject to different interpretations, according to the characteristics of the constitutional and legal systems of the countries concerned; but it would seem that in most cases, in the absence of legislative provision on the matter, an agreement to establish voluntary machinery for disputes settlement would not be contrary to law or public policy, and would therefore be a perfectly legitimate exercise of the parties' freedom to decide on the rules and procedures to govern their relations.

Legislative recognition

In a fair number of countries it is considered good policy to provide for the promotion, in one way or another, of agreed procedures. In one group of countries which have taken measures for that purpose, public policy consists in giving agreed procedures legislative recognition. This is the case in the Federal Republic of Germany, where the law provides that interested parties may agree as to the procedure for settling labour disputes.

At least three other ways of giving legislative recognition to agreed procedures may be noted. One is through legislative provision for the registration of agreements to establish agreed machinery, as in the Conciliation Act, 1896, in the United Kingdom and the Industrial Relations Act, 1946, in Ireland.[54]

Second, the legislation may give precedence to the agreed machinery over the official or state-supported machinery for conciliation or arbitration. This principle has been embodied, for example, in the legislation of Switzerland, where the official machinery cannot in the first instance be called into operation in cases where the parties are bound by an agreement establishing a procedure for settling disputes. In Finland, if the parties have set up a special body for disputes settlement, the national conciliation officer may not intervene in a dispute between them unless that body has failed in its efforts to settle the dispute or the circumstances indicate that it is not able to handle the case successfully.[55] In the United Kingdom the Employment Protection Act, 1975, which provides for the reference of disputes to arbitration by the Advisory, Conciliation and Arbitration Service, with the consent of the parties, stipulates that where an agreed procedure for negotiation or settlement exists the Service may not so refer a dispute to arbitration unless that procedure has been used and has not resulted in a settlement or unless there is a special reason which justifies arbitration as an alternative to that procedure.[56]

In Kenya, Malaysia, Tanzania and Trinidad and Tobago the principle is applied in a modified form. In these countries the legislation requires labour disputes to be reported to the minister of labour, who then considers the steps that should be taken to promote a settlement of the dispute. These steps include the reference of the dispute back to the parties, if they are bound by an agreement establishing a procedure of settlement, in order that the dispute may be dealt with through that procedure (unless it has previously failed to produce a settlement).

A third way of giving legislative recognition to private disputes settlement machinery is by making legally binding or enforceable in court collective agreements establishing such machinery. This method is of especial importance in connection with agreements to submit future disputes to arbitration, in legal systems where the general arbitration law does not apply to labour disputes, being mainly designed for existing disputes of a justiciable character. In countries where labour courts have been established to deal with disputes over the interpretation, application or alleged violation of a collective agreement, such courts would also be competent to settle disputes arising from agreements to establish voluntary machinery (unless the parties have provided for another method of settlement).

In the United States, under the Labour-Management Relations Act, 1947, agreements providing for grievance arbitration are enforceable in the federal courts. Disputes over such agreements may arise not only over the refusal of a party to submit a grievance dispute to arbitration (in particular on the ground that it is not arbitrable under the agreement) but also because the agreement is imperfect or incomplete (if, for instance, it does not name an arbitrator or provide for his or her selection or cover a situation where the parties fail to agree on an arbitrator).

Legislative prescription

The legislation may go farther than giving recognition to agreed procedures and may provide that collective agreements should include stipulations establishing machinery for settling disputes. National practices applying this principle vary as regards the scope of the legislative provisions, the types of collective agreement to which it applies, the types of dispute to be covered by the agreed machinery and supporting provisions.

This practice is followed in the United Kingdom with respect to the nationalised industries. As noted earlier, the various Acts respecting these industries provide for the conclusion of agreements establishing joint machinery for negotiation and disputes settlement (see above, p. 58), but the legislation leaves to the managements and trade unions full freedom to determine the form and procedures of the machinery.

In France,[57] Morocco[58] and Zaire[59] every collective agreement must contain an agreed procedure for settling collective disputes. The legislation in Mauritania[60] provides for a similar requirement with regard to collective agreements which are capable of being extended. The prescribed procedure is conciliation in France and conciliation and arbitration in Mauritania, Morocco and Zaire.

In Trinidad and Tobago[61] every collective agreement must contain provisions concerning appropriate proceedings for avoiding and settling labour disputes; it must also provide for the settlement of differences arising from the application and interpretation of the agreement.

In other countries the agreed procedure prescribed by legislation relates only to the settlement of disputes arising from the interpretation and application of collective agreements or over unsettled grievances. Reference was made earlier to the situation in this regard in the United States (under the Railway Labour Act, relating to air transport, and under the Labour-Management Relations Act, 1947—see pp. 65–66), in Canada (see p. 67), in Denmark (see pp. 62–63) and in the Philippines (see pp. 67–68). This practice is also followed in Ghana, New Zealand, Singapore and Tunisia.

In Ghana every collective agreement must contain a provision for the final and conclusive settlement, by arbitration or otherwise, of all differences concerning its interpretation.[62] In New Zealand every collective agreement (and every arbitration award) must contain a clause for the final and conclusive settlement, without stoppage of work, of all disputes of rights.[63] In Singapore collective agreements must make provision for the settlement of disputes arising out of the operation of the agreement, including provision for the reference of such disputes to a referee, who shall be chosen in the manner provided for in the agreement from a prescribed panel of persons.[64] In Tunisia, when the purpose of a collective agreement is to regulate employer-employee relationships throughout a branch of economic activity, it should include rules for the operation of a joint committee to deal with difficulties arising out of its application.[65]

Another form of legislative prescription for the establishment of agreed procedures for settling disputes is found in Belgium. In this country, as noted earlier, joint committees are now governed by legislation, under which one of their main functions is conciliation in disputes. The procedure of conciliation may be established by a collective agreement between the employers' and workers' organisations represented on a joint committee, or by internal standing order unanimously approved by the committee.

In all the countries mentioned above the task of ensuring compliance with the legislative requirement concerning the establishment of an agreed procedure would normally be an administrative function of the ministry or department responsible for the application of the legislation in question. This is particularly true for Belgium, where the administrative authority is closely involved in the operation of joint committees, especially through the government-appointed chairmen and secretaries. In Denmark, however, in view of the particular character of the legislative requirement, the supervision of its application practically devolves on the Danish Employers' Confederation and the National Confederation of Danish Trade Unions. In Ghana the administrative function is facilitated by the requirement that copies of collective agreements are to be sent to the competent authority.

In some countries, such as Trinidad and Tobago and Zaire, collective agreements are subject to approval by the competent authority. The same applies in Tunisia with respect to a collective agreement which is intended to regulate employer-employee relationships throughout a branch of economic activity. In all these cases a collective agreement will not be approved unless and until its provisions conform or are made to conform with legislative requirements.

In the Philippines the parties to collective agreements cannot make use of state conciliation and arbitration services for settling grievance disputes. In the United States also, under the Labour-Management Relations Act, 1947, federal mediation and conciliation services are not normally available for this type of dispute. Under the Railway Labour Act, as amended in 1936, if the air carriers and their employees fail to establish an agreed procedure the competent authority may set up an adjustment board for the parties concerned.

Another method of ensuring compliance with the legislative requirement is found in Canada and New Zealand. In Canada, if the parties fail to include the prescribed provision in their collective agreement the competent authority is empowered, on application by either party, to frame such a provision, which is deemed to be a term of the agreement. In New Zealand the form and content of the provision is prescribed in the statute and is deemed to be inserted in every award or collective agreement. However, the parties may frame a different clause, which must be submitted to the competent authority for approval. If approved, it replaces the statutory clause.

Administrative action

Administrative action concerning agreed procedures for settling labour disputes may be taken under different types of legislation and public policy and in various forms. In the Federal Republic of Germany the legislation expressly imposes on the labour administration of each Land the function of promoting the establishment of agreed machinery for settling labour disputes (see pp. 60–61). In the United States the Labour-Management Relations Act, 1947, specifically directs the Federal Mediation and Conciliation Service to provide assistance to employers and trade unions in formulating provisions concerning agreed procedures for settling grievance disputes for inclusion in collective agreements.

In Australia, at the federal level, it is provided that in dealing with an industrial dispute the Australian Conciliation and Arbitration Commission shall, where it appears practicable and appropriate to do so, encourage the parties to agree on procedures for preventing or settling, by discussion and agreement, further disputes between the parties, with a view to the agreed procedures being included in an award or in a memorandum of agreement having effect as an award.[66]

Another type of specific legislative mandate for administrative action concerning agreed procedures is found in the Labour Relations and Industrial Disputes Act, 1975, of Jamaica.[67] Under the Act, the Minister of Labour is required to prepare for presentation to Parliament a draft labour relations code containing practical guidance for the promotion of good labour relations in accordance with a number of principles, of which one is "the principle of developing and maintaining orderly procedures in industry for the peaceful and expeditious settlement of disputes by negotiation, conciliation or arbitration".[68]

Even in the absence of such explicit legislative directives, action in favour of agreed procedures may be taken under an administrative policy of the ministry or government department concerned. Such a policy may be initiated with a view to implementing legislative provisions dealing with agreed procedures (i.e. in the form of legislative recognition or legislative prescription), or in support of the general objectives of the government in the field of labour relations. Where, for example, it is the aim of the government to promote industrial peace or better relations between employers and workers, this objective may be considered to justify an administrative policy for the development of agreed procedures. Generally, administrative policy of this kind cannot be mandatory nor rely on methods of compulsion; but legislative support for the implementation of such a policy may be given in appropriate cases in the form of budgetary provisions.

In Australia, during the early part of 1970, the Minister for Labour and National Service and the Attorney-General had a series of discussions with representatives of the central employers' and workers' organisations about establishing procedures for dealing with industrial disputes. The discussions culminated in an agreement on a set of guiding principles to be observed for avoiding and settling disputes.[69] The two central organisations were to advise their respective affiliates to adopt the principles by incorporating the procedures in consent awards or agreements or by exchanges of documents.

In Belgium, from 1919 to 1945, the development of joint committees was promoted by administrative policy. Administrative action was undertaken to persuade the employers and trade unions in an industry to agree on establishing such a committee. The establishment of a committee was thus often the result of negotiations initiated by the government department concerned. The policy was, at the beginning, designed mainly for basic industries, but was later applied to other industries as well (see pp. 58–59). When it was decided in 1945 to place the joint committees on a statutory basis, the role of the Government in their development became more institutionalised, and the work is now being performed by the Collective Labour Relations Service in the Ministry of Employment and Labour.

The wide variety of activities that may be undertaken through administrative policy to promote agreed procedures may be illustrated by the experience in the United Kingdom following the Government's acceptance of the recommendations of the Whitley Committee (1917) to promote the development of joint industrial councils (for both negotiation and disputes settlement) on a voluntary or non-statutory basis. The Ministry of Labour prepared a circular letter addressed to the leading trade associations, which recommended the adoption of the Committee's recommendations; pamphlets were also prepared setting out the Committee's recommendations, with suggestions on the establishment of joint councils. The Joint Industrial Council Division was eventually set up in the Ministry of Labour, which, besides taking on the work already mentioned (see pp. 57–58), also made available to any interested industrial council the services of a civil servant with the necessary experience to be assigned the duties of liaison officer; but he was to act "only as and when required and in a purely advisory and consultative capacity".[70]

In the United States the Federal Mediation and Conciliation Service has long been engaged in a programme to reinforce the role of private arbitration as the principal instrument for maintaining labour peace during the period of a collective agreement. In order to pursue this programme more effectively, the Office of Arbitration Services was set up in 1974 as a separate division within the Service. Probably the most important feature of the programme is assistance to interested parties in the selection of arbitrators, for which purpose it maintains a roster of qualified arbitrators from which names could be supplied to the parties. The programme also includes the organisation of seminars and symposia in order to bring arbitrators up to date about current developments and significant arbitration decisions. The Service has collaborated with interested parties in devising improved or specialised arbitration procedures.[71]

TYPES OF ARRANGEMENT

There exists a wide variety of arrangements for giving practical form to agreed procedures. Nevertheless, as procedures evolve there is often a tendency within a country for certain patterns to emerge respecting the structure of the conciliation and arbitration machinery, the selection and appointment of neutral persons and the scope and modalities of the peace obligation. Before describing some of these arrangements, it may be useful to consider at least two points of a general character.

The first point relates to the two types of collective agreement on the basis of which an agreed procedure is established, namely an exclusively procedural agreement—such as the conciliation agreement in the Federal Republic of Germany and the procedural agreements in the United Kingdom—or a collective agreement which covers, in addition to agreed procedure, substantive terms of employment. In general, the former type of agreement is valid for an indefinite period of time whereas in the case of the latter, which is usually valid for only a fixed period of time, agreement on terms of employment may expire but clauses on the agreed procedure generally subsist. In another situation, unless the agreement is renewed or some other arrangement is made the agreed procedure dies out with the expiration of the agreement. This method is followed in, for example, Canada, the Philippines and the United States, where the negotiations over the arrangements for grievance arbitration may be closely related to the negotiations over wage rates and other economic issues. Most of the arbitration agreements respecting rights disputes in the Federal Republic of Germany and some of the labour peace agreements in Switzerland are also of this type, the collective agreement being usually divided into two main parts: one dealing with the agreed procedure, the other with employment conditions.

Second, in most cases the agreed procedure can be initiated at the instance of one party alone. The agreement of the other party is not essential and the latter is bound to participate in the procedure. For this reason, and in these cases, the agreed procedure may be described as contractual compulsory conciliation/arbitration. With regard to arbitration, however, there are cases in which the consent of both parties is necessary before the procedure can be activated. This is the practice in the coalmining industry in the United Kingdom with respect to national questions, although arbitration is compulsory on pit and district questions.[72] The arbitration machinery in the Ahmedabad textile industry also operated under this type of arrangement from its establishment in 1920 until 1937, when a new agreement made arbitration compulsory. It would seem that at the beginning the parties were not so sure about the wisdom or usefulness of the step they had taken, and that they accepted contractual compulsory arbitration only after a period of mutually satisfactory experience.

Conciliation and arbitration machinery

The traditional form of conciliation and arbitration machinery is a joint body in which the two sides have equal voices or are equally represented. This is, as a rule, the practice in most countries, but grievance arbitration in Canada, the Philippines and the United States is based in most cases on a single arbitrator or umpire.

With regard to the method of settlement employed, agreed procedures fall into three main groups: (a) those in which the agreed procedure consists only of conciliation, particularly when it is used for settling collective or interests disputes (e.g. in France and Belgium, and in some cases in the Federal Republic of Germany and the United Kingdom); (b) those in which the agreed procedure envisages both conciliation and arbitration (as in the case of collective disputes in the labour peace agreements in Switzerland, collective disputes in Mauritania, Morocco and Zaire, rights disputes in Denmark; and in some cases in the United

Kingdom); and *(c)* those in which the agreed procedure consists only of arbitration which is generally of a binding character (as in the case of rights disputes in Canada, New Zealand, the Philippines and the United States).

Agreed conciliation and/or arbitration machinery may be industry-wide, extending over the country as a whole or over only a district or region, covering all establishments in the industry concerned within its territorial scope; or it may be devised for individual companies or enterprises only. Some of the major problems of industry-wide procedures are connected with the application of national or regional collective agreements to individual establishments and the processing of disputes at different stages or levels. While most of the agreed procedures belong to these two main categories, there are some instances of national agreements which apply to various branches of economic activity (such as the agreement between the Federation of Kenya Employers and the Kenya Federation of Labour on the setting up of a National Joint Consultative Council, and the Basic Agreement between the Swedish Employers' Confederation and the Confederation of Swedish Trade Unions).

No attempt, however, can be made to describe all arrangements in all countries. This discussion is therefore limited to examples of some arrangements, especially those representing the main trends, in a few countries.

In the United Kingdom the agreed machinery may be constituted on an ad hoc basis or as a joint standing body. The procedure for manual workers in the engineering industry has been considered the most important example of ad hoc conciliation. A previous agreement provided for conciliation at three levels: a works conference, a local (district) conference and a central (national) conference.[73] This agreement was allowed to expire in December 1971 and a new agreement was signed in March 1976, providing for a simpler procedure consisting of only two levels: domestic and external. If no settlement is reached in the final domestic stage of the procedure, either party may refer the question to an external conference consisting of representatives of the employers' association and local union officials, as well as the management representatives and union shop stewards concerned.[74]

Where the agreed procedure is part of a joint industrial council system, it usually consists of permanent machinery. A relatively simple arrangement is that provided for in the constitution of the Joint Industrial Council for the Food Manufacturers' Industrial Group. When any difference between an employer and a worker cannot be resolved by discussion between them, it goes directly to the Council, where it is considered by a disputes committee. If this procedure does not result in a settlement, the Council may refer the matter to arbitration. The same procedure is followed when the Council fails to reach a decision on any general question.[75]

An example of joint council machinery involving a number of stages is provided by the building industry. Here the procedure calls for the settlement of disputes successively at four levels: the individual site, the local joint committee, the regional conciliation panel and the national conciliation panel. However, along with this joint council system, and in order to expedite the processing of disputes which threaten to cause a work stoppage, the parties have also provided for ad hoc regional and national joint emergency dispute commissions which can hold inquiries without delay at the worksite or elsewhere.[76]

The coalmining industry represents yet another pattern, one involving permanent machinery for conciliation and arbitration. When this industry was nationalised, national and district machinery was already in operation; to this was appended a pit conciliation scheme after nationalisation. At the pit level the conciliation machinery consists of several stages, the last being a disputes committee of the district conciliation board. Failing settlement at this stage, a pit question is referred to a pit umpire appointed by the board. District questions are first considered in joint district conciliation boards in 14 districts; failing settlement, the dispute is referred to a district referee agreed to by both sides of the board. At the national level, questions are discussed at the National Joint Negotiating Committee; unresolved issues can be referred to the National Reference Tribunal for arbitration. The scheme embodies not one but three separate procedures, depending on the appropriate level for the disputed question; there is no system of appeal and a pit question is exhausted when the pit umpire has made his decision; similarly, the last stage of a district question is the district referee.[77]

In Belgium the joint committees generally provide, in the collective agreements they draw up, for the conciliation procedure applicable in case of dispute. These procedures usually entail the submission of disputes to a conciliation committee, which may be regional or national. In the metalworking industry, for example, the applicable collective agreement provides that, if a dispute affects one company alone, it is examined first by the employer and union concerned; if no solution is found by them, it is examined by the regional organisations of employers and trade unions. In the absence of settlement, the dispute is brought before the regional joint conciliation committee, which must meet within seven days. If the dispute concerns the interpretation of a national collective agreement, general commitments agreed by a national joint conciliation committee or general principles affecting the whole or part of an industrial sector, it may be brought before the national joint conciliation committee. Disputes affecting more than one company are immediately brought before this committee.[78]

In Switzerland the agreed procedures generally followed the pattern established by the labour peace agreement of 1937 in the machine and metallurgical industries.[79] However, that agreement was substantially modified in 1974 and 1978. According to the procedure laid down in the agreement of 19 July 1978, general problems affecting all or some of the workers are first examined at the level of the undertaking by management and the works committee; in the absence of agreement, either party may request the employers' and workers' federations concerned to negotiate certain specified matters (general changes in wages, changes in the normal hours of work, introduction and application of systems of job evaluation and payment by results, interpretation and application of the agreement). Closures and transfers of an enterprise and unemployment questions may be presented immediately for discussion by the federations. If the employers' and workers' federations fail to agree, the dispute is to be brought before a conciliation committee composed of two assessors (one chosen by each party) and a chairman chosen by agreement of the parties. If there is no agreement on the designation of the chairman within two weeks, he is selected by the chairman of the central arbitration tribunal, who must also name an assessor if a party fails to do so. Disputes regarding the interpretation of the agreement which go beyond the scope of the individual undertaking and complaints of violation of the agreement are presented, if the parties fail to agree following negotiation, to the central arbitral tribunal, composed of a chairman having judicial status who is appointed by agreement of the parties for the duration of the agreement, and two assessors (one chosen by each of the parties); in the absence of a designation of an assessor, the chairman names the person concerned.

In the Federal Republic of Germany two distinct patterns of arrangements for interests disputes are found in the metal industry and the chemical industry. In the metal industry, under the 1964 agreement, if direct negotiations break down the dispute must automatically be referred to a conciliation board. The board consists of two assessors appointed by each of the parties, with an independent chairman jointly designated by them. For collective bargaining at the regional level, the conciliation authority is the regional conciliation board; for collective bargaining at the national level, the national conciliation board. The conciliation procedure is the same for the regional boards and for the national board; the parties are free to accept or reject the board's proposal as they choose.

In the chemical industry the collective agreement of 1965 provided for conciliation proceedings in two stages: if a dispute was not settled at the Land conciliation board, it was to be submitted to the federal conciliation board. This arrangement was substantially altered by a new agreement that came into force in 1976, under which there is only one conciliation authority instead of two. Members of joint conciliation bodies are henceforth appointed by the federal organisations, each of which is represented on a board by three members. The decisions of conciliation bodies, which are reached by majority vote, are binding.[80]

As regards rights disputes, in about half the 140 arbitration agreements studied in a survey the machinery consisted of arbitration boards with an equal number of employer and employee representatives, and an impartial chairman who took part in the proceedings from their inception. In about a quarter of the agreements the boards were bipartite, and an impartial chairman would be needed only in the case of deadlock.[81]

In Denmark, under the Standard Rules for settling disputes arising from collective agreements (made applicable, by the Labour Court Act, 1934 (now 1973), to all collective agreements not containing adequate rules on disputes settlement) all rights disputes must first be submitted to mediators if either party to the agreement (generally organisations of employers and workers) requests it. There are no rules regarding the composition of the mediation committee, but it generally consists of one member from each side. Mediation committees are usually composed of persons chosen by the employers' and workers' organisations concerned. The final stage of the agreed procedure for settling disputes regarding the interpretation of collective agreements is the submission of the dispute to an arbitration board, on the request of either party, for final decision. The board usually consists of two representatives of each of the parties and an impartial chairman jointly chosen by them.[82]

In Sweden the feature of the peace agreement in the printing industry which has attracted considerable attention is the parties' acceptance of arbitration for settling not only rights disputes but also interests disputes. If in the course of negotiations for a new collective agreement differences should arise which the parties cannot resolve, an impartial chairman must be called in to help to settle the disputed points by conciliation; if he fails, a three-member arbitration board must be constituted with power of binding decision. The peace agreement lays down certain guidelines: the conciliator and the arbitration board must take into consideration, inter alia, the public's justifiable demands for newspapers, the net price index and its development, the wage situation on the labour market in general and for comparable groups, productivity and the justifiable demands of the employees for reasonably good living standards and employment conditions.[83]

The Labour Market Council set up by the Swedish Employers' Confederation and the Confederation of Swedish Trade Unions is a joint organ consisting of an equal number of members from the two sides, but when it acts as an arbitration board for disputes over dismissals on personal grounds a neutral chairman is added. However, when dealing with layoffs for economic reasons it remains a strictly bipartite body; its decisions are taken by majority vote, which the parties concerned may accept or reject.

In the United States, under the steel industry's Experimental Negotiating Agreement, 1973, renewed in 1974 and 1977 (see p. 67), the negotiation of national issues is to be completed by a prescribed date. If no agreement is reached by that date, either party may submit unresolved issues to an impartial arbitration panel for binding decision. The panel would be made up of one union representative, one representative of the steel companies and three impartial arbitrators selected by both sides. Of these three impartial arbitrators, at least two would be persons thoroughly familiar with collective bargaining agreements in the steel industry.[84]

Arbitration boards are also used in some industries for the settlement of grievance disputes, but in most cases the preference is for a single arbitrator, who may be appointed on an ad hoc basis or as a permanent arbitrator or umpire (i.e. for a fixed period of time). The relative merits of ad hoc and permanent arbitration systems have been a subject of controversy in the United States and are tied up with the nature of grievance arbitration and the precise role of the arbitrator in this type of arbitration. One school of thought holds that the role of the arbitrator is essentially judicial in character, and his function is limited to adjudicating on the issues presented to him. According to this view the arbitrator, in making his decision, ought to stay within the four corners of the agreement from which the grievance arose. Another school of thought would give the arbitrator a larger role, deriving from the very nature of the collective agreement, which is considered to be only a partial or inconclusive meeting of minds. In this situation, grievance settlement is seen to be more than simply a process of contract interpretation; it is considered to become an integral part of a continuing process of agreement-making. In this process the arbitrator's function is thought to be both creative, by way of mediation and counselling, and adjudicatory.[85]

The view of grievance arbitration as being limited to adjudication has commonly found practical expression in the system of ad hoc appointment which is followed in the majority of cases, especially those of smaller establishments.[86] The usual avenue for the other, broader view is the system of permanent arbitrator, although some parties which have recourse to permanent appointment expressly limit the arbitrator's function to adjudication. General Motors has adopted the permanent system limited to adjudication, while Ford is a notable example of the permanent umpire with a larger counselling and adjudicatory function.[87]

Selection and appointment of independent conciliators and arbitrators

In a few cases conciliation bodies may function without third-party chairmen. This is the case, for example, with regard to the external conferences for manual workers in the engineering industry in the United Kingdom. The Model Conciliation Agreement in the Federal Republic of Germany also envisages (Section 2(3)) a situation in which the parties' spokesmen act as chairmen of a conciliation board. As a rule, however, agreed procedures utilise the services of neutral or independent persons as impartial chairmen, arbitrators or umpires, and this arrangement is invariably followed where the agreed procedure consists of arbitration (although the majority decision of a joint body may be made final and binding).

While the joint committees in Belgium have state-appointed chairmen, elsewhere parties to agreed procedures control the selection of neutral persons to serve therein. Where permanent appointments are involved, the parties may name the impartial chairman or umpire in the collective agreement setting up the agreed procedure. Otherwise, and invariably in cases of ad hoc appointments, the collective agreement provides for the method in which the neutral person is to be selected or appointed. The usual arrangement is for the neutral person to be appointed by mutual agreement, often with provision for an alternative method in the event of failure to agree; existing practices differ in some respects but are essentially variations of this arrangement.

In one situation the parties to the dispute make the appointment. In case of a board with a member from each side, the two members may be the ones to appoint the chairman. In either case, in order to facilitate the process, the selection may be made from a previously agreed list or panel.

Where a joint board is concerned, the chairman may be appointed before the commencement of the proceedings, so that he participates in the proceedings right from the start; and he may arbitrate the disputed issues by his power of a casting vote or by his decision. Under another arrangement the two partisan members are first given an opportunity to reach agreement on a joint award and only if they fail to do so will the neutral member be called in; he or she may have been designated in advance or the process for his or her appointment may be started only when the need for his or her services arises.

Variations also exist as regards the alternative method of appointment if the parties concerned are unable to reach mutual agreement. Under the Model Conciliation Agreement in the Federal Republic of Germany the neutral person may be chosen by lot from the names of two persons proposed by each of the two sides. In Denmark and the United Kingdom the usual alternative method consists in designating a public authority to appoint the neutral member. In

Denmark this authority is usually the Chairman of the Labour Court, and in the United Kingdom often the Secretary of State for Employment. There have been cases in the latter country where the choice was left to the Lord Chief Justice or the Speaker of the House of Commons.

In the United States it is usual for the parties in grievance arbitration, when they are unable to agree on the selection of an arbitrator, to seek the assistance of the Federal Mediation and Conciliation Service, the American Arbitration Association or the local (state) mediation agency. The normal practice is for the parties to request any of these bodies for a list of qualified arbitrators, from which the parties make their choice by agreement or by a process of elimination.

National practices regarding the persons usually selected as impartial chairmen, arbitrators or umpires in agreed procedures are affected by the number of cases in which their services are usually required, by the existence of labour courts or voluntary state arbitration machinery which may also deal with disputes within the ambit of the agreed procedures, by the prevailing system of collective bargaining and by other factors. The availability of persons actually holding judicial or other government positions for service in agreed procedures would be a matter of administrative tradition and practice, if not the subject of special arrangements, where constitutionally possible.

It is common practice in Denmark for judges of the regular courts to be chosen as chairmen of arbitration boards. The labour peace agreement in the Swiss machine and metallurgical industries specifies that the chairman of the conciliation or arbitration committee shall have judicial status. In the Federal Republic of Germany the chairmen of the conciliation boards may also be judges, as well as high-ranking government officials, university professors, Members of Parliament or other well known personalities. In the United Kingdom the choices are also usually made from well known personalities and university professors as well as lawyers.

Under the system of comprehensive enterprise-level bargaining in the United States the number of grievance disputes tends to be high and the demand for the services of arbitrators a continuing one. Since the end of the Second World War labour arbitration has practically developed into a profession; where previously civic-minded citizens served as arbitrators free of charge, today's arbitrator is usually paid a fee. However, thousands of arbitrators still practise arbitration on a part-time basis, while relatively few can be considered to be full-time arbitrators. A large proportion of practising arbitrators are university professors (for example, in industrial relations, economics, finance or law). A good number of them are lawyers, some of whom had previously served in an impartial capacity in government.[88]

Notes

[1] See ILO: *La negociación colectiva en América latina*, op. cit., p. 31.

[2] For the text of the agreement, see idem: *Basic agreements and joint statements . . .*, op. cit., pp. 171–186.

[3] Royal Commission on Trade Unions and Employers' Associations, op. cit., para. 32.

[4] Ian G. Sharp: *Industrial conciliation and arbitration in Great Britain* (London, George Allen and Unwin, 1950), pp. 2–3. Mundella was an influential employer in the Nottingham hosiery trade.

[5] ibid., pp. 185–186. Kettle was a local lawyer and judge.

[6] In 1868 Mundella observed in a lecture, "It is well to define what we mean by arbitration. The sense in which we use the word is that of an arrangement for open and friendly bargaining . . . in which masters and servants meet together and talk over their common affairs openly and freely." See A. J. Mundella: *Arbitration as a means of preventing strikes* (Bradford, 1868), cited in Sidney and Beatrice Webb: *Industrial democracy* (London and New York, Longmans, Green, 1902), p. 223, note 2.

[7] Cited in Sharp, op. cit., p. 292.

[8] The Board of Trade was responsible for administering the Act until the establishment of the Ministry of Labour.

[9] In fact, only a few boards took advantage of registration. See Sharp, op. cit., p. 293.

[10] ibid., p. 328.

[11] See Léon Delsinne: "La conciliation des conflits du travail en Belgique", in *Revue de l'Institut de sociologie* (Brussels, Université libre de Bruxelles, Institut de sociologie Solvay), Jan.–Mar. 1939, pp. 15–35.

[12] ibid., p. 25.

[13] A. Delpérée: "Joint committees in Belgium", in *International Labour Review*, Mar. 1960, pp. 185–204.

[14] ILO: *Legislative Series (LS)*, 1945—Bel. 5.

[15] ibid., 1968—Bel. 1.

[16] idem: *Conciliation and arbitration in industrial disputes*, op. cit., pp. 216 ff.

[17] idem: *LS*, 1949—Swi. 1.

[18] Alexandre Berenstein: "Le règlement des conflits collectifs du travail en Suisse", in *Revue syndicale suisse* (Berne), Apr. 1975, pp. 101–114.

[19] For the full text of the 1969 agreement, see ILO: *Basic agreements and joint statements . . .*, op. cit., pp. 217–220. For the main changes included in the 1978 agreement, see idem: *Social and Labour Bulletin* (Geneva), Sep. 1978, pp. 239–240.

[20] idem: *LS*, 1946—Ger. 4. Promulgated by the Control Council of the Occupying Powers.

[21] It may, however, be noted that even at the time of the Weimar Republic there was already legislative recognition of agreed disputes settlement procedures. Under the 1923 Order respecting conciliation (ibid., 1923—Ger. 6), an agreed conciliation machinery had precedence over the official or state-supported conciliation machinery. This legislative recognition was actually based on practices which had begun to develop even before the First World War, but the process of development was held up by the outbreak of the war. See idem: *Conciliation and arbitration in industrial disputes*, op. cit., p. 244.

[22] For the text of the agreement, see idem: *Basic agreements and joint statements . . .*, op. cit. pp. 63–65.

[23] Thilo Ramm: "Labor courts and grievance settlement in West Germany", in Benjamin Aaron (ed.): *Labor courts and grievance settlement in Western Europe* (Berkeley and Los Angeles, University of California Press, 1971), pp. 134–135.

[24] ILO: *LS*, 1972—Ger. FR 1, paras. 76 and 87.

[25] See footnote 4 to ibid., 1934—Den. 1B.

[26] ibid., 1934—Den. 1B.

[27] ibid., 1973—Den. 1.

[28] Cases involving the interpretation of the main collective agreements, e.g. those between the Danish Employers' Confederation and the National Confederation of Danish Trade Unions, belong to the Labour Court.

[29] See Walter Galenson: *The Danish system of labor relations: A study in industrial peace* (Cambridge, Mass., Harvard University Press, 1952), pp. 209–232; and Per Jacobsen: "Denmark", pp.174–203, in R. Blanpain (ed.): *International encyclopaedia for labour law and industrial relations* (Deventer, Kluwer, 1977).

[30] This Basic Agreement replaced the 1960 Main Agreement (see ILO: *Basic agreements and joint statements . . .*, op. cit., pp. 28–32), which contained similar provisions on the settlement of disputes relating to dismissal.

[31] See Folke Schmidt: "The settlement of employment grievances in Sweden", in Aaron: *Labour courts and grievance settlement in Western Europe*, op. cit., pp. 236–238.

[32] ILO: *LS*, 1928—Swe. 3.

[33] Schmidt, op. cit. p. 227.

[34] R. W. Fleming: *The labor arbitration process* (Urbana, Ill., University of Illinois Press, 1965), pp. 2–4.

[35] ibid., pp. 6–8. See also William Gomberg: "Special study committees", in John T. Dunlop and Neil W. Chamberlain (eds.): *Frontiers of collective bargaining* (New York, Harper and Row, 1967), pp. 235–251; and Paul M. Herzog and Morris Stone: "Voluntary labour arbitration in the United States", in *International Labour Review*, Oct. 1960, pp. 301–326.

[36] ILO: *LS*, 1935—USA 1.

[37] ibid., 1926—USA 1.

[38] ibid., 1934—USA 1.

[39] ibid., 1936—USA 1.

[40] Quoted in Fleming, op. cit., pp. 18–19.

[41] ILO: *LS*, 1947—USA 2.

[42] Charles J. Morris: "The role of interest arbitration in a collective bargaining system", in B. Aaron et al.: *The future of labor arbitration in America* (New York, American Arbitration Association, 1976), p. 199.

[43] ILO: *Conciliation and arbitration in industrial disputes*, op. cit., pp. 525–527.

[44] Morris, op. cit., p. 269.

[45] See I. W. Abel: "Basic Steel's Experimental Negotiating Agreement", in *Monthly Labor Review* (Washington, DC), Sep. 1973, pp. 39–42; see also Morris, op. cit., pp. 270–276.

[46] See ILO: *Social and Labour Bulletin*, June 1977, pp. 141–142.

[47] idem: *LS*, 1944—Can. 1.

[48] ibid., 1948—Can. 1.

[49] ibid., 1953—Phi. 1.

[50] See C. D. Calderon: "From compulsory arbitration to collective bargaining in the Philippines", in *International Labour Review*, Jan. 1960, pp. 1–24.

[51] ILO: *LS*, 1974—Phi. 1A.

[52] See "The Ahmedabad experiment in labour-management relations", in *International Labour Review*, Apr. and May 1959, pp. 343–379 and 511–536.

[53] See ILO: *Basic agreements and joint statements* . . ., op. cit., pp. 104–106 and 107–109.

[54] idem: *LS*, 1946—Ire. 1, Sections 59–65. The Act provides for the registration of qualified joint industrial councils, defined to mean associations which are substantially representative of workers of a particular class, type or group and their employers, which have as their object the promotion of harmonious relations between such employers and such workers, and the rules of which provide that, if a trade dispute arises between such workers and their employers, a strike or lockout will not be undertaken in support of the dispute until the dispute has been referred to the association and considered by it.

[55] Act respecting mediation in labour disputes (ibid., 1962—Fin. 1), Sections 15–16.

[56] ibid., 1975—UK 2, Section 3.

[57] Industrial Disputes Act (ibid., 1957—Fr. 2A).

[58] Decree respecting conciliation and arbitration in collective labour disputes (ibid., 1946—Mor. 2A, Sections 28–29; 1948—Mor. 2A).

[59] Labour Code (ibid., 1967—Congo (Kin.) 1), Section 273.

[60] Labour Code (ibid., 1963—Mau. 1), Book I, Section 63.

[61] Industrial Relations Act, 1972 (ibid., 1972—Trin. 1), Section 43.

[62] Industrial Relations Act, 1965 (ibid., 1965—Ghana 2), Section 12.

[63] Industrial Relations Act, 1973 (ibid., 1973—NZ 1), Section 115.

[64] Industrial Relations Ordinance, 1960 (ibid., 1965—Sin. 1, Section 24); Industrial Relations (Amendment) Act, 1968 (ibid., 1968—Sin. 2, Sections 6–7).

[65] Labour Code (ibid., 1966—Tun. 1), Sections 37 and 42.

[66] Conciliation and Arbitration Act, 1972, Section 20 (ibid., 1972—Aust. 1); amendment of the Conciliation and Arbitration Act, 1904–70.

[67] ibid., 1975—Jam. 1.

[68] Section 3(1) *(b)*. The draft labour relations code becomes effective upon its approval by Parliament. However, any violation of its provisions is not punishable, although those provisions may be taken into account in the determination of any question to which they are relevant.

[69] ILO: *Basic agreements and joint statements* . . ., op. cit., pp. 3–6.

[70] Sharp, op. cit., p. 340.

[71] Federal Mediation and Conciliation Service: *Twenty-seventh annual report: Fiscal year 1974* (Washington, DC. 1974), pp. 45–46.

[72] *The Times* (London), 20 Feb. 1974, p. 5 (article on the Coal Board's statement of evidence presented to the Pay Board Relativities Inquiry).

[73] A. I. Marsh and W. E. J. McCarthy: *Disputes procedures in Britain*, Research papers, No. 2 (Part 2) (London, Royal Commission on Trade Unions and Employers' Associations/HMSO, 1968), pp. 10–33 and 97–100.

[74] ILO: *Social and Labour Bulletin*, June 1976, pp. 123–124.

[75] Joint Industrial Council for the Food Manufacturers' Industrial Group: *Constitution and working agreement* (London, 12th revised edition, Dec. 1969), Section 3.

[76] Marsh and McCarthy, op. cit., pp. 52–54.

[77] ibid., pp. 73–85 and 115–121.

[78] R. Blanpain: "Belgium", pp. 205–206, in Blanpain: *International encyclopaedia for labour law and industrial relations*, op. cit.

[79] ILO: *Basic agreements and joint statements . . .*, op. cit., pp. 217–220. See also p. 60 above.

[80] idem: *Social and Labour Bulletin*, Mar. 1976, p. 37.

[81] Ramm, op. cit., pp. 135–136.

[82] See Jacobsen: "Denmark", pp. 176–186, in Blanpain: *International encyclopaedia for labour law and industrial relations*, op. cit.

[83] Schmidt, op. cit., pp. 236–237.

[84] Abel, op. cit., pp. 40–41.

[85] Herzog and Stone, op. cit., pp. 311–312.

[86] ibid., pp. 312–317.

[87] Fleming, op. cit., pp. 13–17.

[88] Herzog and Stone, op. cit., p. 318.

GOVERNMENTAL SYSTEMS OF CONCILIATION

5

The previous chapter reviewed conciliation and arbitration procedures set up by the parties themselves, whether of their own volition or pursuant to legislation requiring them to do so. This and the next two chapters review systems of conciliation and arbitration set up by governments. The present chapter is concerned with types of conciliation system and their structure, while the next describes the functioning of these systems.

It will be recalled that the term "conciliation" is used in this book to designate procedures whereby a third party assists the parties to a dispute to settle the dispute by agreement, although this process is sometimes designated by the term "mediation", and although, furthermore, in some countries "conciliation" and "mediation" are two distinct procedures, the latter being a more active form of assisting the parties to find an agreed solution (see p. 15 above). As previously indicated, the term "conciliation" is used here to cover this kind of disputes settlement procedure in general, although references will be made to conciliation and mediation where appropriate in connection with those countries which distinguish between the two procedures.

TYPES OF GOVERNMENTAL CONCILIATION SYSTEM

Conciliation is the most widely used method of settling labour disputes under government auspices. A distinction may be made between different governmental systems of conciliation according to the form in which conciliation is carried out and according to the method by which it is applied.

Forms of conciliation

As a rule, conciliation is carried out either: *(a)* by an individual, known under various official designations in different countries, who will hereafter be generally referred to as "individual conciliator" or simply as "conciliator"; or *(b)* by a body consisting of several members, variously designated as a board, council or committee of conciliation, which will hereafter be generally referred to simply as "conciliation board".

As regards the form in which conciliation is carried out, governmental systems of conciliation fall into three main groups: *(a)* those in which the legislation makes provision only for the services of individual conciliators; *(b)* those in which the legislation makes provision for conciliation boards only; and *(c)* those in which provision is made for both forms of conciliation.

The services of individual conciliators are more widely utilised than those of conciliation boards. The historical trend appears to be towards an extension of the system of individual conciliators, either involving the elimination of the conciliation board procedure (e.g. in Pakistan, the Philippines and Sri Lanka) or in conjunction with an existing conciliation board system (e.g. in Kenya, Mauritania, New Zealand and Zambia). Several Latin American countries (e.g. Mexico, Panama and Venezuela) have developed a system of administrative conciliation carried out by individual conciliators attached to the ministry of labour which is parallel to and distinct from the collegiate form of conciliation by tripartite boards provided for in the legislation. In Canada also the pre-eminent role of the conciliation board under earlier enactments has been supplanted by that of the individual conciliator (conciliation officer, conciliation commissioner and mediator), whose position was first provided for in the Industrial Relations and Disputes Investigation Act, 1948.

The systems of individual conciliators and of conciliation boards have their respective advantages, disadvantages and problems. While it is not possible to go into this question in detail here, it may be pointed out that an individual conciliator can take action more readily, more expeditiously and more decisively than a conciliation board. The procedure before an individual conciliator is also generally considered to be more flexible than the conciliation board procedure, since a conciliator may be in a better position to adjust his approach to the varying circumstances of the cases in which he is involved. It is also possible under the system of individual conciliators to entrust the work of conciliation to a specialised staff, which is important in countries where a considerable amount of conciliation has to be undertaken owing to the number of disputes that normally arise during the year. A major problem of the system is that its effectiveness depends on the selection of conciliators with the necessary qualifications (see also pp. 99–102); it takes time to build up a body of qualified conciliation personnel and it requires expenditure of money and effort. When the work of conciliation is entrusted to persons who do not possess the necessary qualifications, the result may be that they will not only fail in their attempts to settle disputes but that they will compound the difficulties between the parties and make the process of settlement more problematical.

The principal advantage of the system of conciliation boards derives from the inclusion of employers' and workers' representatives on these boards, since this may give the parties greater confidence that their respective points of view will be adequately taken into consideration in the course of the proceedings. It may also account for the observation made by an Ecuadorian expert to the effect that the conciliation carried out by the Conciliation and Arbitration Board has become in practice a formal hearing to which the parties do not attach much importance.[1] The real conciliation is effected by officials of the Ministry of Labour; the conciliation procedures before the Board serve to authorise the declaration of a strike or to pave the way for arbitration. It is interesting to note, however, that in the case of Colombia individual conciliators appointed by the parties must be assisted by three representatives of the workers and three of the employers, "all of whom must know the situation of the enterprise and must receive the necessary assistance to act".[2] At the same time the employers' and workers' members of a board can bring to their task the benefit of their practical knowledge and experience. When these members are not directly concerned with the disputes before the board, they can play an extremely valuable role in helping to bring about a settlement. A unanimous recommendation by the employers' and workers' members as to the terms on which the dispute should be settled almost carries with it the certainty of acceptance by the parties. A possible difficulty is that, in practice, unanimity between the employers' and workers' members may seldom be obtained and that in many cases reference to a conciliation board may become an empty formality. The problem, then, is how to increase the likelihood of the employers' and workers' members of conciliation boards reaching agreement on a common recommendation, instead of their preparing majority and minority reports. Another difficulty, which has been observed in Latin America in particular, is the cumbersome nature and excessively rigid and formalistic procedure of the conciliation boards. The fact that many Latin American boards proved to be slow-moving in practice has been regarded as the main reason for the appearance of the system of conciliation by individual officials of the ministries of labour.[3]

Voluntary and compulsory conciliation

It has become normal to distinguish between systems of voluntary conciliation and systems of compulsory conciliation. In voluntary conciliation the parties are free to use or not to make use of the government's conciliation facilities. When one of the parties to a dispute requests conciliation, it may be provided if the other party does not object. When no request for conciliation is made by either party, conciliation may be offered but the parties are not bound to accept it. In voluntary systems the provision of conciliation by the government is mainly conceived of as assistance or service to industry, and the term "service" may figure in the official title of the governmental organ concerned. Examples of voluntary conciliation systems include those in Austria, Belgium, Italy, Japan, the United Kingdom and the United States, as well as in a number of countries where the conciliation system has been patterned on the British model (e.g. Ghana, Kenya, Sri Lanka and Trinidad and Tobago). In Canada and New Zealand, while conciliation is compulsory (see below), the separate mediation procedure is voluntary. Conciliation by individual conciliators in Ireland and Japan and administrative conciliation in Mexico are also voluntary.

In compulsory systems parties to disputes are required to make use of the governmental conciliation machinery. However, it must be emphasised that compulsory conciliation differs from voluntary conciliation only in the method by which the procedure is set in motion; the substantive object of conciliation in either case remains the same, i.e. a settlement of the dispute on the basis of the parties' agreement. In compulsory conciliation (as in voluntary conciliation) the parties are not bound to accept a conciliator's suggestions or proposals for settlement; the conciliator can only persuade the parties to make mutual compromises in order to reach agreement.

Conciliation may be made compulsory by a provision making it obligatory to submit a dispute to the statutory conciliation procedure or requiring the parties to participate in conciliation proceedings; or by a provision empowering the conciliation authority to compel the parties' attendance in such proceedings; or by a combination of any such provisions (e.g. in Australia, the United Republic of Cameroon, Colombia, Denmark, Finland, France, Luxembourg, Malaysia, New Zealand, Norway, the Philippines, Singapore, Sweden and Zambia). In Canada the use of compulsory conciliation at the federal level dates back to the beginning of the century; provincial legislation (with the exception of Saskatchewan) has also followed the compulsory approach.

In most of these countries the sanction for compulsory conciliation consists in penalising as an offence a refusal without good cause to appear in conciliation proceedings after the party concerned has been duly summoned. In the Philippines attendance in conciliation proceedings is part of the statutory procedure of collective bargaining, and failure to bargain collectively in accordance with that procedure is dealt with as an unfair labour practice. In Sweden, if a party fails to appear after having been called in by a conciliator the latter can request the other party to report the matter to the Labour Court, which can order the defaulting party to fulfil its obligation under pain of a penalty.

One of the reasons for compulsory conciliation—probably the main reason in most of the countries concerned—is that it can provide an opportunity for the peaceful settlement of a dispute before either party resorts to industrial action. For this reason it is often required that advance notice of an intention to declare a strike or lockout be given to the conciliation authority concerned, thus enabling the latter to initiate the conciliation procedure even if neither of the parties has requested conciliation. The objective of strike or lockout prevention is more evident in another method of making conciliation compulsory: a provision making it illegal to declare a strike or lockout without prior resort to the statutory conciliation procedure or unless that procedure has been exhausted (e.g. in Argentina, Bolivia, Canada, Colombia, Costa Rica, the Dominican Republic, Guatemala, Guinea, Lebanon, Mauritania, Mexico, Panama, Tunisia, Turkey and Venezuela). Many countries with systems of compulsory arbitration (for which several of the above-mentioned countries provide in certain cases) also make provision for prior compulsory conciliation. Doubts regarding the value of compulsory conciliation relate mostly to the difficulties involved in winning the confidence of the parties, its possible detrimental effects on good faith bargaining and the higher costs involved in operating compulsory schemes.[4]

In a few countries both voluntary and compulsory methods of conciliation are employed. As indicated earlier, in Canada and New Zealand the law distinguishes between mediation and conciliation, the first being voluntary and the second compulsory. In Mexico the procedure before individual conciliators is voluntary, while that before boards of conciliation and arbitration is compulsory.

ADMINISTRATIVE FRAMEWORK FOR CONCILIATION

When a government decides to make provision for the settlement of labour disputes through conciliation, it has to make policy decisions as to the authority to be entrusted with the responsibility for that function and as to the necessary arrangements by which such responsibility may be most effectively put into practice. In some cases the administrative responsibility for conciliation may be granted directly to the body or persons responsible for conciliation: here the conciliator or the conciliation board has generally no function other than disputes settlement; a request or application for conciliation is generally made direct to the conciliator or conciliation board as the appropriate conciliation authority. This is the case, for example, with regard to the Australian Conciliation and Arbitration Commission, the regional labour tribunals in Brazil, the Federal Conciliation and Arbitration Board in Mexico and, generally, the permanent conciliation boards in various countries.

On the other hand, assistance in the settlement of disputes by way of conciliation may be provided under the responsibility of an administrative authority having wider responsibilities. This body may be given a number of powers and functions in connection with labour disputes (or in the field of labour relations generally), including the power to appoint conciliators or to establish conciliation boards, to decide whether or not to intervene in a dispute or to take any of the steps prescribed in the legislation. Furthermore, reports of disputes or notices of strikes or lockouts are to be given to this body. Thus national practices regarding the administrative authority for conciliation fall into the following two main patterns.

Administrative responsibility exercised by the ministry of labour

Unless the legislation expressly allocates the administrative responsibility for conciliation otherwise, that responsibility is generally held to be a part of the general administrative responsibility of the government ministry or department responsible for labour affairs (hereinafter to be generally referred to simply as "ministry of labour" or "labour ministry"). This is the position where no special legislation concerning the settlement of labour disputes has been enacted (e.g. Italy); but in fact the legislation in many countries specifically assigns the administrative responsibility for conciliation to that ministry.

This used to be the position in the United Kingdom. Under the Conciliation Act, 1896, the Ministry of Labour (or its predecessor, the Board of Trade) might take such steps as might seem expedient to induce the parties to a difference to meet together. On application of either of the parties the Minister of Labour might appoint a person or persons to act as a conciliator or a conciliation board.[5] Similar powers were vested in the Minister under the Industrial Courts Act, 1919.

The exercise of these powers required some kind of administrative organisation. This originated as a small section in the Board of Trade. In the course of time it evolved into the Industrial Relations Department, one of the principal units of the Ministry of Labour. Although conciliators were at first appointed on an ad hoc or part-time basis, the function of conciliation came to be the full-time responsibility of the industrial relations officers of that Department. As well as conciliation, its main functions included assistance in the formation and maintenance of agreed machinery for negotiation and disputes settlement, advice on personnel management and joint consultation and administration of wages councils policies.[6]

While the responsibilities of the Minister of Labour as regards conciliation and arbitration under the Conciliation Act, 1896, and the Industrial Courts Act, 1919, had been transferred to another authority, the Advisory, Conciliation and Arbitration Service (see p. 94), with the result that the Ministry's Industrial Relations Department had ceased to exist, the administrative framework for conciliation under those Acts served as a model for a number of the former British territories. It would appear that among the first countries to be influenced by the British model was Canada, where the matter is now governed at the federal level by Part V (Industrial Relations) of the Canada Labour Code.[7] Under this legislation, failure to conclude collective agreements is to be reported to the Minister of Labour, who decides whether or not and in what form conciliation is to be provided; he is also empowered to appoint mediators to carry out functions for the promotion of industrial peace. The administrative organisation which grew out of these provisions was for a good number of years the former Industrial Relations Branch of the Department of Labour, but in 1967 it was divided into a Conciliation and Arbitration Branch and an Employee Representation Branch. The Conciliation and Arbitration Branch, which remains one of the principal divisions of the Department, administers its conciliation and arbitration services as well as a preventive mediation service. The Department's industrial relations functions have been brought together into the Federal Mediation and Conciliation Services group and placed under the responsibility of the Assistant Deputy Minister of Labour.[8]

In Ghana, Jamaica, Kenya, Malaysia, Singapore and Trinidad and Tobago, as well as in Argentina, the Dominican Republic and Jordan, the ministry of labour is also expressly identified in the legislation as the administrative authority for conciliation. Among its powers is usually that of appointing conciliators or conciliation boards. In Malaysia the responsibility for conciliation is assigned to the Department of Industrial Relations of the Ministry of Labour and Manpower.[9]

It appears that in some other countries the administrative organisation for conciliation is the labour ministry's department of labour, which has general responsibility for the administration of labour legislation and is headed by a commissioner of labour. In Nigeria, Sri Lanka, the Sudan and Tanzania the legislation directly vests in that official certain functions in connection with the settlement of disputes, although the general responsibility for the administration of disputes settlement procedures rests with the minister of labour.

In another group of countries the legislation does not specifically allocate the administrative responsibility for conciliation to the ministry of labour but to an organisation within the ministry, generally the directorate or inspectorate of labour (e.g. in El Salvador, Madagascar, Mali, Mauritania, Senegal and Venezuela). Like the departments of labour mentioned in the previous paragraph, these administrative organs also perform other labour administration functions.

In Mexico the Labour Act, 1931, which established a system of conciliation through permanent boards, was silent as to the authority of the Department of Labour and Social Welfare with regard to conciliation. This, however, did not prevent that Department from developing administratively a voluntary conciliation system, which was institutionalised in 1953 with the establishment of an organisation known as the Corps of Conciliation Officials and later transformed into the Department of Conciliation.

In Indonesia the Industrial Relations Department was established by ministerial decree in the Ministry of Manpower and Transmigration, which is entrusted with general administrative responsibility for matters relating to the prevention and settlement of labour disputes. The specific duties of the Department include the promotion of good relations between employers and workers and the collection of information concerning labour relations.

Administrative responsibility assigned to another authority

In a number of countries the administrative responsibility for conciliation is assigned to bodies specially created by statute or to national officials whose positions have been similarly established. In some countries these agencies are organised under the ministry of labour, while in others they have been set up as autonomous organs, although often linked for certain purposes to the ministry of labour (e.g. in Denmark, Finland, Ireland, Japan, Luxembourg, Mauritius, New Zealand, Norway, Sweden, the United Kingdom and the United States).

Among the agencies functioning under a ministry of labour is the Central Conciliation Office in Austria, established under the Collective Labour Relations Act, 1973.[10] The Central Conciliation Office acts as a conciliation board for the settlement of labour disputes in the federal sphere; it also supervises the conciliation offices established in the different provinces, especially for the purpose of ensuring uniformity in their activities; and it has been given a number of other functions with regard to collective bargaining and certain other aspects of collective labour relations.

In Belgium conciliation used to be a function of the labour inspectorate. In July 1969 a Royal Order was issued creating a new office in the Ministry of Employment and Labour to deal specially with collective labour relations.[11] The preamble to the Royal Order listed a number of considerations which led to the establishment of the new office, some of which related to the special qualities required of officials charged with the function of conciliation. It was also considered that while the legislation concerning collective agreements and joint committees should permit the development of labour systems adapted to the needs of each industry as well as of good labour relations which should contribute to industrial peace, it was evident that the realisation of these aims depended on the means which were placed for that purpose at the disposition of the Ministry of Employment and Labour; and that in consequence it was necessary and urgent to endow that Ministry "with a flexible instrument capable of coping with all situations".

The chosen instrument was a new office known as the Collective Labour Relations Service. Under the Royal Order its main functions are to contribute to the orderly development of collective labour relations and to administer the legislation concerning collective agreements and joint committees; and to assist in the prevention of labour disputes, undertake conciliation and submit reports to the Minister on labour relations in particular branches of economic activity, industrial sectors or undertakings. It has a technical division for each of these functions.

In Finland conciliation was formerly carried out by district conciliation officers under the administrative supervision of the Ministry of Social Affairs. The situation was changed by an Act of 1962, under which the work of conciliation remains administratively under that Ministry. However, in addition to district conciliation officers the Act created the post of national conciliation officer.[12] This Act was amended in 1970[13] to provide also for mediation in disputes involving civil servants and for two national conciliation officers. Among their duties are: to co-operate with the labour-market organisations in furthering the relationships between employers and workers and their organisations; to direct the work of conciliation in labour disputes throughout the country; to undertake conciliation in disputes affecting the areas of jurisdiction of two or more district conciliation officers; and to act as chiefs to the district conciliation officers. Each of the national conciliation officers acts as the other's deputy and one of them is designated by the Council of State to be the head of the conciliation office and to take decisions on questions of competence arising in connection with conciliation.

In Israel the Settlement of Labour Disputes Law, 1957, provides for the appointment by the Minister of Labour of a Chief Labour Relations Officer.[14] Under the Law notices of disputes are to be given to this official, who decides whether conciliation proceedings are to be initiated in any labour dispute, who assumes the function of conciliation of any dispute or assigns that function to a labour relations officer and who is also the authority who appoints ad hoc arbitration boards.

In Panama the Labour Code of 1971[15] provides for conciliation under the Ministry of Labour and Social Welfare, which is to be carried out by the expert conciliation staff of its Labour Relations Department. However, some conciliation and adjudication bodies still exist for the settlement of individual disputes. Formerly, under the Labour Code of 1947, conciliation was undertaken only by ad hoc conciliation boards set up by labour judges, and there was no provision for conciliation under the responsibility of an administrative authority.

In the Philippines, before the promulgation of the Labour Code of 1974, there was already a Bureau of Labour Relations in the Department of Labour whose function included conciliation in interest as well as rights disputes. Under the Labour Code[16] its conciliation functions extend to all labour disputes (including intra-union and inter-union conflicts) except those arising from the implementation or interpretation of collective agreements. It has also the function of registering legitimate labour organisations and of certifying any such organisation as the exclusive collective bargaining representative in a collective bargaining unit. It also administers a voluntary arbitration service.

In Tunisia, under an enactment of 1976 concerning the settlement of labour disputes, the responsibility formerly exercised by the labour inspectorate in regard to conciliation is now carried out by the Central Conciliation Office and regional conciliation offices. These are new administrative bodies within the Ministry for Social Affairs, which have been created to relieve the labour inspectorate of some of its burden.[17]

Among the autonomous bodies responsible for conciliation is the Labour Court in Ireland, created by the Industrial Relations Act, 1946.[18] In spite of its official title it is really an administrative body, functioning independently of any other state authority. It consists of an independent chairman and an equal number of employers' and workers' members. While its main function is the investigation of labour disputes, the Labour Court is authorised to appoint industrial relations officers and conciliators. Beside disputes settlement, its functions include the administration of policies concerning joint industrial councils and joint labour committees (wage boards).

In Japan two parallel systems of labour relations commissions have been established by the Trade Union Law, 1949, and its various amendments: one for the private sector and local public enterprises, and the other for the maritime industry.[19] Each system consists of the Central Labour Relations Commission and prefectural or local labour relations commissions. Each commission consists of an equal number of members representing employers, workers and the public, the chairman being elected by all the members from among the public members. The functions of each commission include disputes settlement, certification of trade unions (as being in compliance with law) and investigation of unfair labour practices. The Trade Union Law also provides for the establishment in each commission of an office under a director to handle the administrative affairs of the commission.

In Luxembourg a Joint Conciliation Board has been established within the National Labour Conference. Besides assistance in the prevention and settlement of labour disputes, the Board has the duty of exercising constant supervision over all conditions of employment, in close collaboration with the labour inspectorate, and of formulating proposals concerning measures calculated to prevent social disturbances.[20]

In Mauritius the Industrial Relations Act, 1973,[21] provides for the establishment of the Industrial Relations Commission, consisting of a chairman and from three to six members appointed by the Minister of Labour after appropriate consulatations with employers' and workers' organisations. One of the principal functions of the Commission is to provide a conciliation service to assist employers, employees and trade unions. It is also charged with the investigation of questions on union recognition and union security in the form of an agency shop.

In New Zealand in 1970, pursuant to a request of the New Zealand Employers Federation and the New Zealand Federation of Labour, the Government established the Industrial Mediation Service, independent of any government department.[22] It was originally set up under an amendment to the former Industrial Conciliation and Arbitration Act and its continuance is provided for in the new Industrial Relations Act, 1973.[23] It consists of a number of mediators whose general function is "to assist employers, unions, and workers to carry out their responsibilities to establish and maintain harmonious industrial relations". The establishment of the Industrial Mediation Service marked a notable departure from the previous government policy of almost exclusive reliance on the system of compulsory conciliation and arbitration.

In Sweden the Act respecting co-determination at work, 1976,[24] which became effective in January 1977, provides for a new administrative framework for conciliation. Formerly conciliation was carried out by mediators appointed for each of the eight districts into which the State was divided, who performed their function under their own responsibility. The above-mentioned Act makes conciliation the responsibility of an administrative organ—the State Conciliators' Office—created by the Act. The general functions of the Office include the monitoring of labour market conditions and the establishment of policies in accordance with which the conciliators must provide the social partners with advice and information on negotiations and collective agreements.

In the United Kingdom the former Industrial Relations Department of the Ministry of Labour has been replaced by the Advisory, Conciliation and Arbitration Service as the administrative organisation for conciliation. It was first established administratively in January 1975 after government consultations with employers' and workers' organisations, and was placed on a statutory basis in the Employment Protection Act, 1975.[25] Created as an independent agency, it is directed by a council consisting of a full-time chairman and nine other members, of whom three represent employers, three represent workers and three are neutral members, being persons knowledgeable in labour relations. The Service is "charged with the general duty of promoting the improvement of industrial relations, and in particular of encouraging the extension of collective bargaining and the development and, where necessary, reform of collective bargaining machinery" (Section 1. While the promotion of collective bargaining has long been administrative policy in the United Kingdom, it was given statutory basis for the first time in the Employment Protection Act, 1975). Besides conciliation, its specific functions include administering voluntary arbitration, providing advice on labour relations questions, making inquiries into such questions in general or in relation to a particular industry or undertaking, and issuing codes of practice containing practical guidance for the improvement of labour relations.

In the United States the Act of 1913 creating the Department of Labour contained a provision authorising the Secretary of Labour to mediate in labour disputes and to appoint commissioners of conciliation for that purpose. The conciliation work of the Department rapidly expanded and a special division known as the United States Conciliation Service was set up in 1917 to be responsible for that function. This body was abolished by the Labour-Management Relations Act, 1947, which established in its stead the Federal Mediation and Conciliation Service as an independent agency. It was set up as a separate agency largely at the behest of employer groups which felt that, if conciliation were to remain a function of the Department of Labour, conciliators would inevitably reflect what many employers considered to be a pro-labour bias of the Department.[26] The Service, which is headed by a director, is generally responsible for implementing the policy with regard to the fostering of collective bargaining; besides mediation and conciliation and the administration of a voluntary arbitration service for grievance disputes, it has developed a preventive mediation programme to promote the general objectives of the Labour-Management Relations Act, 1947.

In Denmark a different type of arrangement exists. The main responsibility for conciliation is entrusted to three mediators who together constitute a body known as the Mediation Board (or, subsequently, the Conciliation Board). The three mediators elect one of their number as chairman, for a year at a time; the chairman acts as administrative director of the Board. It is the duty of the Board, at the invitation of the chairman, to discuss the general situation in the country as regards conditions of employment and especially wages. The Board specifies the labour questions in which each of the three mediators is to intervene, by means of standing orders or as cases arise. Its other functions include receiving notices of proposed stoppages of work and submitting an annual report on its activities to the Minister of Labour.

FACTORS AFFECTING THE DEVELOPMENT OF
ADMINISTRATIVE ORGANISATIONS FOR CONCILIATION

It may be noted from the preceding discussion that, considered by function, administrative organisations for conciliation generally fall into one of two categories. In one category the functions of the organisation include those relating to labour law administration and to disputes settlement. Organisations of this type are always established as administrative units of the ministry of labour, usually as a department, directorate or inspectorate of labour. In the second category the functions involved are mainly in the field of labour relations. These functions may or may not be limited to the prevention and settlement of disputes. The organisation concerned may or may not be an integral part of the labour ministry.

There appears to be a long-term trend towards the establishment of administrative organisations falling into this second category. In many cases conciliation was first assigned to a body of the first category, and subsequently an organisation in the second category was created to which that function was transferred. However, in practically all countries which have this category of organisation (except Canada, Denmark, the United Kingdom and the United States) the organisations in question have been set up only during the past 30 years or so. It will have been noted that while those in Argentina, Belgium, Finland, Israel, Japan, Lebanon, Luxembourg, Malaysia, Mexico and the Philippines have been in existence for some years, those in Mauritius, New Zealand, Panama, Sweden and Tunisia were created only recently. It would seem that the establishment of bodies of the second category, whether by legislation or by administrative action on the part of the minister of labour, represents a policy decision that the stage has been reached for conciliation to be placed under the responsibility of an administrative agency which specialises in that function or in disputes settlement and possibly in other aspects of labour relations policy as well.

Among the factors on which such a policy decision depends, one relates to the type and frequency of labour disputes in the country concerned. As a rule, disputes which justify the establishment of a specialised body for conciliation are interests or collective disputes. In some countries such disputes are in many cases of national or major importance because of the centralised or nation-wide character of the negotiations involved. In many other countries it appears to be the frequency and regularity with which such disputes are being brought before the government conciliation machinery that has been the primary consideration in judging whether there is a real need for a specialised conciliation or disputes settlement agency.

This factor is to a great extent dependent on a system of enterprise or company-level bargaining. Most cases of specialised government conciliation services are to be found in countries where such systems of collective bargaining prevail (e.g. Canada, Mexico, the Philippines and the United States), or where a substantial proportion of collective negotiations takes place at the level of the undertaking, company, plant or section thereof, notwithstanding the development of industry-wide or occupation-wide bargaining (e.g. in Belgium and the United Kingdom).

Sweden provides an interesting example of an administrative organisation for conciliation being set up to meet the needs of a new situation. As indicated above, conciliation in this country was formerly carried out by eight district mediators who performed their function on their own responsibility (there was, however, a mediation office in the Social Welfare Board which co-ordinated their activities). Their services under such arrangements were considered sufficient for the number of interests disputes which normally arose under the prevailing system of centralised and industry-wide bargaining. The Act respecting co-determination at work, 1976, has not modified this system of bargaining, but it has extended collective bargaining to the enterprise level in a manner that was not possible under previous legislation. Briefly, the right of co-determination to which workers are entitled under the Act is to be assured through negotiations and collective agreements with individual employers.[27] It was presumably to deal with an increased number of disputes resulting from the anticipated expansion of negotiations that the State Conciliators' Office was created by the Act.

In a number of countries the administrative organisation for conciliation has also been given responsibility for other disputes settlement procedures under government auspices. In Ireland the functions of the Labour Court include the administration of a voluntary conciliation and arbitration service as well as the investigation of labour disputes and adjudication in certain cases. In Japan the responsibility of the labour relations commissions extends to conciliation and arbitration as well as to the administrative investigation of unfair labour practices. In the United Kingdom the Advisory, Conciliation and Arbitration Service also administers a voluntary arbitration service, as does the Conciliation and Arbitration Branch of the Canada Department of Labour, the Bureau of Labour Relations in the Philippines and the Federal Mediation and Conciliation Service in the United States.

The functions of administrative organisations for conciliation may not be limited to disputes settlement. A second major factor affecting their development is the scope of the government's labour relations policy. If this policy includes other aspects of labour relations besides the prevention and settlement of disputes, it may be considered that such a policy can be better implemented through a specialised labour relations agency. Thus, apart from conciliation and arbitration, its functions may include preventive mediation, promotional action for various purposes and the provision of information, advice and assistance in connection with such purposes. These may include the promotion of collective bargaining, grievances procedures inside undertakings, agreed conciliation and arbitration machinery, joint consultation and workers' participation in management decision-making, sound personnel policies and practices and generally good labour relations. It will have been noted that in a number of countries, including Belgium, Canada, Indonesia, Malaysia, Sweden, the United Kingdom and the United States, the administrative organisation for conciliation is also responsible for certain other aspects of labour relations policy such as those indicated above.

It is also important to note that technical support for conciliation can be more effectively organised and provided through an administrative organisation which has a specialised staff for such work, especially for the collection of information and documentation and the research activity connected with it. The value of such technical support for conciliation is always important, but the need for it would be greater where most or a substantial portion of the collective bargaining that takes place is carried out at the undertaking or plant level. This system of bargaining can involve a multitude of issues concerning wage rates, wage differentials, bonus systems, hiring practices, workload and manning levels, work organisation, physical working conditions, and so on. In dealing with actual cases, conciliators would need to have as full and as up-to-date information as possible concerning such questions. It would be a function of the headquarters staff of the administrative organisation to help them to meet that need.

ARRANGEMENTS CONCERNING INDIVIDUAL CONCILIATORS AND CONCILIATION BOARDS

National practices concerning specific arrangements regarding individual conciliators and conciliation boards show great diversity. In the case of conciliation boards, legislative or administrative provisions have to be made for the board as a body as well as for the chairman and members. While for this reason practices with regard to conciliation boards are more varied, differences in national practices concerning individual conciliators tend to be more significant.

Types of individual conciliator

In most of the national systems which utilise the services of individual conciliators, the work of conciliation is normally carried out by one of two types of official, namely: (a) those who combine the function of conciliation with other duties in the field of labour administration and law enforcement; or (b) those who are appointed especially with a view to performing conciliation and/or labour relations functions.

Officials of the first type include those regularly appointed as labour officers or labour inspectors, and in principle they are engaged in conciliation work on a part-time basis. It has been argued that the performance by labour inspectors of conciliation and arbitration functions may be incompatible with, and may consequently hamper them in, the performance of their duties.[28] In this connection the ILO Labour Inspection Recommendation, 1947 (No. 81), and the Labour Inspection (Agriculture) Recommendation, 1969 (No. 133), provide that the functions of labour inspectors should not include that of acting as conciliator or arbitrator in proceedings concerning labour disputes. In view of this and other factors there appears to be a tendency, whenever conciliation is carried out on an individual basis, towards entrusting this function to officials of the second type. These officials may be formally designated as mediators, conciliators, conciliation officers or conciliation commissioners (e.g. in Argentina, Belgium, Canada, Denmark, Finland, Honduras, India, Japan, Mexico, New Zealand, Norway, Pakistan, Panama, the Philippines, Singapore, Sweden, Thailand and the United States); or as industrial relations or labour relations officers (e.g. in Ireland, Israel, Kenya, Lebanon, Malaysia, Mauritius, Uganda and the United Kingdom).

In most of these countries the conciliators are regularly appointed officials serving on a full-time basis. In Denmark, however, in view of the seasonal character of collective bargaining the office of mediator is a part-time instead of a full-time activity. In Japan each labour relations commission has to appoint and keep a panel of conciliators; persons who have been appointed to the panels include present and former officials of the executive offices of the commissions, university professors, lawyers and journalists, who also undertake conciliation on a part-time basis.

In most countries permanent conciliators are appointed for particular districts or are assigned to regional offices under a superior officer, and they deal with disputes arising within the territorial limits of their respective districts or regional offices. In these cases provision is generally made for conciliation in disputes extending beyond the limits of one district or regional office or in disputes of major or national importance. In some countries, including the United Kingdom and the United States, a number of top conciliators are assigned to the headquarters staff of the national conciliation service.

In Finland and Norway there are also district conciliators, but the main responsibility for conciliation is entrusted to national conciliation officials. In Denmark the three mediators who constitute the Mediation Board are also appointed for the whole country. Each mediator normally carries out his mediation work without the assistance of the other two. In practice, the chairman of the Board, who has come to be known as the National Mediator, handles the cases involving the two main employers' and workers' confederations and their affiliated organisations. Another mediator traditionally handles disputes in the agricultural industry and the third mediator handles other disputes. In addition there are a number of submediators who assist the three mediators and who are also appointed for the country at large.

Commonwealth practice in Australia represents yet another type of arrangement. In this country the members of the Australian Conciliation and Arbitration Commission are grouped into panels. A panel is assigned the responsibility for dealing with disputes in a particular industry or group of related industries. The competence of each panel and of each panel member is co-extensive with that of the commission, i.e. over the country as a whole. Some countries (e.g. India, Ireland and Jordan) authorise the appointment of conciliators for specific industries or for disputes of a particular character.

In a number of countries provision is made for the appointment of conciliators for particular disputes on an ad hoc basis. In France, for example, the chairman of a conciliation board may invite the parties to a dispute to appoint a mediator. Mediation proceedings may also be initiated by the Minister of Labour on request by one of the parties to a dispute or on his own motion. If the parties cannot agree on the appointment of a mediator, the latter is chosen by the authority concerned from a list of mediators which has been previously established for the purpose.[29] Substantially similar provisions authorising the appointment of a mediator, in cases where the parties cannot agree on submitting a dispute to arbitration, have been embodied in the Labour Code of the Ivory Coast.[30]

In some countries the method of ad hoc appointment makes it possible to utilise the services of qualified persons other than permanent conciliators. In Canada, where normally a conciliator is selected from the permanent staff, the Minister of Labour may appoint an ad hoc conciliation commissioner for a particular dispute. In Sweden it is also possible, under the provisions concerning the appointment of special conciliators, to make use of the services of private persons. In the United Kingdom the Advisory, Conciliation and Arbitration Service may appoint a person other than an officer or servant of the Service to assist in settling a dispute.[31]

Qualifications and appointment of conciliators

The question of conciliators' qualifications is very largely a matter of administrative practice, and legislative provisions dealing with it are found in only a few countries.

In Belgium the Royal Order of 23 July 1969 creating the Collective Labour Relations Service emphasises in its preamble the importance of appointing as conciliators persons possessing the essential personal qualities on which the success of their mission depends. They should have, in particular, sufficient independence to fulfil their delicate task, a special aptitude in the matter of human relations and a deep understanding of labour relations and labour law.

In France persons to be considered for inclusion in the national or regional list of mediators are to be nominated on account of their moral authority and their competence in economic and social matters.

In Japan conciliators of the labour relations commissions must be persons who have the knowledge and experience necessary to render assistance in the settlement of labour disputes.

In Panama the task of conciliation must be carried out by officials who have been trained for the purpose, and who have had special experience in labour law, labour relations and individual and group psychology.

As may have been noted, the legislative provisions in question are far from uniform. They serve to emphasise the importance of certain qualifications in regard to the situation in the country concerned. Moreover, the qualifications are stated in general terms only for the guidance of the appointing authority. Administrative practices provide more details on what are usually deemed to be the necessary qualifications of conciliators.

These qualifications are determined by the fact that, from the nature of the individual conciliator's function, his relationship with the parties to disputes in which he is involved is highly personal and subjective; in order to be effective he must have the trust and confidence of both the parties to a dispute. The qualifications are of two main types: *(a)* personal qualities or attributes, and *(b)* technical or professional qualifications.[32]

It has been noted that independence and impartiality are the two attributes which every conciliator should possess, regardless of other qualifications. A conciliator must also have a strong belief in the importance and usefulness of conciliation, otherwise he can readily fall into the danger of performing conciliation simply as a bureaucratic routine.[33]

Other personal qualities which have been mentioned as being important in a conciliator include the ability to get along well with people, honesty, sincerity, power of analysis, evenness of temper, mental alacrity, perseverance and patience. The parties to disputes in which a conciliator has intervened must see him as a person of experience, responsibility, mature judgement and practical-mindedness. For his work of persuasion, he needs a good command of language, including the ability to communicate with the parties in language that they understand.[34] Physical fitness is also necessary for the work of conciliation.

The technical qualifications relate to educational attainments, knowledge and experience—the qualifications that make a person "professionally" competent to perform conciliation. A would-be conciliator is generally required to have attained a certain level of formal schooling and to have had some previous work experience or training related to conciliation. In many countries new conciliators are often recruited from government services concerned with labour or labour relations. In the United States it is common practice for the Federal Mediation and Conciliation Service to appoint as new mediators persons with a background in trade unionism or personnel management.[35]

Besides possessing a thorough knowledge of local laws and regulations concerning labour and labour relations, a conciliator needs to be sufficiently familiar with the practical aspects of his country's labour relations system: the structure and characteristics of the trade union movement and of employers' organisations, collective bargaining practices and negotiation procedures, typical collective bargaining issues, pattern of labour disputes, and so forth. Where negotiations take place at the undertaking, plant or shop level, he also needs to know something about labour relations questions and practices within the undertaking, including payment systems. When an official is to be appointed with a view especially to performing conciliation or labour relations functions, it is possible to take into account through the appointment procedure the qualifications which, in accordance with the policy of the appointing authority, a conciliator should possess.

However, the question of a conciliator's technical qualifications does not end with his initial appointment. It is often considered that a conciliator's professional competence is best advanced by his experience of handling actual cases. In more and more countries great importance is thus attached to training programmes to enhance the competence and technical qualifications of the permanent conciliation staff. For newly appointed conciliators the training may include observing or assisting in conciliation proceedings conducted by experienced conciliators. In the United States the programme of the Federal Mediation and Conciliation Service includes the continued training of experienced mediators, in the form of annual seminars, workshops and regional conferences.[36]

The procedure for the appointment of government conciliators is important not only for the purpose of ensuring that qualified persons are appointed but also as a means of according official recognition to the importance of their functions and responsibilities. The appointment may be made in accordance with the normal procedure provided for in the public service or civil service regulations of general application, which is followed in many countries, or under a special procedure. Under the former system one of the questions to be considered is the classification of the post of conciliator, in particular with regard to hierarchical ranking or official status and compensation. Among the countries in which conciliators are appointed under a special procedure are Belgium, Denmark, Finland, Norway, Panama, Sweden, the United Kingdom and the United States.

In Belgium the Royal Order establishing the Collective Labour Relations Service also contains regulations concerning the appointment of officials charged with conciliation. It considers that the mission of conciliators requires, in view of its particular character, special guarantees of reliability, confidence and exceptional merit, which should be left to the appreciation of the appointing authority. The Royal Order specifies certain qualifications for the different posts in the service and provides for the direct appointment of persons who fulfil those qualifications, without their going through the normal recruiting procedure.

In Denmark the three mediators and the submediators are appointed by the Minister of Labour on recommendation of the Labour Court. Each mediator or submediator is appointed for a term of three years at a time, subject to reappointment for similar terms. In Panama official mediators are appointed in accordance with the rules made by the Minister of Labour, preferably on the basis of competitive examinations. Similar provisions obtain in other Latin American countries but they are not always observed in practice.

The importance of the office of conciliator is emphasised in some countries by the fact that he is appointed by the Head of State or by the Cabinet, usually for a fixed number of years at a time. In New Zealand, for example, mediators are appointed by the Governor-General, while in Norway the State Mediator and the district conciliators are appointed by the Crown. In Finland the two national conciliation officers are appointed by the President of the Republic, while the district conciliators are appointed by the Council of State. In Sweden, before the Act respecting co-determination at work, 1976, the district conciliators were also appointed by the Crown; there is no indication in that Act that this arrangement has been modified.

In the United Kingdom it is the Advisory, Conciliation and Arbitration Service which is given the power to appoint its officials who are to be entrusted with conciliation. This power is exercised with the consent, as to numbers, manner of appointment and terms and conditions of service, of the Secretary of

State for Employment, such consent having been approved by the Minister of State for the Civil Service Department.

Another factor relating to the appointment of conciliators is the question of their acceptability to the employers' and workers' representatives who are to make use of their services. The ultimate test of a conciliator's acceptability in this respect is his conduct and performance in the actual work of conciliation, but in a few countries the selection procedure includes advance assurance that a proposed candidate for appointment is acceptable.

In Denmark, as indicated above, the three mediators are appointed by the Minister of Labour on the recommendation of the Labour Court. The recommendation made by the Labour Court must be agreed to by at least one of the members of the Court elected by the employers and by one of the members elected by the workers.

In France the list of mediators is drawn up after consultation with, and an examination of the suggestions of, the employers' and workers' organisations which are most representative at the national level and which are represented on the Central Collective Agreements Board.

The workers' and employers' members of the Labour Court in Ireland, of the labour relations commissions in Japan and of the Council of the Advisory, Conciliation and Arbitration Service in the United Kingdom also have their say in the appointment of industrial relations officers or conciliators.

Ad hoc conciliation boards

A conciliation board is generally established either on an ad hoc basis for the purpose of dealing with an existing dispute, or as a permanent body to which disputes may be referred as they arise. Among the countries which utilise ad hoc boards are Bolivia, Canada, Colombia, Costa Rica, Ecuador, Guatemala, India, the Ivory Coast, Japan, Jordan, Kenya, New Zealand, Peru, Turkey, Uruguay, Venezuela and Zaire. In Switzerland an ad hoc board may be established by the Federal Government for settling a dispute extending beyond the limits of a canton, but cantonal conciliation boards are generally permanent bodies. As a rule, ad hoc boards have no function other than conciliation.

The discretionary power to establish a conciliation board is vested in Canada in the Department of Labour and in Switzerland in the Department of Public Economy. In Japan a labour relations commission performs its mediation function through mediation committees, while in New Zealand the convening of a conciliation council is a function of the conciliator (the conciliator in New Zealand is a permanent official whose main function is to preside in a conciliation council). In most of the other countries listed above a conciliation board may be set up by the competent labour administration authority or labour inspector (e.g. in Bolivia, Ecuador, Peru, Turkey, Uruguay and Venezuela) or by the competent labour judge (e.g. in Costa Rica).

Ad hoc boards include, besides the independent chairman, members representing employers and workers. Each side may have one representative (e.g. in Canada, Colombia, Costa Rica, Guatemala, Switzerland, Turkey and Zaire) or two representatives (e.g. in Bolivia, Ecuador, the Ivory Coast and Venezuela), as specified in the legislation. In India, Japan, Jordan and Kenya the legislation simply provides that the members of a conciliation board representing the employers and workers shall be equal in number. In Japan a mediation committee also includes a number of members representing the public interest.

The New Zealand legislation contains rather detailed provisions concerning the employers' and workers' assessors in a conciliation council. While the number of assessors for each side may not exceed a prescribed maximum, it is possible for one side to have more assessors than the other. In this case, however, the conciliator, who acts as chairman of the council, is to determine the assessors' voting rights so as to preserve equality of voting between the two parties.

The employers' and workers' members of an ad hoc conciliation board may be designated by the parties themselves (e.g. in Bolivia, Colombia, Ecuador, Turkey and Venezuela); or may be appointed by the competent authority on nomination by the parties to the dispute (e.g. in Canada, India and New Zealand). They may also be selected from lists or panels of employers' and workers' representatives which had been previously established for the purpose (e.g. in Costa Rica, Guatemala, Switzerland and Zaire). Names are included in the list or panel generally on nomination or recommendation by employers' and workers' organisations.

The panel system is also used in the selection of the members of a mediation committee in Japan. For this purpose three panels of not more than five members each are installed in each labour relations commission, representing employers, workers and the public interest respectively. Members of the employers' and workers' panels are appointed on nomination by employers' and workers' organisations, while the public members are appointed with the consent of the employers' and workers' members of the commission. However, the members of a mediation committee are not necessarily selected from these panels; they are designated by the chairman of the commission from the members of the commission itself or from the panel members.

In Canada, Japan and Turkey the chairman of the board is elected after the appointment of the employers' and workers' members. In Turkey he is appointed by agreement of the two members, and in Canada on the basis of their joint nomination. Provision is made in both countries for cases in which the two members cannot agree on the selection or nomination of a chairman. In Japan the chairman of a mediation committee is selected by the employers' and workers' members from among the members representing the public interest. In Switzerland the chairman is selected from a panel nominated by the Federal Council.

In most of the other countries the chairman of the conciliation board is the same authority which has appointed the members—the labour administration authority, labour inspector, labour judge or, as in the case of New Zealand, the conciliator concerned. It may be noted that in the last-named country the office of conciliator is similar to that of government officials who specialise in conciliation in other countries; appointed by the Governor-General for a given term at a time, he is principally concerned with the settlement of interests disputes, his general functions being to convene conciliation councils and to take other steps to promote the voluntary settlement of such disputes.

Permanent conciliation boards

Permanent conciliation boards are found in Austria, Brazil, Ecuador, Egypt, France, Honduras, Indonesia, Iran, the Libyan Arab Jamahiriya, Luxembourg, Mauritania, Mexico, Morocco, Paraguay and Tunisia. In most of these countries the organ concerned has been set up primarily as a conciliation body for collective or interests disputes. In Mexico, besides this type of organ, bodies have also been established as conciliation and arbitration boards. In Brazil, Honduras and Indonesia the bodies concerned also exercise both conciliation and arbitration functions.

In many countries the legislation provides for the establishment of permanent conciliation boards on a local territorial basis, the territorial unit being often a political or administrative subdivision (canton, province or department) and sometimes a judicial district or region. In Austria, France, Mexico, Morocco and Tunisia the conciliation system includes local bodies and also central, national or federal or inter-regional boards, which deal with disputes extending beyond the territorial limits of a local body. The National Conciliation Office in Luxembourg, and the board for the settlement of disputes set up in Egypt in 1964, exercise national jurisdiction. In Egypt, however, the board may assign all or part of its functions to local committees.

In Mexico the Federal Conciliation and Arbitration Board and every local conciliation and arbitration board include special committees established for different branches of activity; a board sits in plenary session when dealing with a dispute affecting all the industries represented on it, and acts through the special committee concerned when dealing with disputes affecting particular branches of activity only.

The membership of permanent conciliation boards tends to be larger than that of ad hoc boards. In most countries the number of board members is fixed in the legislation, always on the principle of parity between employers' and workers' representatives, who range in number from one to three for each group. In France and Morocco the number of representatives from each group must not be less than nor more than the figures prescribed in the legislation. In Austria the number of members is left to the discretion of the Minister of Social Administration.

Various methods are followed in associating employers' and workers' organisations in the selection of employers' and workers' representatives. They may be designated by specified employers' and workers' organisations (e.g. in Egypt) or by the most representative organisations for each side (e.g. in France). They may be appointed by the competent authority on recommendation of the appropriate organisations (e.g. in Austria) or from names on lists submitted by them (e.g. in Brazil). They may be selected by drawing lots from such lists, or through election by the employers and workers concerned (e.g. in Mexico). In Luxembourg the membership of the board, when dealing with a particular dispute, is augmented by the inclusion of the representatives of the parties directly involved in the dispute.

In certain countries the government or the public interest is represented on the board by a number of members in addition to the chairman. A board includes, in Austria, one or more vice-chairmen; in Brazil, two members without connection with occupational interest; and in France, not more than three representatives of the public authorities. In some other countries (e.g. Egypt, Indonesia, Iran, the Libyan Arab Jamahiriya and Mauritania) the government members are specified in the legislation, invariably including one or more representatives of the ministry of labour or a local administrative unit thereof, while the other members may be representatives of other ministries (e.g. in Indonesia) or of the local government (e.g. in Egypt, Iran and Mauritania).

In Austria the chairman and vice-chairmen of conciliation boards are appointed by the Minister of Social Administration after consultation with appropriate employers' and workers' organisations. In Brazil the chairmen of regional labour councils are appointed by the President of the Republic from among lawyers whose qualifications include a specialised knowledge of labour relations. In most of the other countries the chairmen are representatives of the ministry of labour or of a national or regional labour office or inspectorate. In Iran and Tunisia the chairmen of the local boards are the heads of the local government, and in the Libyan Arab Jamahiriya they are judges of the courts of first instance.

Stages of conciliation

In countries which use the services either of individual conciliators or of conciliation boards (but not of both) the procedure of conciliation is generally carried out in only one stage. In countries in which both forms are employed the procedure may consist of two or more stages. Under the more general pattern the first of these stages normally consists of the intervention of an individual conciliator, a dispute being referred to a conciliation board if he fails to achieve a settlement. In a number of countries (e.g. Indonesia, Iran, the Ivory Coast, Venezuela and Zaire) the reference of a dispute to a conciliation board is obligatory following a conciliator's unsuccessful attempt to deal with it. National practices in other countries are more varied.

In Mexico the intervention of an individual conciliator may be by-passed by the initiation of the pre-strike conciliation procedure before a conciliation and arbitration board. It is also possible in New Zealand for a dispute to be dealt with directly by a conciliation council without the parties benefiting from the services of a mediator. In India and Jordan, on the other hand, while a dispute may be referred to a conciliation board after the conciliation officer stage, the decision to do so is a matter of discretion on the part of the government. In the Ivory Coast, if a conciliation board fails to settle a dispute, either of the parties may request the mediation procedure if they are unable to agree on submitting the dispute to arbitration. In Zambia, after the labour officer stage, the Government has to appoint a conciliator or a conciliation board to deal with a dispute; but this step may be dispensed with if the parties request that the dispute be referred to the Industrial Relations Court.

The situation in Canada is altogether different. Under the compulsory conciliation procedure, the Minister may refer a dispute either to a conciliation officer, to a conciliation commissioner or to a conciliation board. He may therefore directly refer a dispute to a conciliation commissioner or to a conciliation board instead of appointing a conciliation officer to deal with it. If he appoints a conciliation officer and the latter is unsuccessful, the Minister may appoint a commissioner or a board to deal further with the dispute but he is not obliged to do so. In addition to the compulsory conciliation procedure, during which the parties may not declare a strike or lockout, the Minister is authorised to appoint a mediator whose intervention does not in any way affect the parties' freedom of industrial action. In principle, the Minister may appoint a mediator to deal with a dispute before setting the compulsory conciliation procedure in motion; but it appears that, in practice, he appoints a mediator after that procedure has been applied without positive results, when the parties have recovered their right to strike or lock out and when in fact a work stoppage may have occurred.

The system in France is an exception to the general pattern described above. In that country, if a dispute is not settled by the agreed conciliation procedure it has to be brought before the appropriate conciliation board. There is a possibility for a second stage consisting of the intervention of a mediator, but this depends on the discretion of the competent authority (i.e. the chairman of a regional conciliation board or the Minister of Labour in case of a dispute referred to the national board).

It may also be noted that in Ghana, although conciliation is undertaken only by individual conciliators, the procedure may be carried out in two stages. If a conciliator who was initially appointed to deal with a dispute fails in his efforts to bring about a settlement, the Minister of Labour has the choice of directing that the dispute be referred to arbitration or of appointing the Chief Labour Officer or some other senior official of the Ministry as an additional conciliator to make further endeavours to bring about a settlement.

Notes

[1] H. Valencia: "Ecuador", p. 235 in Blanpain: *International encyclopaedia for labour law and industrial relations*, op. cit.

[2] G. Gonzalez Charry: "Colombia", p. 109, ibid.

[3] See E. Córdova: "Labour legislation and Latin American development: A preliminary review", in *International Labour Review*, Nov. 1972, p. 471.

[4] For a discussion of the possible disadvantages of the compulsory system in Canada, see John D. Misick: "Compulsory conciliation in Canada: Do we need it?", in *Industrial Relations* (Quebec), 1978, No. 2, pp. 193–204.

[5] Sharp, op. cit., pp. 293–294.

[6] Ministry of Labour: *Industrial relations handbook* (London, HMSO, 1961), pp. 133–137.

[7] This Code, an Act consolidating federal labour statutes, was enacted in 1972. Part V (Industrial Relations), which was proclaimed in 1973, replaced the former Industrial Relations and Disputes Investigation Act, 1948. See Canada Department of Labour: *The Labour Gazette*, Anniversary issue 1975, p. 601.

[8] ibid., pp. 597–601 and 607–612.

[9] Dunston Ayadurai: "Collective bargaining and labour arbitration in Malaysia", in ILO/Friedrich-Ebert-Stiftung, op. cit., pp. 53–84.

[10] ILO: *Legislative Series (LS)*, 1973—Aus. 2.

[11] "Arrêté royal créant un Service des relations collectives du travail et fixant le statut du personnel de ce service", in *Moniteur belge* (Brussels), 30 July 1969, pp. 7411–7416.

[12] ILO: *LS*, 1962—Fin. 1.

[13] ibid., 1970—Fin. 5.

[14] ibid., 1957—Isr. 1.

[15] ibid., 1971—Pan. 1, Sections 437 and 440.

[16] ibid., 1974—Phi. 1A.

[17] idem: *Social and Labour Bulletin*, Dec. 1976, pp. 325–326.

[18] idem: *LS*, 1946—Ire. 1.

[19] Ministry of Labour: *Japan Labour Laws 1968* (Tokyo, Institute of Labour Policy, 1968), pp. 15–28.

[20] Grand-Ducal Order regarding the control of employment and conciliation (ILO: *LS*, 1944—Lux. 2).

[21] *Government Gazette of Mauritius* (Port Louis, Government Printer), 24 Dec. 1973, Legal supplement, pp. 244–313.

[22] *Employer* (Wellington), Feb. 1973; *New Zealand Federation of Labour Bulletin* (Wellington), Dec. 1973.

[23] ILO: *LS*, 1973—NZ 1, Section 64.

[24] ibid., 1976—Swe. 1.

[25] ibid., 1975—UK 2.

[26] Herbert R. Northrup and Gordon F. Bloom: *Government and labor* (Homewood, Ill., Richard D. Irwin, 1963), pp. 275–276.

[27] Inter alia, a workers' organisation has the right to negotiate with an employer on any matter concerning the relations between him and any of his employees who is a member of the organisation. The employer must negotiate on his own initiative with the workers' organisation before he decides on any important change in his operations and, at the request of the workers' organisation, on certain other matters. If the workers' organisation so requests, where a collective agreement on wages and general working conditions has been concluded, a collective agreement shall also be concluded on co-determination with workers on questions relating to the conclusion or termination of contracts of employment, the supervision and distribution of work and the operation of the company in general.

[28] ILO: *Record of proceedings*, International Labour Conference, 30th Session, Geneva, 1947, p. 510.

[29] Act No. 57-833, to promote the settlement of collective labour disputes, dated 26 July 1957 (ILO: *LS*, 1957—Fr. 2).

[30] ibid., 1964—IC 1.

[31] As a matter of administrative practice, the intervention by such a person is described as "mediation", while "conciliation" is reserved for the intervention by the permanent staff. See Advisory, Conciliation and Arbitration Service: *Annual report 1976*, para. 15.

[32] ILO: *Prevention and settlement of industrial disputes in Asia*, Labour-management relations series, No. 15 (Geneva, 1962), pp. 245–246.

[33] idem: *Conciliation in industrial disputes*, op. cit., pp. 24–25.

[34] ibid., p. 27.

[35] William E. Simkin: *Mediation and the dynamics of collective bargaining* (Washington, DC, Bureau of National Affairs, 1971), pp. 60–65.

[36] ibid., pp. 71–73.

FUNCTIONING OF GOVERNMENTAL SYSTEMS OF CONCILIATION

6

The previous chapter reviewed the different types of governmental systems of conciliation and certain administrative arrangements concerning their establishment. The present chapter discusses the functioning of these systems. It considers in particular the conciliation proceedings, special arrangements for conciliation in major disputes, fact-finding and so-called preventive mediation.

CONCILIATION PROCEEDINGS

National legislation seldom specifies the manner in which conciliation proceedings under government auspices are to be initiated, conducted and terminated. There are instances in which the question of the intervention of the government conciliation service in the settlement of labour disputes has been the subject of collective agreements. An interesting example is the agreement on rules for negotiation concluded in 1964 between the Danish Employers' Confederation and the National Confederation of Danish Trade Unions.[1] Various provisions of the agreement deal with the dates on which mediation by the state Conciliation Board is to be requested and on which it is to be concluded, as well as with the steps which the Board may take at various stages of the negotiations. A more recent example is the Cyprus Industrial Relations Code, 1977, concluded under the auspices of the Ministry of Labour and Social Insurance by the central employers' and workers' organisations, which provides that in the event of a breakdown of direct negotiations the parties may either jointly or separately submit the dispute to the Ministry for mediation.[2]

Agreements establishing private machinery for the settlement of disputes which does not terminate in a binding settlement (i.e. where the agreed procedure is in the form of conciliation or advisory arbitration) may stipulate that unsettled disputes should be referred to the state conciliation machinery. For example, under the disputes procedure in the gelatine and glue industry in the United Kingdom, if the Joint Industrial Council fails to settle a dispute recourse shall be had to the official conciliation machinery.[3]

Collective agreements providing for the submission of disputes to the government conciliation service are less common than those establishing private machinery for conciliation or arbitration discussed in the preceding chapter. However, they are not without significance because thereby the parties themselves establish the conditions under which they seek the assistance of the government conciliation service. For example, a common feature of the collective agreements noted above is that they all provide for a labour peace obligation.

Such a contractual undertaking would be important in countries where the parties' freedom of industrial action remains intact during or after conciliation proceedings before the official machinery, but it does not become superfluous or useless even in countries where the legislation prohibits strikes and lockouts during the pendency of such proceedings. This is not only for the reason that the parties may be more inclined to comply with an obligation to abstain from industrial action which they have voluntarily imposed upon themselves than with a legislative interdiction making the declaration of a strike or lockout unlawful. Over and above this psychological factor is the fact that the consequences of violation of a contractual obligation differ from those arising from violation of a legislative prohibition. A contractual peace obligation can immeasurably strengthen a policy of discouraging strikes and lockouts until peaceful methods of settlement have been tried.

When is a dispute deemed to exist?

One of the questions relating to the making of appropriate regulations with regard to conciliation proceedings is that of determining when a labour dispute should be deemed to have arisen for the purposes of intervention by the conciliation authority. The legislative definition of labour dispute does not shed much light on this question, since such a definition invariably deals with the matters which can be the subject of dispute, not with the question of when a dispute should be deemed to have come into existence. There have been two main approaches to this question.

Under the earlier of these two approaches, the conciliation authority could intervene or be asked to intervene in a dispute if a strike or lockout was being threatened or had actually occurred. This was the approach which prevailed before collective bargaining became the subject of legislation or public policy. It is related to the view referred to earlier which equated the concept of labour dispute with the occurrence or likelihood of a strike or lockout. On the other hand, the second approach relates the arising of a dispute to the process of collective bargaining or direct negotiations between the parties.

The two approaches were reflected in the Conciliation Act, 1921, of Denmark,[4] which provided that if there were reason to fear a stoppage of work, or if a stoppage of work had occurred, the conciliator within whose competence the case lay might convene the parties to the dispute for negotiations. The Act also established a further condition for the intervention by the conciliator: negotiations must already have been carried out between the parties or been declared terminated without a settlement by either party. Under an amendment in 1958[5] the conciliator could assist at an earlier date in bringing about new agreements, even if the negotiations that had taken place had not been declared terminated.

The second approach underlies labour relations policy in the United Kingdom and has been embodied in the legislation of an increasing number of countries (e.g. Austria, Canada, the Dominican Republic, Ghana, Greece, Peru, the Philippines, Singapore, Thailand, Trinidad and Tobago, Turkey, the United States and Zambia). As a rule, the assistance of the conciliation authority in settling a dispute may be requested or offered if direct negotiations between the parties have broken down or reached an impasse.

Under certain circumstances there are no practical differences between the two approaches. Where, for example, the parties' negotiations become dead-locked, the trade union may give a strike notice, on the basis of which the conciliation authority will intervene. However, under the second approach it is not necessary for a party, if it feels that direct negotiations have become fruitless, to threaten a strike or lockout before it can call on the assistance of the government conciliation service. It would seem that, whatever other advantages may be claimed for it (it may, for example, be argued that the second approach is more in conformity with a policy of promoting collective bargaining), the second approach would enable the government conciliation service to adopt a flexible policy in the timing of its intervention in labour disputes. For certain parties or under certain circumstances it may be desirable to wait until the process of direct negotiation has reached a critical stage; for other parties or under different circumstances an earlier intervention may be preferable. The service can adjust its approach according to the circumstances of each case.

Initiation of proceedings

According to the ILO Voluntary Conciliation and Arbitration Recommendation, 1951 (No. 92), "Provision should be made to enable the [conciliation] procedure to be set in motion, either on the initiative of any of the parties to the dispute or ex officio by the voluntary conciliation authority." While this is generally the case under systems of voluntary conciliation, in countries where conciliation is compulsory the regulations usually require the conciliation proceedings to be instituted by either of the parties.

A common method of initiating the proceedings is by request or application of a party to the dispute. The initiation of the proceedings on the parties' request is by no means limited to systems of voluntary conciliation. The method of formal application is usually followed where either of the parties is required to submit the dispute to the statutory conciliation procedure. In a number of Latin American countries (e.g. Bolivia, Costa Rica, Ecuador, Guatemala, Haiti, Panama and Venezuela) the statutory procedure is set in motion by the submission of a statement of claims with the competent authority by the trade union or workers concerned.

The applicable rules in a number of countries (e.g. Australia, Benin, Canada, Chad, Gabon, Ghana, Indonesia, Israel, the Ivory Coast, Kenya, Madagascar, Malaysia, Norway, Senegal, Singapore, Tanzania, Thailand, Trinidad and Tobago, Turkey, Uganda, the United States, Zaire and Zambia) provide for the sending of a report, notice or information to the competent authority as to the existence of a dispute, the breaking off of negotiations or the failure to conclude a collective agreement. The competent authority may be the individual conciliator or the conciliation board which is to undertake the conciliation in the dispute; or the minister of labour or head of the conciliation service or labour administration office who is to consider the report and determine what action to take on it. In the latter case the legislation may enumerate the steps which the conciliation authority is to consider in deciding what action to take on the report. Such measures may include asking the parties for more particulars or referring the dispute back to the parties for further negotiation or for consideration through an agreed procedure. If the minister or other person responsible decides that conciliation should be provided, he assigns a conciliator or appoints a conciliation board to deal with the dispute.

The report of the dispute thus serves as a basis for the initiation of conciliation by the authority concerned. A similar function is performed by the sending of advance notice of a proposed strike or lockout, which is required in some countries (e.g. Denmark, Mexico, Norway, Pakistan, Sweden and the United States). In Mexico the strike notice is to be accompanied by a statement of demands; both set in motion the statutory pre-strike conciliation procedure.

The formula for government intervention in the United Kingdom in the settlement of labour disputes is embodied in the words "when a dispute exists or is apprehended". Under this formula the occurrence of a strike or lockout is the most palpable evidence that a dispute exists, but a dispute may also be found to exist or is apprehended because of a request or report from either or both of the parties, or by advance notice of a proposed strike or lockout or in some other way. A similar practice is followed in India, Ireland and Sri Lanka.

Conduct of proceedings

Legislative provisions dealing with conciliation proceedings give only a very limited view of the manner in which such proceedings are actually conducted in practice. Very often, the legislative provisions are supplemented by regulations issued by the competent authority or by administrative policies and guidelines. Whatever the scope of such provisions, regulations and guidelines, practices in the conduct of conciliation proceedings largely depend on the conciliators or conciliation boards themselves. However, apart from legislative provisions, available information on conciliation practices in many countries is rather negligible.

The legislative provisions in question invariably refer to the object of conciliation: to bring about an amicable settlement of a dispute. In many cases the provisions are of a general character, and are sometimes limited in certain countries to a simple statement of that objective.[6] More often, however, the legislation also refers, with varying degrees of detail, to one or more aspects of the proceedings. It is not uncommon, for instance, to fix by legislation a maximum period for the duration of conciliation proceedings. This is the case in several Latin American countries which have tried to reflect in their labour legislation that concern for the expeditious handling of labour disputes that was mentioned before. The maximum period ranges from nine days in Honduras to 30 in Venezuela. In Chile, Panama and Peru the relevant provisions refer to 10, 12 and 20 days respectively.

It may be that, because of the nature of the conciliation process, it is not advisable for the conduct of conciliation proceedings to be regulated by legislation except in general terms or with the barest essential details. Provisions of a general character leave plenty of room for flexibility in the administration and practice of conciliation and this may be considered an advantage. Administrative regulations and policies may be laid down to supplement legislative regulations and provide more details. They can be more readily modified than legislation to reflect the results of experience.

Parties' attendance and representation

As was noted earlier, where conciliation is compulsory the law may require the parties to attend the proceedings or may empower the conciliation authority concerned to compel their attendance. In most countries the parties may designate any person to represent them in the proceedings, as they wish; but in a few countries the parties' choice of their representative is subject to some limitation or condition. In Denmark, for example, they may not be persons from outside the employers' or workers' organisations or establishments concerned. In New Zealand no practising barrister or solicitor, under a power of attorney or otherwise, is allowed to appear before a conciliation council. In Norway practising barristers and solicitors are not allowed as authorised representatives of the parties without the consent of the conciliator. In some countries (e.g. France, Pakistan and Zaire) the legislation requires that the parties' representatives should be authorised to negotiate and conclude or sign an agreed settlement.

It is generally considered good practice that the parties' representatives should have such authority, but in countries where this condition is not prescribed in the legislation there may be cases in which it is not followed. Among such cases are those in which the companies involved in the negotiations are divisions or subsidiaries of larger undertakings, where any settlement negotiated by the local management is subject to the general approval of the headquarters. This may not involve any particular difficulty where the headquarters concerned is located within the same country, but it may become a real problem in the case of subsidiaries of multinational enterprises. On the workers' side, it is not unusual in some countries, including in particular Canada and the United States, for the terms of settlement negotiated by a union negotiating committee to be submitted for ratification by the membership. It appears to be accepted practice in these cases that the reservation of the power of the parties' representatives to negotiate a final agreement should be made clear at the very outset of the conciliation proceedings.

Conciliation meetings

A conciliator usually begins his intervention in a dispute by holding preliminary meetings with the parties, in order to advise them of his intervention in the dispute, to obtain background and other relevant information from them and to establish the basis for future meetings with them. Depending on the parties' experience of collective bargaining or conciliation, the conciliator may also decide to arrange such preliminary meetings with a view to giving the parties appropriate information in connection with the future negotiations or the procedure he intends to follow. From the conciliator's point of view, these initial contacts can serve a vitally important purpose—they are a means by which he can prove his "acceptability" to both parties and establish his relationship with them on a wholesome, positive note. These initial contacts (which may be conducted by telephone or take the form of visits to the parties' offices or separate meetings in the conciliator's office) are to be distinguished from the conciliation meetings which are devoted to a substantive discussion of the issues in dispute.

In general, conciliation boards are limited to holding joint meetings in which both parties are present. Beside joint meetings, conciliators in many countries may hold separate meetings with each of the parties.

Separate meetings are carried out in two main ways. In the first place they may take place in connection with a joint meeting. They may be held before or after a scheduled joint meeting, which may be suspended so that the conciliator can meet with each party separately. The process may involve the conciliator's shuttling back and forth between the two sides, until he decides that the joint meeting should be resumed. In the second place the conciliator may hold a meeting with each of the parties at different times and places; he may decide to do so if it is not advisable in the existing circumstances to bring the parties together in a joint meeting, or if it is not possible to schedule a joint meeting immediately or for tactical considerations.

For the conciliator joint and separate meetings serve different purposes. A joint meeting is essentially a discussion between the two parties under his chairmanship and guidance. In a separate meeting the conciliator sheds his role as chairman and engages in a dialogue or confidential discussion with the party present. The scope of the initiatives that the conciliator can take in a joint meeting is limited by the fact that he should observe the strictest neutrality between parties. While it is also necessary for him to be absolutely neutral and impartial in a separate meeting, this type of meeting gives him broader scope for taking initiatives than a joint meeting. In a separate meeting he can give information or advice or make suggestions to one of the parties which he cannot do in a joint meeting without running the risk of being suspected of partiality by the other party.

The practice of holding separate meetings has developed under different types of legislative provision. In Israel and Zambia the legislation expressly provides that the conciliator may hold separate (as well as joint) meetings. In Panama the holding of separate meetings may be implied from the provision that the conciliator is to act as an intermediary between the parties. In most countries, however, the practice has developed under general provisions directing the conciliator to meet, confer with, consult, communicate with or hold open discussions with the parties. Indeed, it may be said that unless the legislation expressly provides or clearly implies that the conciliator shall hold only joint meetings, it would be possible for a conciliator to hold separate meetings with the parties and for the conciliation service to promote this practice among its staff.

A separate meeting is of necessity more informal than a joint meeting. However, national practices differ over the degree of formality observed by conciliators or conciliation boards in the conduct of joint meetings. The question of formality is dealt with in the legislation of New Zealand and Panama. In the former country the conciliation council is not bound to proceed with its inquiry in any formal manner or sit formally as a tribunal. In Panama the conciliation procedure is to be flexible in nature, free from formalities and simple in its mode of functioning.

Greater informality in conciliation meetings is associated with what is known as the "conference method" of discussion, and greater formality with what may be described as a semi- or quasi-judicial method. In the conference method, after the presentation of its case by each party, there is a continuous interchange between the two sides; the procedure may involve prolonged discussions extending over a number of joint meetings or sessions. In the semi-judicial method each side is given the opportunity, one after the other, to present its case as fully as possible and the parties generally address themselves to the conciliator or chairman of the board rather than to each other.

The conference method is generally associated with proceedings before individual conciliators and the semi-judicial method with proceedings before conciliation boards; but there may be cases in which the proceedings before individual conciliators more nearly approach the semi-judicial method, and proceedings before conciliation boards that more nearly approach the conference method. In this regard, national practices are greatly influenced by legal traditions and the extent to which lawyers participate in conciliation proceedings, either as individual conciliators or as the chairmen of conciliation boards and as representatives or counsel of the parties. The legal tradition may find expression in the regulations governing the procedural aspects of board proceedings, and not infrequently such proceedings are referred to in the legislation as "hearings".

The role of the individual conciliator and that of the chairman of a conciliation board in presiding over a joint meeting are essentially the same. However, while a conciliator controls the procedural aspects of the meeting, the chairman of a board may have less power in deciding procedural questions. This again is a matter of practice which is seldom expressly dealt with in the legislation; in some countries the board has the power to fix its own rules of procedure, while in other countries the question is dealt with by administrative regulations. In New Zealand, where the matter is governed by legislation, procedural questions before a conciliation council are decided on the basis of a majority of the assessors present at a meeting; if they are equally divided, the conciliator has a casting vote.

Gathering and obtaining information

While meetings serve as the avenue by which conciliators and conciliation boards perform their substantive responsibility of assisting the parties in the settlement of disputes, their principal vehicle in discharging that responsibility consists of information which they possess or are able to obtain, on the basis of which they form conclusions regarding the facts and on the merits of the issues involved and the possibilities, which in turn provide the basis for their decisions in taking initiatives which will lead the parties to agreement, particularly their suggestions, proposals or recommendations for settlement.

In a typical case, each party to a dispute will put forward all the documents and information it has been able to obtain in support of its claim or contention. As a rule, however, a conciliator or a conciliation board is not limited to acting solely on the basis of information supplied by the parties. As the parties are biased sources of information, any information from one party is often incomplete.

There are, however, important differences in regard to the manner in which individual conciliators and conciliation boards obtain information and make use of it. An individual conciliator has to rely on personal effort to obtain as much information as possible concerning a dispute, whereas the individual members of a conciliation board are generally under no such obligation. The task of a conciliator in gathering information on the basis of personal effort has to be distinguished from the exercise of any powers of investigation which may be vested in him by legislation; they are different things, but one does not exclude the other.

A conciliator starts gathering information when he decides to intervene in a dispute or is assigned to deal with it. However, much of the relevant information that a conciliator may use in a particular dispute can be obtained in advance. This is true, for example, with regard to the movement of wages in general and in particular industries, occupations and areas and to comparative wage rates and employment practices. In certain countries it is the duty of conciliators to keep abreast of developments concerning such questions, particularly those which are typically the subject of collective bargaining negotiations, and generally of the developments which affect the relations between employers and workers. The information a conciliator will collect in connection with a particular dispute will thus be mainly to supplement that which he already possesses or has obtained beforehand.[7]

While the collection of advance information has developed largely on the basis of administrative policies and regulations (e.g. in the United Kingdom and in former British territories), they have been the subject of specific legislative mandates in a few countries. In Denmark, for example, the law requires the mediators to keep in touch at all times with the general situation as regards employment, especially wages, and to meet as often as necessary to discuss the situation. In New Zealand one of the functions of a mediator is to maintain a close liaison with the parties in industry and to carry out relevant studies and surveys. In Norway and Sweden conciliators have to follow with close attention the conditions of work within their respective spheres.

In some countries conciliators are aided in keeping themselves abreast of significant developments by information supplied by the headquarters office of the conciliation service; and it may also be possible for a conciliator to request headquarters for information on a specific, troublesome point in connection with a dispute which is currently engaging his attention. It was noted earlier that this assistance from headquarters is a form of needed technical support for conciliators and that this is one of the most important aspects of the problem of administrative arrangements for conciliation. The value of technical staff in the central headquarters who can collect and analyse information and send necessary material to conciliators cannot perhaps be overemphasised.

While individual members of conciliation boards are not in the same position as individual conciliators as regards the collection of information by personal effort, conciliation boards and individual conciliators have the same possibility of obtaining relevant information from the parties in joint meetings, by requesting them to supply such information. There is also the further possibility for an individual conciliator to obtain information on the basis of similar requests in separate meetings. In many countries the conciliator or the board can use only voluntary methods of gathering information from the parties. They can thus obtain only such information as the parties are willing to offer, of their own volition or in response to requests.

In order to enable them to obtain such information as they may need, conciliators and conciliation boards are given powers of investigation in certain countries (e.g. Canada, Colombia, Denmark, Finland, France, India, Indonesia, Israel, the Ivory Coast, Lebanon, Malaysia, Mauritania, New Zealand, Norway, Peru, the Philippines, Sri Lanka, Sweden, Tunisia and Zaire). There is no uniform formula for the grant of investigatory powers. It may consist of a general authority to require the parties to submit the necessary information (e.g. in Colombia, Denmark, Finland, Lebanon, Malaysia, Norway, Peru and Sweden). In other cases certain specific powers may be granted, either alone or in combination with a general authority to require the submission of information.

The grant of specific powers may include any or more of the following: *(a)* the power to compel the attendance of the parties and of witnesses in order to give evidence, or the power to authorise the examination of witnesses; in some countries the legislation specifies experts among the persons who may be compelled to attend; *(b)* the power to take testimony under oath and to swear in witnesses; *(c)* the power to compel the production of books, records and other documents; and *(d)* the power to make ocular inspection of factories and workplaces.

In certain countries which make use of the services of individual conciliators and conciliation boards and where it is possible to carry out conciliation in two stages, the grant of investigatory powers is generally limited to the procedure that may be utilised at the second stage, although this stage may not eventually be resorted to. For example, in Canada, Indonesia and New Zealand powers of investigation are given to a conciliation commissioner or a conciliation board but not to a conciliation officer or a mediator; and in France and the Ivory Coast such powers are given to a mediator but not to a conciliation board or a labour inspector (acting as a conciliator).

An investigation need not necessarily take place in connection with a conciliation meeting. In Norway, for example, the legislation authorises a conciliator to collect information (i.e. by citing the parties, experts or witnesses to be present and give evidence) even if one or both of the parties fail to appear. It also appears that in India, Malaysia and Sri Lanka a distinction is made between investigation and conciliation (i.e. promoting the settlement of a dispute); the conciliator has to investigate a dispute as the first part of his intervention in it and will normally undertake conciliation only after such investigation.

In New Zealand a person is not bound to give evidence before a conciliation council with regard to trade secrets, profits, losses, receipts, and so forth, or to produce books in connection with his business. If he decides to give such evidence or produce such books, he may, if the conciliator thinks fit, do so in the presence of the conciliator alone, without the parties' assessors.

From a mere reading of the legislative provisions granting powers of investigation to conciliators and conciliation boards it is not possible to deduce the reasons underlying them in the countries concerned; and probably the actual reasons would vary from country to country. It seems, however, that a grant of these powers is related in certain cases to provisions which authorise conciliators and conciliation boards to present proposals or recommendations for settlement to the parties (e.g. in Denmark, Finland, France, the Ivory Coast and Norway); or which require them to submit reports including such recommendations (e.g. in Canada, India, Mauritania, Sri Lanka and Tunisia). In these cases the making of proposals or recommendations for settlement would require an assessment of the facts upon which they are to be grounded and it would be important that the process of fact-finding be carried out as fully and as objectively as possible.

Confidentiality of information

The expression "confidentiality of information" is here used to denote the principle under which it is the duty of conciliators and conciliation boards to observe secrecy with regard to confidential information given by the parties in the course of conciliation proceedings. The expression "confidential information" includes information which is declared to be so by a statute or administrative regulation as well as information which the person giving it asks the board or conciliator to treat as confidential.

The legislation in a number of countries provides expressly for confidentiality of information (e.g. Denmark, Finland, France, India, Indonesia, Israel, Mauritania, New Zealand, Norway, the Philippines, Sweden and Zaire). In many countries the provisions in question are a corollary to provisions concerning investigatory powers. National law regarding the scope of confidential information varies from country to country. The duty to observe secrecy is qualified by divers conditions in different countries.[8]

What is the position in countries where there are no legislative provisions dealing with confidentiality of information? What is the position where such provisions exist but are of a limited character, with respect to confidential information not covered by them?

In considering these questions it may be useful to ask what are the purposes of the legislative provisions in question. These purposes appear to be mainly two, of which the first is to protect the interests of persons giving confidential information. This purpose is more clearly perceived in connection with information obtained through compulsory process, or which a party is legally required to submit, even if he was not willing to do so. If the disclosure of such information (for example, a trade secret) can lead to his prejudice in his relations with third parties or the public, he is entitled to be protected by law from such a result.

The second purpose, which is perhaps more important from the point of view of disputes settlement, is to protect the integrity of the conciliation process itself and to enhance its effectiveness. The parties to labour disputes need to be encouraged to give conciliators and conciliation boards such information as they may need for the performance of their function, and the principle of confidentiality of information is one of the most practicable means to achieve that purpose. While this purpose may also be served by legislation, it does not always have to depend on legislative sanction; it is more a matter of collective discipline within the conciliation service concerned and of individual discipline among the members of its staff.

It may be noted that, unless otherwise provided by law, conciliation meetings are held in private. They are as private as the direct collective bargaining sessions between the parties, of which they are essentially and logically an extension. They do not lose their character as a strictly private affair between the participants when the conciliation proceedings are brought to an end. Public policy would require that the private character of conciliation meetings be fully respected and not abused.

In this connection, Norwegian legislation expressly requires that conciliation proceedings should be held *in camera*. On this basis it provides that the matters dealt with in conciliation proceedings are to be regarded as confidential. This rule, however, may be taken as a statement of good practice in conciliation, which is valid and relevant wherever this method of settlement is applied, and not as a regulation arising from specifically Norwegian circumstances and requirements—although, in the absence of a statutory or regulatory declaration as to the scope of confidential information, this may be limited to such information as the party giving it requests to be so treated.

For the individual conciliator, confidentiality of information is an essential aspect of separate meetings with the parties. It is through such meetings that he can obtain from each of the parties valuable information which will advance the negotiations. It is not information concerning material facts only, but may be information on their attitudes on the issues and on the concessions they would be willing to make. It includes in particular information affecting the parties' bargaining position, which a party would be willing to convey to the conciliator but not to the other party. The principle of confidentiality of information in separate meetings encourages a party to give confidential information while protecting its negotiating position vis-à-vis the other party. There is a provision in Finnish legislation enabling a party to make it a condition that information given to the conciliator is not to be revealed without his consent to the other party; but this provision may also be taken as a statement of good and accepted practice in conciliation and is not peculiar to Finnish conditions.

It may not therefore be supposed that, in the absence of legislative provisions on the matter, conciliators and conciliation boards are not duty bound to observe secrecy with regard to confidential information; and it may be assumed that in many countries the matter is governed by administrative regulations, either developed purely as a matter of administrative policy or to supplement legislative provisions. In Japan, for example, Article 6 of the Enforcement Order for the Labour Relations Adjustment Law, 1946, provides that "The conciliator shall not disclose any secret information obtained in performing his functions."[9] Note may also be taken of a provision contained in the existing regulations of the United States Federal Mediation and Conciliation Service, according to which "Labour and management or other interested parties participating in mediation efforts must have the assurance and confidence that information disclosed to commissioners and other employees of the Service will not subsequently be divulged, voluntarily or because of compulsion."[10] The regulations also indicate that all files, reports, letters, memoranda, minutes, documents or other papers in the official custody of the Service or any of its employees, relating to or acquired in its or their official activities under the Labour-Management Relations Act, 1947, are regarded as confidential: "No such confidential records shall be disclosed to any unauthorised person, or be taken or withdrawn, copied or removed from the custody of the Service or its employees by any person, or by any agent or representative of such person without the prior consent of the Director."[10]

Irrespective of law or regulations, confidentiality of information is a matter of vital personal importance for those who are engaged in the practice of conciliation on a professional basis or as a life career. A conciliator who fails in his duty with regard to confidential information will sooner or later find that his indiscretion has acquired notoriety and that his future usefulness as a conciliator has been immeasurably and perhaps irremediably damaged. While the practice of conciliation may not be regarded as a profession in the same way as law or medicine, an increasing number of people who regularly work as conciliators acquire the conviction that they are bound by certain rules or standards of professional conduct. The Association of Labour Mediation Agencies in the United States adopted in September 1964 a code of professional conduct for labour mediators which provides in part as follows:

Confidential information acquired by the mediator should not be disclosed to others for any purpose or in a legal proceeding or be used directly or indirectly for the personal benefit or profit of the mediator.

Bargaining positions, proposals and suggestions given to the mediator in confidence during the course of bargaining for his sole information should not be disclosed to [the] other party without first securing permission from the party or person who gave it to him.[11]

In order to be encouraged to give confidential information required for conciliation, employers and trade unions should be aware of the rules regarding confidentiality. Such awareness may derive from the publicity given to the relevant legislation or regulations. In addition, when dealing with an actual case, conciliators and chairmen of conciliation boards may make it a practice, on an appropriate occasion, to inform the parties of these rules.

Getting the parties to agree: role of the conciliator

The substantive responsibility of a conciliator or a conciliation board to assist parties in labour disputes to reach an agreement which will settle the dispute involves an exercise of independent judgement. In view of the important differences in the way in which individual conciliators and conciliation boards perform that responsibility and exercise judgement, it may be useful to consider their respective roles separately.

As regards individual conciliators, apart from legislative provisions couched in broad and general terms, there are very few provisions dealing specifically with the manner in which they are to perform their functions. Moreover, such provisions as do exist relate invariably to procedural matters only, particularly the steps which a conciliator may take at various stages of the negotiations.

In Finland it is provided, inter alia, that, after thoroughly acquainting himself with the circumstances of the dispute, the conciliator must endeavour to induce the parties to determine the precise matters in dispute. In Sweden it is provided that the negotiations conducted by the conciliator must, in the first place, have the object of bringing about an agreement in accordance with the offers or proposals made by the parties themselves. Other provisions, in Finland, Sweden and various other countries, are to the effect that the conciliator may urge the parties to accept appropriate concessions and adjustments for the purpose of bringing about a compromise. All these provisions suggest basic guidelines which are followed by conciliators in many countries, even though nothing might be said about them in the legislation or even in administrative regulations.

The first step therefore is for the conciliator to help the parties in clarifying the issues and to limit the discussions as far as possible to those issues which the parties accept as the real problems in dispute. It may be noted that clarification of the issues is essential not only for the parties, in order to avoid a situation where they talk about different things, but also (and no less importantly) for the conciliator himself, who can be misled in his efforts if he does not understand clearly the precise issues which separate the parties.

After the issues have been clarified, the conciliator will seek to encourage and induce the parties to make offers, proposals and counter-proposals which can serve as a basis of agreement and he also assists either party in formulating its proposals or counter-proposals. In this phase of the proceedings the conciliator must maximise the role of the parties' negotiators and minimise his own functions.[12] This phase involves the application of techniques of conciliation and persuasion that are largely a reflection of the personality and individual inclination of each conciliator. For this reason, although the techniques employed by conciliators may be similar in their objectives, they will differ in certain important respects and especially in detail from conciliator to conciliator.

If the parties are not able to reach agreement on the basis of their own proposals and counter-proposals, the conciliator may submit to the parties his own proposal for settling the dispute. If various issues are involved, his proposal may amount to what is called a "package deal". In other words, the conciliator's proposal will be one to settle the dispute as a whole.

Generally, a conciliator may present his proposal verbally or, with the help of notes or written figures, on an informal basis. In addition, in certain countries the legislation provides for the conciliator to make formal written proposals or recommendations for settlement directly to the parties (e.g. in France and the Scandinavian countries) or to submit reports to the competent authority containing such recommendations, which are then transmitted to the parties (e.g. in Canada, the Ivory Coast and Sri Lanka).

In many countries the question of whether or not he should present a proposal for settlement is addressed to the discretion of the conciliator, and he may decide against doing so. This appears to be the practice generally where the conciliator's proposals are presented to the parties verbally or informally. In Denmark, where the conciliator's proposal may take the form of a draft settlement, the conciliator must refrain from presenting such a draft to the parties if he considers it likely that the proposal will be rejected by one of the parties.[13]

The parties are free to accept or reject the conciliator's proposal. In this connection, the legislation in Denmark and Norway provides for the possibility of the proposals being submitted to a vote of the members of the organisations involved in the negotiations. In some countries the parties are given the right to state within a prescribed number of days whether they accept or reject the proposal, and it is deemed to have been accepted by both parties if during the said period none of them has refused the proposal, as in France,[14] or has interposed an objection to it, as in the Ivory Coast,[15] or if no reply is received from them, as in Sri Lanka.[16]

Getting the parties to agree: role of the conciliation board

The substantive responsibility of a conciliation board to assist the parties in labour disputes to reach an agreed settlement may be considered in connection with the three steps a conciliator may take, as discussed above. These steps may be briefly restated as follows: *(a)* clarifying the issues; *(b)* attempting to get agreement on the basis of the parties' proposals and counter-proposals; and *(c)* if no agreement is possible through the second step, submitting a proposal or recommendation for settlement for consideration by the parties.

It appears that the first step is also generally followed by conciliation boards. In Costa Rica and Guatemala, for example, the first business of a conciliation board is to have the disputed claims clearly specified and recorded in a brief minute. Generally, after each side has presented its case, the chairman of the board attempts to narrow down the area of disagreement.

In most countries the conciliation boards are given wide latitude in discharging their substantive responsibility and are not restricted from taking the second step. For this purpose, however, the board can normally make use only of joint meetings and of information supplied by the parties as well as information obtained by compulsory process. The question of taking this step may be the subject of a decision by the board itself, which will be affected by various factors, including the time-limit for conciliation. Among such factors will also be the feasibility of convening the members of the board for the necessary number of meetings or hearings. It would therefore appear that this step is not often followed by conciliation boards.

Most of the more specific legislative provisions dealing with the substantive responsibility of conciliation boards are concerned with the third step, i.e. submitting a proposal or recommendation for settlement. In contrast with conciliation by an individual conciliator, where there is only a single source of third party proposals, in a conciliation board the members and the chairman are potential sources of such proposals. However, in some countries (e.g. Bolivia and Venezuela) the chairman is barred by the legislation from expressing an opinion on the merits of the dispute. According to the legislation in Mexico, members of the board, including the chairman, may during conciliation proceedings make whatever suggestions they may deem necessary for the amicable settlement of the dispute. In most other countries the board as a whole has to come to a decision on the proposals to be presented to the parties. This would require that the members discuss the proposals among themselves or in a session at which the parties are not present. Although national practices differ as to the manner in which the board's proposals are to be arrived at, they fall broadly into two main patterns.

Under one pattern the decision on the proposals must be taken unanimously. This pattern involves two different situations, depending on the role of the chairman. In the case, for example, of Bolivia and Venezuela, referred to above, the chairman takes part in the discussion only as a presiding officer. In the other situation, where he can express an opinion on the merits of the dispute, he can take an active part in the discussions and be an advocate of a particular proposal. In practice, however, since his objective is to gain a unanimous decision, his role may be reduced to that of reconciling the divergent views of the employers' and workers' members of the board.

Under the second pattern (e.g. in Canada, Egypt, India, Japan and Turkey) the board takes a decision by majority vote of its members. Where, as may often be the case, the employers' and workers' members are equally divided, the chairman can decide the issue by his casting vote. In practice, however, it is likely that in these cases the primary objective of the chairman is to obtain a unanimous decision of the employers' and workers' members.

While the parties are free in all these countries to accept or reject the board's proposals for settlement, in Mauritania[17] and Zaire[18] there are provisions similar to those in the Ivory Coast referred to above, under which the parties are deemed to have accepted the proposals if none of them interposes their objection thereto within a prescribed number of days of their reception of the proposals.

Termination of proceedings

Conciliation proceedings are terminated by the parties' coming to an agreement which settles the entire dispute. Under national practices an agreement reached by conciliation in interests or collective economic disputes may take different forms.

On the principle that the negotiations in conciliation proceedings are an extension of the process of direct negotiations between the parties, in which the conciliator is assisting the parties to reach a collective agreement, in some countries a conciliated settlement may take the form of a collective agreement, drawn up and signed by the parties (e.g. Austria, Canada, Denmark, Finland, Ghana, Greece, Indonesia, Malaysia, Norway, the Philippines, Singapore, Sweden, Thailand, the United Kingdom and the United States). Under this practice a collective agreement reached by conciliation will differ in no material respect from one which is the product of direct negotiations between the parties, although it may refer to the fact that it was reached by conciliation. The conciliator, however, might assist in drafting the agreement and also sign it, either as a witness or as a participant in the proceedings.

In New Zealand the conciliator (as chairman of the conciliation council) is to record in writing the terms of settlement, which must be signed by him and by one or more authorised assessors from each side. The conciliator must notify the terms of settlement to the Industrial Commission, which is to embody the terms in a collective agreement and register it.

The settlement reached by conciliation may take other forms besides that of a collective agreement. In these cases the primary figure in the execution of the instrument is generally the conciliator or the conciliation board itself. In some countries the conciliator draws up the agreement or a memorandum of its terms, which must be signed by the parties (e.g. India, Pakistan, Sri Lanka and Trinidad and Tobago) and attested by his signature (e.g. Israel). Under this practice the agreement or memorandum of settlement may list the various claims of the union and, opposite each claim, the way in which it has been disposed of.

The legislation in a number of French-speaking countries refers to the settlement reached by conciliation as a conciliation agreement and prescribes certain formalities with regard to it. In France, for example, the chairman of a conciliation board or the mediator must draw up a record of the agreement, which must be communicated to the parties. In Senegal the agreement is entered in the procès-verbal or record of proceedings drawn up by the conciliator and signed by him and by the parties. A similar practice is followed in most Latin American countries, where a certification of the recorded agreement is issued to the parties by the conciliation board. In Lebanon the settlement is also entered in the record of proceedings and signed by the mediator and the parties.

Where it is not possible to obtain a settlement of a dispute by conciliation, the proceedings may be terminated by the parties agreeing to submit the dispute to another method of settlement. In this connection the legislation of a number of countries provides that the parties should be encouraged or asked to agree to submit an unresolved dispute to binding arbitration, without a strike or lockout. In the United States the parties may also be asked to submit to the employees concerned the employer's last offer of settlement for approval or rejection in a secret ballot.

In the case of an unsettled dispute where the parties do not agree to submit it to another method of settlement, the termination of conciliation proceedings will depend on whether the parties are free to take industrial action or whether further action may be taken by the competent authority with regard to the dispute. Where the party's freedom of industrial action is suspended during conciliation, the proceedings may be terminated in accordance with the relevant legislative provisions (i.e. on the duration of conciliation proceedings or of the period of suspension of the right to strike or lock out). In some countries a formal act of the conciliator, conciliation board or competent authority is required for the termination of conciliation proceedings.

Recourse to further conciliation where the compulsory conciliation procedure has been exhausted is encouraged in a number of countries. While further conciliation may be taken by the ordinary conciliation staff, in Canada it is carried out by officials designated as mediators. In a number of countries provisions concerning reports by conciliators or conciliation boards containing their recommendations for settlement may have specially in view the possibility of further conciliation. For this purpose the competent authority may authorise the publication of the report so that the pressure of public opinion may be exerted upon the parties to work out a settlement in further negotiations, which may be undertaken before the same or a different conciliator.

In other cases conciliators and conciliation boards are required to submit reports, which will be their final act in the conciliation proceedings concerning a particular dispute, to enable the competent authority to decide whether the dispute is to be referred to compulsory arbitration. In certain countries the reference to compulsory arbitration, which may or may not be accompanied by some formality, is automatic, and the conciliation proceedings are terminated thereby. In the Philippines certification that conciliation has been unsuccessful is a prerequisite for recourse to statutory arbitration.

CONCILIATION IN MAJOR DISPUTES

In many countries special arrangements have been made for dealing with "disputes of major importance", a category of dispute variously defined. The main criteria used in defining these disputes relate either to the magnitude of the dispute or to its adverse effects.

One of these criteria, which is perhaps the most widely used, is the territorial scope of the dispute. This criterion is applied in countries where the governmental system of conciliation consists of a central headquarters structure and a field or regional structure. As noted earlier, under the practice in many countries a conciliator may be appointed or a conciliation office or permanent conciliation board set up for a particular region. Under this arrangement a dispute which extends over the territory of two or more regions may be considered as a major dispute which is beyond the competence of the regional conciliator, office or board. Major disputes in this category will include those arising from negotiations of a national or inter-regional scope, in which the parties are generally employers' associations or a combination of employers and national unions.

A second criterion, also based on the magnitude of the dispute, is the number of establishments and/or workers directly involved. This criterion is applied in countries where there are no regional conciliators, conciliation offices or conciliation boards. It is also followed in countries where a regional office extends over a relatively large territory, covering a number of the constituent states or political subdivisions. In the United States, for example, there are only seven regional offices of the Federal Mediation and Conciliation Service, but each office covers from 4 to 14 states. Disputes arising from national or regional industry-wide negotiations would necessarily fall into the category of a major dispute under this criterion. In other cases the question of whether a dispute is to be considered as a major one is approached on a pragmatic basis and often with flexibility.

A third criterion, based on the possible adverse effects of the dispute, is whether or not it may have important regional or national repercussions. This criterion relates to a situation where an establishment forms an important link in a large-scale production chain. Because of its strategic position, a stoppage of work in that establishment can bring about the shutdown of production in other and larger enterprises which depend upon it for certain essential supplies or components. Under this criterion a dispute may become of major importance even if it directly involves only a single undertaking or a relatively small number of workers.

125

A fourth criterion is the nature of the activity of the undertaking involved in the dispute. A stoppage of work in the undertaking may result in the deprivation of essential services and cause hardship to the community. Under this criterion disputes involving essential services or public utilities are generally considered to be of major importance. These disputes, hereafter referred to as "essential services disputes", may arise from negotiations at the national, regional, undertaking or plant level. The expression "essential service" or "public utility" is generally defined in the legislation and includes public transport, communication, water supply, generation and distribution of energy, and hospital services; but in certain countries the competent authority is empowered to make additions to the list.

A fifth criterion is the possibility that a work stoppage in connection with a dispute may have pervasive adverse effects on the nation or the economy as a whole. Major disputes under this criterion include those which are of far-reaching social importance (e.g. in Denmark); those which may seriously threaten national economic activities or the daily life of the nation (e.g. in Japan) and those which may endanger national health and safety (e.g. in the United States). These disputes, hereafter referred to as "emergency disputes", usually involve whole industries, may arise from national or multi-employer negotiations, and are not limited to disputes involving essential services but may involve important manufacturing industries, such as the production of steel or vehicles, coalmining, commerce, and so forth.

The special arrangements applicable to these various types of major dispute include special treatment within the normal conciliation procedure (e.g. through the intervention of central or special conciliators or conciliation bodies), special rules designed to postpone a threatened work stoppage for a given period to allow conciliation or fact-finding efforts to bear fruit, and the prohibition of work stoppages with compulsory arbitration of the dispute. The last two kinds of arrangement—involving the postponement or prohibition of work stoppages—are in many countries restricted to the fourth and fifth types of major dispute mentioned above (essential services and emergency disputes). These various kinds of special arrangement will be discussed in the following pages, with the exception of the prohibition of work stoppages and compulsory arbitration, which are treated in Chapter 7.

Regulation of strikes and lockouts in major disputes

The primary concern of governments in dealing with major disputes, especially essential services and emergency disputes, is to prevent or avoid work stoppages. In various countries there are obligatory strike and lockout notice periods and compulsory conciliation procedures which are of general application and operate to postpone work stoppages in ordinary as well as major disputes. In some countries various measures have been devised specifically in connection with major disputes to postpone a threatened work stoppage or to limit its adverse effects.

In India, as well as in Japan, advance notice of a proposed strike or lockout is prescribed in disputes affecting a public utility or public welfare work but not in other cases. In Japan, furthermore, emergency action may be decided upon not only by reason of a dispute's being related to a public welfare work but also because of its large-scale character or of the special nature of the activity involved. In such a case the Prime Minister may decide to apply the emergency dispute procedure; if he does so, the parties may not resort to a strike or lockout for 50 days from the publication of his decision, and notice of a strike or lockout may not be given until after that period has expired.

In the United States a similar cooling-off period is prescribed in cases of emergency disputes under both the Railway Labour Act, 1926, and the Labour-Management Relations Act, 1947. The emergency procedure provided for in each of these enactments involves the intervention of an ad hoc fact-finding body, which is discussed further below. It may suffice at this point to note that the cooling-off period under the Railway Labour Act, 1926, begins after the creation of the fact-finding body and continues for 30 days after it has submitted its report. Under the Labour-Management Relations Act, 1947, the President may, after receiving the report of the fact-finding body, apply to a federal court for an order to enjoin a strike or lockout, which would last for a period not exceeding 80 days.

In Turkey the Council of Ministers may order the suspension of a threatened lawful strike or lockout which is likely to be prejudicial to the national economy or the safety of the nation, for a maximum period of 30 days. Upon receiving an advisory opinion from the Central Court of Arbitration, the Council of Ministers may extend the suspension for up to 60 days.

In Denmark, when a conciliator intervenes in a dispute, he can always require the parties, as a condition of his mediation, to postpone a proposed work stoppage for a period of not more than two weeks. In addition, where the stoppage will affect essential public institutions or services or will have far-reaching social significance, the three conciliators acting together can require a further postponement for a similar period.

In Finland, when a threatened work stoppage would affect essential services or prejudice the general public interest to an appreciable extent the Minister of Social Affairs may prohibit it for a maximum period of 14 days, "with the object of reserving a sufficient time for mediation".

In Norway the state conciliator may also prohibit a work stoppage until the conciliation proceedings have been terminated, if he considers that it will prejudice the public interest in view of the nature of the undertaking or the extent of the dispute. Ten days after the issuance of the prohibition either party may demand that the proceedings be terminated, and the proceedings must then be terminated within four days.

Public policy in Belgium has centred on limiting the effects of a work stoppage in essential services disputes; there is no total suspension but rather a partial operation of the essential service involved. Under an Act of 19 August 1948 each joint committee is required to define those services and operations at enterprise level which fulfil "vital needs" and which must be maintained in the event of a labour dispute.[19]

Once a committee has agreed on the services and operations to be maintained during a strike or lockout, its decisions are put into effect by a subcommittee appointed by the joint committee. Details are left to plant-level arrangements; however, if the employer and workers concerned cannot agree, the subcommittee is authorised to designate those persons judged to be indispensable for meeting vital needs. The use of the procedure was illustrated in the strike by petroleum workers in January 1973; the stoppage was maintained in non-essential service establishments, but hospitals, clinics, medical institutions, food manufacturing and preserving plants continued to receive supplies.[20]

The use of disputes settlement procedures as a means of preventing work stoppages, and not only for settlement, is naturally a much greater object of concern where major disputes which may adversely affect the well-being of the community are involved. Such disputes may be referred in a good number of countries to compulsory arbitration, either under systems of general application or under those specially designed for essential services disputes. In certain countries only voluntary settlement procedures (conciliation, voluntary arbitration and fact-finding) can be used for settling major disputes. In this context the application of conciliation and fact-finding procedures becomes of critical importance. There is much more concern for effective conciliation than would otherwise be the case.

Statutory conciliation procedures in major disputes

Government intervention by way of conciliation in the settlement of major disputes may take the form of statutory procedures or non-statutory procedures. The statutory procedures fall into two main groups: *(a)* the normal arrangements; and *(b)* the special legislative procedures.

As a rule, the normal arrangements for governmental systems of conciliation have been designed for dealing with all types of interests or collective disputes, including those of major importance. In many countries such arrangements consist of a central structure and a regional structure, in which the central structure is competent to deal with disputes extending beyond the spheres of two or more regional conciliators, conciliation offices or conciliation boards.

Under one pattern this arrangement is provided for in the legislation itself, as in the case of the national conciliators and district conciliators in Finland and Norway, and of the national and regional conciliation offices or boards in various countries (e.g. Austria, Bolivia, France, Mexico, Switzerland and Tunisia.

A variation of this pattern may be found in Senegal, where the Minister of Labour is empowered, in the case of a dispute extending beyond the spheres of two or more regional inspectorates, to appoint as conciliator for that dispute a labour inspector or an official of the Ministry of Labour specially charged with the settlement of disputes. Exceptionally, he is also empowered to make a similar appointment even in the case of a dispute which is confined within the limits of a regional inspectorate; otherwise, the dispute would normally be dealt with by the labour inspector for the region concerned.

Where the general responsibility for conciliation is assigned to the minister of labour or to a national conciliation or labour relations office, the establishment of a field structure to function alongside the headquarters structure may be the result of executive or administrative decision. It is usual, under this pattern, for the headquarters office to have a number of senior or top-flight conciliators who can be assigned to major disputes occurring in any part of the country.

In the United States the mediators handle cases individually in most disputes, but the Federal Mediation and Conciliation Service has developed the practice of forming a panel of two or more mediators for a dispute of major importance. While a panel may consist of two field mediators or of the regional director and a field mediator, for more difficult cases a three-man panel is constituted by the addition of a mediator from the national headquarters. For this purpose, the Service maintains at its Washington office from three to five national representatives; but either of the three highest-rated officials of the Service may also serve as a panel member. Usually, when a national representative enters the negotiations, he simply joins the parties and the other mediators at the regular location of the negotiations; but sometimes a decision is made to request the parties to move the negotiations to Washington, either at the time the national representative enters into the case or sometimes after he has worked with the panel.[21]

The arrangement under which the general responsibility for conciliation is assigned to national conciliators or to national offices may not include a regional structure. This is the case, for example, in Denmark; in that country major negotiations take place in Copenhagen, where the headquarters of the main employers' and workers' organisations and the offices of the conciliators are located.

In some countries where the conciliation procedure may consist of two stages, the second stage may involve a more active form of intervention or the mediation of a higher official and may be utilised in particular for disputes of major importance (e.g. in Canada, France, Ghana, Indonesia and the Ivory Coast).

As regards special statutory conciliation procedures, these are mainly of two types: *(a)* those established for particular industries, usually undertaken by specialised agencies; and *(b)* those established for emergency disputes, which may be, though are not necessarily, of an ad hoc character. Examples of the first type include the procedures for the maritime industry in France and Japan, which are essentially parallel arrangements to the procedures for the private sector in general; and the procedure for rail and air transport in the United States, under the Railway Labour Act, 1926, as amended. Under this Act the responsibility for mediation is vested in the National Mediation Board; this body consists of three members and thus differs in structure from the Federal Mediation and Conciliation Service.

Special statutory procedures for dealing with emergency disputes are found in Denmark, Japan, Sweden, Turkey and the United States. In Denmark, as noted earlier, the three conciliators acting together may extend the period of postponement of a threatened work stoppage; in this case the conciliator who has been dealing with the dispute will continue normally to deal with it. If, however, in the opinion of the conciliator concerned, the dispute is of considerable social importance, the three conciliators may decide that all of them shall intervene in it.

In Japan, in considering whether the emergency adjustment procedure shall be applied to a dispute, the Prime Minister is required to ask in advance the opinion of the Central Labour Relations Commission. When the Prime Minister decides on emergency adjustment, the Commission is to exert its utmost efforts to settle the dispute and is to deal with it in preference to all other cases. It may try to settle the dispute by conciliation (i.e. through individual conciliators) or by mediation (i.e. through a mediation committee); but it may also undertake fact-finding or such other measures as it deems necessary for settling the dispute.

In Sweden the State Conciliators' Office normally chooses one of its conciliators to mediate in a dispute. However, in disputes of major importance the Government may set up a conciliation board (generally consisting of three neutral members) or appoint a special conciliator.[22]

In the United States, under the Labour-Management Relations Act, 1947, if a court order is issued at the instance of the President enjoining a strike or lockout in an emergency dispute for a period of up to 80 days, the Federal Mediation and Conciliation Service continues to be responsible for assisting in the settlement of the dispute by conciliation or mediation. It will act in the case according to the general powers and functions conferred upon it by the Act, including the formation of a mediation panel or the personal involvement of the Director of the Service.

In Turkey, when the Council of Ministers orders the suspension of a lawful strike or lockout, the dispute is referred to the Central Conciliation Board, which meets under the chairmanship of the Prime Minister or his representative, and includes the President of the Labour Division of the Court of Appeal, another president of a division of the Court selected by the Council of State and an independent mediator selected by the employers' and workers' confederations having the largest membership. The Board must give its decision containing its recommendations for the settlement of the dispute within the time-limit fixed for the suspension of the strike or lockout. The Board's decision is taken by an absolute majority of its total membership.

Certain features of the systems described above may be noted. In Canada, Japan and Sweden the competent authority has a number of choices, when voluntary arbitration is not available, in dealing with a major dispute. In Canada, as noted earlier, the initial choice is between a conciliation officer, a conciliation commissioner and a conciliation board and at the second stage the choice is between the last two. In Japan the choice is between conciliation, mediation, fact-finding or some other measure; and in Sweden between a conciliation commission and a special conciliator.

Another approach that may be noted, which is followed in Canada, France, Israel, the Ivory Coast, Japan Sweden and the United Kingdom, is the possibility of appointing an ad hoc conciliator or mediator. In most of these countries this approach permits the utilisation of the services of highly qualified and eminent persons other than the permanent staff.[23] In the United States a private person of outstanding qualifications may also be appointed a member of a mediation panel.

The United States is not the only country to use the panel method of mediation. Very similar to the United States mediation panel are the bodies constituted in Denmark when the three conciliators act together in a dispute and the conciliation commission in Sweden. All these bodies are composed of independent neutral persons who are specialists in conciliation and who work together as a team in seeking a settlement of the dispute; they are to be distinguished from conciliation boards which include employers' and workers' representatives, each of whom has his own voice and vote in the deliberations of the board.

The problem of moral authority in statutory procedures in major disputes

In prolonged disputes, Sidney and Beatrice Webb noted, many years ago, "the intervention of an eminent outsider is found the best lever for collective bargaining. His social position or official status secures for the proceedings, even among angry men, a certain amount of dignity, order, and consideration for each other's feelings . . .".[24]

The Webbs were evidently referring to the moral authority of the conciliator. The problem of moral authority is inherent in the role of individual conciliators. It is naturally of much greater importance where major disputes are concerned, which usually involve important trade unions and employers' associations. The officials of these organisations who make up their respective negotiating committees are frequently important people in the world of business and labour. Third parties who conduct meetings with them, who try to persuade them and reason with them to reach a settlement, need to possess a moral authority corresponding to the importance of the dispute and of the organisations involved and to the standing of the parties' negotiators in their respective organisations.

For conciliators in the permanent service of the government, the problem of moral authority is one of official status, as well as of qualifications, experience and reputation. The method of appointment, hierarchical ranking, post classification, rate of compensation and other conditions of service are the outward signs of official status, but this is essentially a recognition of the importance of the functions involved and of the required qualifications. While the question of the official status of government conciliators arises in different national conditions, the practices in various countries reveal a fundamental uniformity in the need to accord appropriate official status to government conciliators who are normally called upon to mediate in major labour disputes.

In the United States the national representatives of the Federal Mediation and Conciliation Service are better known locally as "trouble-shooters". They have been selected from among the field staff as mediators who have demonstrated skills in the more difficult cases. One purpose of the assignment of a national representative to a dispute is to make available the special skills that he has demonstrated. It has also been noted that "the status symbol of selection as national representative may add something in some negotiations. The fact that the case is receiving official 'Washington attention' may be important to the intangible elements of mediation".[25]

High-level administrative officials of the ministry of labour or of the national conciliation service may also act as conciliators in major disputes, and when they do they bring to their task the moral authority of their office. Under the legislation in some countries conciliation may be undertaken by the Commissioner of Labour (e.g. in Sri Lanka and the Sudan); by the Director of the National Labour Department (e.g. in Brazil); by the Chief Labour Relations Officer (e.g. in Israel); or by the Chief of the Labour Industrial Relations Service (e.g. in Lebanon). In Ghana the Chief Labour Officer or some other senior officer of the Ministry of Labour may be designated by the Minister as an additional conciliator to undertake further conciliation in a dispute.

In some other countries the practice by which high-level officials of the governmental conciliation service personally intervene in major disputes has developed administratively. In the Philippines the Director of the Bureau of Labour Relations is himself often an active conciliator in disputes of national importance. It is not unusual in the United Kingdom for the Chairman of the Advisory, Conciliation and Arbitration Service to be personally involved as a conciliator in important disputes. In the Federal Mediation and Conciliation Service in the United States the National Director, the Deputy National Director and the Director of Mediation Services occasionally act as members of mediation panels; in rare cases the Director himself may be directly involved in a dispute from the beginning of the intervention of the Service.

Another way in which governmental conciliation services in a number of countries are able to bring the moral authority of persons of high repute or high social standing to bear upon the parties in major disputes is through the ad hoc appointment of a conciliator or mediator. As was previously noted, this practice is followed in Canada, France, Israel, the Ivory Coast, Japan, Sweden and the United Kingdom. In Canada superior court judges, prominent lawyers and university professors have been appointed as conciliation commissioners. Among the persons who have been appointed as special conciliators in Sweden are those who have gained special prestige in the public service.

Non-statutory procedures

What happens when every available statutory conciliation procedure has been exhausted and the dispute remains unsettled, where there is no possibility of referring the dispute to voluntary or compulsory arbitration? Is there to be no alternative to the parties' engaging in a trial of strength, which may mean a work stoppage of undue proportions, possibly causing great prejudice to the country? Some countries have found such an alternative in further conciliation through non-statutory procedures.

Most cases of non-statutory conciliation involve the intervention of prominent politicians who hold high public office. The official most often called upon in this regard is the minister of labour, where the conciliation service is under his ministry or he is given the power to appoint conciliators. (It may be noted that, in some countries, the minister of labour is himself expressly authorised in the legislation to act as a conciliator. This is so in the Dominican Republic, Malaysia, Singapore and Trinidad and Tobago.)

Other ministers may also be brought in as non-statutory conciliators in major disputes, such as those responsible for specific economic sectors or for nationalised industries, in regard to disputes affecting those sectors or industries. District governors and city mayors may also be involved extra-officially in important negotiations taking place within their respective jurisdictions.

There have been cases where even heads of government have intervened personally in disputes of exceptional importance in order to induce the parties to reach a settlement by conciliation. In the United States a dispute in the coalmining industry in 1978 led to the intervention of the President; before the fact-finding procedure under the Labour-Management Relations Act, 1947, was invoked, conciliation proceedings were held under White House auspices with the Secretary of Labour as Chairman.[26]

In the Federal Republic of Germany the Chancellor was urged by the printers' union to intervene personally in the newspaper industry dispute of March 1978, which was accompanied by strikes in four newspapers, followed by a national lockout by the employers.[27]

It can be argued that high government officials are in a better position than the technical or professional conciliation staff to assert the public interest in disputes of major importance, and can thus more effectively marshal the pressure of public opinion upon the parties to induce them to reach a settlement. In their task of conciliation the moral authority of their office is certainly a favourable factor, which becomes more important when officials owe their office to popular suffrage. Nevertheless, in countries where non-statutory procedures are utilised they are probably resorted to only in exceptional cases.

As regards the United States, the 1962 Report of the President's Advisory Committee on Labour-Management Policy stated as follows:

In all but a relatively few exceptional cases the federal, state and local mediation services provide the only appropriate form of government service. . . . In the case of major industries, involving whole or important segments of critical industries, extraordinary measures may be found necessary. Normal mediation may prove unequal to the task of removing a strike threat or ending an actual strike.[28]

Probably the principal reason against frequently resorting to non-statutory procedures is that they will undermine the effectiveness of the statutory procedures and the authority of the technical conciliation staff. However, the decision whether a high public official should intervene in a particular dispute is one left to his discretion, since he is under no legal or statutory obligation to do so. His decision will be affected by various factors, including the degree of public pressure for his intervention in the dispute, his real chances of obtaining a settlement if he does intervene, the possible effects of the success or failure of his intervention on his personal prestige, and his talent or liking for conciliation.

FACT-FINDING

As a distinct method of disputes settlement, the procedure of fact-finding seeks to assist in clarifying the facts concerning a dispute for the benefit of the parties to the dispute and usually also of the public. The body carrying out the procedure is invariably given compulsory powers of investigation and has to submit a report containing its findings of fact, which are usually made available to the public. It is the hope that the findings of fact and any recommendation for settlement that the report may contain will help the parties in further efforts to negotiate an agreement or will enable the public to form an opinion about the dispute which will exert pressure upon the parties to reach a settlement.

While fact-finding as a distinct procedure for the settlement of disputes is sometimes resorted to for ordinary disputes, it is mainly used in connection with major disputes of one type or another.

In countries which utilise both conciliation and fact-finding, the two procedures may be sufficiently differentiated in the legislation. However, the practices in various countries have tended to blur the distinction between them or have made them hardly distinguishable from each other. For one thing, conciliation bodies have been given powers of investigation while fact-finding bodies may also make recommendations for settlement. A particular procedure may be labelled as conciliation or mediation in the legislation of a country while it could also probably be designated as fact-finding. The fact-finding procedures discussed below are those which are so designated in the legislation or are mainly designed for investigation, in particular procedures entrusted to bodies established as courts or boards of inquiry.

Among the earliest enactments which dealt in some detail with fact-finding as a distinct method of settling labour disputes were the Industrial Disputes Investigation Act, 1907, in Canada and the United Kingdom Industrial Courts Act, 1919. The procedure was introduced, along with voluntary conciliation and arbitration, in most of the former British territories, but was abandoned in a number of these countries after they became independent, in favour of compulsory conciliation or compulsory arbitration. Besides Canada and the United Kingdom, the countries in which the existing legislation provides for fact-finding in the settlement of labour disputes include Ghana, India, Ireland, Jamaica, Japan, Kenya, Malaysia, Nigeria, Uganda and the United States. In general, the effectiveness of the system has been more visible in societies in which the mass media are well developed and public opinion plays a significant role. However, experience with fact-finding is very limited outside the English-speaking world.

National practices in the use of fact-finding procedures fall into three main patterns. Under one pattern, which is followed in Ireland, the United Kingdom and the United States, fact-finding is the only available method of settling disputes when conciliation does not lead to a settlement (and the parties cannot agree on submitting the dispute to arbitration). Under the second pattern, which is followed in the private sector in Japan, fact-finding is one of a number of voluntary settlement procedures which may be applied in a major dispute. Under this pattern, the competent authority may judge that, in view of the circumstances of a particular dispute and the issues involved, it should be referred to conciliation; or it may decide that fact-finding would be a more appropriate procedure.

The first and second patterns may also be applied in countries with systems of compulsory arbitration which are limited to the settlement of disputes in essential services. Fact-finding may then be used or may be made available along with conciliation in disputes outside the scope of compulsory arbitration (i.e. non-essential services disputes). Unless otherwise specified in the legislation, the question whether the first or second pattern is followed will depend on the discretion of the competent authority.

Under the third pattern, fact-finding may be used in the settlement of disputes which can also be referred to compulsory arbitration. This pattern assumes that the competent authority has the discretion to decide whether or not compulsory arbitration should be applied to any dispute. It will then have the choice, in regard to a particular dispute, either of submitting it to compulsory arbitration or of using the fact-finding procedure. The choice will naturally depend on the government's policy with respect to compulsory arbitration in relation to collective bargaining and voluntary settlement of disputes.

In Ireland the investigation of labour disputes is the most important function of the Labour Court. A conciliation officer is usually appointed to mediate in a dispute and the Court will deal with it if he fails to obtain a settlement. The Court, however, is competent to deal directly with a dispute without appointing a conciliation officer and may do so in disputes of major national importance.

In Canada the Minister of Labour is empowered, whenever a labour dispute exists or is apprehended, to appoint an industrial inquiry commission to which he may refer any matter under consideration. He will not, however, make use of this procedure when he has decided to apply the compulsory conciliation procedure and this has not been exhausted.

In the United Kingdom fact-finding by a court of inquiry is used with reserve, generally after the failure of attempts at conciliation and where the Secretary of State for Employment considers that the public interest requires such action.[29] It was probably according to the same principles that fact-finding was introduced in the former British territories, but its use in Ghana, India, Jamaica, Kenya, Malaysia and Nigeria will now be affected by the system of compulsory arbitration in these countries (in Uganda the board of inquiry procedure is an intermediate step to compulsory arbitration).

Fact-finding is one of a number of procedures that may be considered in an emergency adjustment in Japan. In the United States it has been designed to play a principal role in the settlement of emergency disputes and in disputes in the health care industry; the Labour-Management Relations Act, 1947, did not originally apply to non-profit hospitals, but this exemption was repealed by amendments introduced in 1974 and the Act now applies to all private hospitals or the health care industry in general.[30] By these amendments the Federal Mediation and Conciliation Service is authorised to appoint a board of inquiry for the settlement of a dispute in any health care institution, whenever a threatened or actual strike or lockout will substantially interrupt the delivery of health care in the locality concerned.

In general the fact-finding procedure is instituted ex officio by the competent authority, irrespective of the parties' wishes. In Ireland the Labour Court itself, which is a tripartite body, carries out the investigation when it decides to intervene in this way in a dispute. In Japan, if the Central Labour Relations Commission decides to use fact-finding in an emergency dispute it will presumably also decide in what form the procedure is to be undertaken. In the other countries mentioned above the general practice is for the competent authority to appoint an ad hoc body to undertake the investigation, designated as a court of inquiry (e.g. in India and the United Kingdom) or as a board or commission of inquiry.

An ad hoc court or board of inquiry may consist of a chairman and several members, but it may also be a one-member body (e.g. in Canada, Ghana, India, Malaysia, Nigeria, Kenya, Uganda and the United Kingdom). The chairman and members are usually independent persons but in the United Kingdom a court of inquiry may include employers' and workers' representatives not connected with the industry involved in the dispute.

The terms of reference of a fact-finding body are usually to inquire into the causes and circumstances of the dispute in question, including any matter which appears to be connected with or related to it (e.g. in Ghana, India, Jamaica, Kenya, Malaysia, Nigeria, Uganda and the United Kingdom) or to inquire into the issues involved in the dispute (as under the United States Labour-Management Relations Act, 1947) or to investigate such a dispute (as in Ireland and under the United States Railway Labour Act, 1926). The powers of investigation granted to fact-finding bodies are generally similar to those enjoyed by arbitration tribunals or adjudicatory bodies, and the proceedings before them are characterised by a certain degree of formality approaching that of judicial proceedings. In effect, the fact-finding procedure is midway between conciliation and arbitration.

In Ireland the Labour Court, after having investigated a dispute, makes a report setting forth its opinion on the merits of the dispute and the terms on which, in the public interest and with a view to promoting industrial peace, it should be settled, due regard being had to the fairness of such terms and the prospects of their being accepted by the parties. The Court communicates its recommendation to the parties, who are free to accept or reject it, and may also cause it to be published.

An ad hoc board of inquiry is invariably required to make a report containing its findings of fact. In Canada and in the health care industry in the United States, if the dispute has not been solved in the meantime the report has also to include recommendations for settlement; although the United Kingdom Industrial Courts Act, 1919, and the United States Railway Labour Act, 1926, are silent on the matter, in practice courts or boards of inquiry set up under those Acts have included recommendations in their report.

In health care disputes in the United States the report is prepared for submission to the parties. In other cases the report is submitted to the competent authority (i.e. the authority which appointed the board or court of inquiry), which may cause it to be published (in the United Kingdom the report of a court of inquiry is also to be laid before Parliament). In practice, if a report is not accepted by both parties it provides a basis for further negotiations with the assistance of a government conciliator, which may result in a collective agreement substantially embodying the recommendation or with modifications.

The United States Labour-Management Relations Act, 1947, prescribes a more elaborate procedure for emergency disputes. When the President considers that an actual or threatened strike will affect the nation's health or safety, he may appoint a board of inquiry, which must report to him within such time as he has prescribed. While the report must include a statement of facts, the Act expressly provides that it is not to contain any recommendation for settlement. Upon receiving the report the President has its contents published and may cause a petition to be filed before the competent court to enjoin any threatened strike or lockout. Upon issuance of the court order the President reconvenes the board of inquiry; and if at the end of 60 days the dispute has not been settled, the board submits a second report. This report states the current position of the parties and the efforts which have been made for the settlement of the dispute. The report, which the President also makes available to the public, must include as well the employer's last offer of settlement. Within the succeeding 15 days a secret ballot is taken of the employees concerned to ascertain whether they accept the employer's last offer. Upon the certification of the results of such a ballot (within five days of the ballot) or upon a settlement being reached, whichever occurs first, a petition must be filed with the court for the discharge of the injunction.

PREVENTIVE MEDIATION

In more and more countries the labour relations policy of the government is becoming concerned not only with the settlement of labour disputes but also with their prevention, as well as with the promotion of better relations between employers and workers and their organisations. To a large extent this is a comparatively recent development, which may be better understood in the light of earlier governmental approaches to labour relations.

Evolution of governmental approaches to labour relations

It is a well known fact that today's problems of labour relations came in with the Industrial Revolution—with the factory system of production, the growth of a proletariat and the development of trade unions. However, when governments first attempted to deal with these problems, they had no previous relevant experience to guide them and there was little understanding of the nature of the emerging relations between employers and workers. With the benefit of hindsight it can now be seen that the policy of governments during the early decades of the Industrial Revolution was to wait for events to happen; measures were adopted mainly as a reaction to serious labour troubles and largely for reasons of law and order.

Until quite recently the role of the government in labour relations was mainly concerned with regulating by law the rights and obligations of employers and workers and with preventing and settling disputes. The approach to the prevention of disputes was essentially that of preventing strikes and lockouts by means of legislative restrictions, together with the use of the procedure of settlement itself as a means of preventing and terminating work stoppages.

From the end of the nineteenth century a broader view of labour relations policy began slowly to evolve. With the development of permanent conciliation offices a body of officials came into being with specialised experience and knowledge of the problems. As they could give closer attention to these problems, they became valuable for purposes other than those connected with regulatory powers and with disputes settlement. After the Second World War it became increasingly recognised that a government could do much more to promote better labour relations and co-operation in industry without resorting to authoritative intervention or legal compulsion.

This development was essentially an outgrowth of experience and a response to felt needs. Experience itself showed the inadequacy of a governmental approach that was almost exclusively concerned with the making of regulations and the resolution of conflict. But it was also very much due to the fact that studies and research had led to a fuller knowledge and understanding of labour relations problems. It became clear, from this accumulated body of experience and knowledge, that the causes of industrial strife or industrial peace are profound and complex; that they are often rooted in attitudes, sentiments, a sense of human values and even prejudices and misconceptions; that the problems are both great and small and in practice are often a matter of minor detail in the process of day-to-day relations; that many of the problems do not always erupt into disputes and are beyond the reach of legislative regulation; and that the problems have to be attacked from these various angles, through consciously organised efforts and by various methods of action.

The development may also be seen as an integral part of that larger process of evolution affecting all social institutions and institutional processes. In many countries the unions have adopted a more constructive policy in their dealings with managements and employers' associations, and vice versa. Collective bargaining has come to be recognised not only as a method of regulating wages and conditions of employment but also as a basic institutional process by which the parties organise their continuing relationship on a stable, orderly basis. The parties themselves are continually evolving methods and practices concerning the forms of their mutual relationship and for dealing with specific issues and problems. In many of the countries concerned the government has not remained indifferent to these developments, which make for better relations between the parties, but has recognised that their encouragement and promotion are good policy.

The importance of this policy was recognised in the ILO Labour Administration Recommendation, 1978 (No. 158), which states, in its Paragraph 8(2):

The competent bodies within the system of labour administration should assist in the improvement of labour relations by providing or strengthening advisory services to undertakings, employers' organisations and workers' organisations requesting such services, in accordance with programmes established on the basis of consultation with such organisations.

A government programme for the improvement of labour relations may include at least three types of activity. In the first place, there are those activities intended for the benefit of the general body of workers, employers, trade unions and employers' associations. These activities do not have any particular collective bargaining relationship specifically in view, and it is up to employers, trade unions or employers' associations to take advantage of any activity of interest to them. Among these activities are the collection, analysis and dissemination of information, especially objective data and statistics for collective bargaining; the investigation of specific labour relations problems and the publication of the results; the preparation of codes of practice or similar documents containing practical guidance for the improvement of labour relations; the provision of advice on specific questions such as those concerning personnel policy or communications; the training of management and trade union representatives; and collaboration with research and training institutions on these matters.

In contrast with these activities of a general character, the other two types of activity are designed for the benefit of particular parties in a specific situation. This may be a dispute situation arising from the failure of the parties to negotiate a collective agreement or to adjust a worker's grievance by joint discussion. When a government conciliator intervenes in the dispute, he may not only perform the traditional conciliator's role (i.e. helping the parties to reach an amicable settlement of the dispute) but also seek to assist in improving the parties' relationship in other ways. Even where there is no policy as regards the use of conciliation with a view to the latter objective, participation in conciliation proceedings under the skilful guidance of a conciliator can be, for both the parties, a wholesome educational experience. It can help them to expand their appreciation of the collective bargaining process, to develop their skills and habits of negotiation and mutual dealings, to enlarge their understanding of mutual problems and to modify attitudes that cause unsatisfactory relations. It may be thought that, if such results are possible in the casual use of conciliation, far better results can be achieved if there is a policy under which conciliation is aimed consciously at the improvement of labour relations—so that, whenever a conciliator intervenes in a dispute and to the extent that the circumstances of the case permit, he will strive by appropriate methods to make their participation in the proceedings before him as fruitful and as instructive as possible for the parties.

Assistance may also be provided to the parties in a particular situation, between whom there is at a given moment no existing dispute, in order to help them to resolve a current problem in their relationship. The objective of this type of activity is to help the parties to avoid future disputes between them or to prevent disputes from arising. For the purposes of this study, this type of activity is described as "preventive mediation", although this expression may not necessarily be the term in use in a particular country.

For the sake of simplicity, the government organ undertaking preventive mediation activities will be generally referred to in the following pages as the "labour relations service".

Basis, scope and aims of preventive mediation

The preventive mediation programme of a labour relations service may be based on express legislative provisions supplemented by administrative policy, or solely on administrative policy. The legislative provisions may be of a general character or may relate to specific objectives or activities. Provisions of the second type will be referred to further in appropriate places in the latter part of this section. As regards general provisions, examples may be found in Australia, Belgium, Canada, New Zealand, Sweden, the United Kingdom and the United States.

In Australia the first in the list of the stated chief objects of the Conciliation and Arbitration Act is "to promote goodwill in industry".

In Belgium one of the functions of the Collective Labour Relations Service is to assist in the prevention of labour disputes. Among the specific duties of conciliators are those of attempting to prevent labour disputes and of following their commencement, evolution and termination.

Part V (Industrial Relations) of the Canada Labour Code contains a Part entitled "Promotion of industrial peace". Under this Part the Minister, where he thinks it expedient, may do such things as to him seem likely to maintain or secure industrial peace and to promote conditions favourable to the settlement of industrial disputes or differences (Section 197).

In New Zealand the general function of a mediator is to assist employers, unions and workers to carry out their responsibilities to establish and maintain harmonious industrial relations. Among his other functions the mediator must use his best endeavours to prevent industrial disputes.

In Sweden, under the Conciliation and Arbitration Act, 1920, it was the duty of a conciliator, on request, to assist employers and workers to conclude agreements likely to establish good relations between them and to prevent strikes and lockouts.[31] Under the Act respecting co-determination at work, 1976, the duty of conciliators to provide employers and workers with advice and information concerning negotiations and collective agreements is to be performed under policies laid down by the State Conciliators' Office.[32]

In the United Kingdom Part I of the Employment Protection Act, 1975, is entitled "Machinery for promoting the improvement of industrial relations".[33] This is the part of the Act which provides for the establishment of the Advisory, Conciliation and Arbitration Service. Under the Act the Service is charged with the general duty, among others, of promoting the improvement of industrial relations (Section 1(2)).

In the United States it is inter alia the policy, under the Labour-Management Relations Act, 1947,[34] that "certain controversies which arise between parties to collective bargaining agreements may be avoided or minimised by making available full and adequate governmental facilities for furnishing assistance to employers and the representatives of their employees in formulating for inclusion" in collective agreements certain types of provisions "and other provisions designed to prevent the subsequent arising of such controversies" (Section 201(c)). A main object of the assistance provided by the Federal Mediation and Conciliation Service in the settlement of labour disputes is to prevent or minimise interruption to the free flow of commerce.

Even without express legislative provisions the governments in many countries are concerned with industrial peace and the promotion of harmony and understanding between employers and workers. Such objectives are often the subject of solemn pronouncements and exhortations on the part of national leaders, and in some countries they have been embodied in administrative policies and programmes which have received parliamentary confirmation in budgetary provisions.

The administrative policy in question may relate to the establishment and functions of the administrative organisation which is responsible for labour relations. In Malaysia, for example, among the functions of the Ministry of Labour's Department of Industrial Relations are those of assisting in the prevention and settlement of trade disputes and of advising those who seek advice in industrial relations matters.

Preventive mediation is invariably applied in cases where there already exist collective bargaining relationships, whether newly or recently established or of longer duration. The consent of both the parties is always a precondition to the provision of assistance through preventive mediation. Such assistance is not, however, always based on a joint request of the two parties; it may be requested by only one party, or it may be offered.

Countries in which preventive mediation activities are being undertaken have followed different paths in the development of the programmes. Preventive mediation is a delicate task, and the development of a programme is affected by the availability of trained and qualified personnel to perform the work. While there is a great deal of variation in the range of national programmes, in the activities being undertaken and in the areas of emphasis, a composite view of national practices gives a fairly good idea of the potential scope of preventive mediation.

In the United Kingdom the Advisory, Conciliation and Arbitration Service took over the work of the former Ministry of Labour for the development of Whitley Committee machinery (see p. 57). On the basis of the recommendations of the Royal Commission on Trade Unions and Employers' Associations, the Employment Protection Act, 1975, gave the Service a distinct and wide-ranging mandate to provide advice to employers and their associations and to workers and trade unions on matters concerned with labour relations and employment policies and to undertake inquiries concerning labour relations questions. In developing its advisory work the Service has both long-term and short-term aims. In the long term its purpose is to help management and unions to create constructive relationships in which change can take place smoothly and differences can be resolved before they become disputes, while in the short term it aims to help the parties to deal with current difficulties. Its advisory work arises largely from requests for information or assistance with some specific problem. Usually an adviser visits the undertaking which is the subject of the request, for discussion with the parties. The visit may be a short one lasting about half a day to discuss an issue or to provide information on some specific point. In requests for assistance with a particular project or programme of work, the advisory work may consist of a series of planned visits spreading over some months.[35]

In the United States the development of a preventive mediation programme by the Federal Mediation and Conciliation Service began after the passage of the Labour-Management Relations Act, 1947. As the programme developed in its early years, it was directed mainly to small- and medium-sized plants where the labour relations climate was known to be bad. It now includes the provision of assistance and advice to managements and trade unions in the process of exploring and solving problems before they reach the crisis stage and the promotion of non-crisis bargaining.

The National Labour-Management Panel made a careful study of preventive mediation in 1963–64, and in its second report dated 30 December 1964 to the Director of the Federal Mediation and Conciliation Service the Panel gave its enthusiastic support to an expanded programme of preventive mediation. Inter alia the Panel noted that:

As desirable as is the avoidance of immediate conflict, of even greater value is the fashioning of long-range solutions to basic problems, solutions that take account of the interests of the public as well as those of the immediate parties.

However successful and effective traditional bargaining has been, management and labour today are confronted with bargaining problems far more complicated than ever before. . . . For such problems time and study are among the essential ingredients needed, and the normal period of contract bargaining, by itself, does not provide enough of either.

The attitude of the parties and their relationship to each other will determine, in the final instance, whether solutions will be earnestly sought and effectively achieved. Time, study and painstaking exploration can create effective attitudes.[36]

Preventive mediation is undertaken by the mediators of the Federal Mediation and Conciliation Service as part of their normal functions. It may be performed on a formal or informal basis, but in either case the assistance or advice is given in agreement with the parties concerned. The assistance provided includes assistance in early negotiations and in the establishment of joint labour-management committees to deal with specific problems, as well as special educational programmes for supervisors and union representatives.[37]

Assistance in bilateral negotiations

One type of preventive mediation activity consists of assistance to the negotiations which the parties are undertaking for the conclusion of a collective agreement, through the provision of an impartial chairman to preside over their joint conferences. There is no existing dispute, and the role of the impartial chairman is not that of a conciliator in an actual dispute who is helping the parties to find a solution to the conflict. The role of the impartial chairman is to assist the parties so that the negotiations will lead to an agreement and will not end in deadlock. Of course, the negotiations do not always result in complete agreement.

In Sweden the collective bargaining system is characterised by the rather extensive use it makes of impartial chairmen. Most of them are chosen from outside the official conciliation staff, but it is not unusual for a district conciliator to be selected for this task. An impartial chairman usually enters the negotiations right at the beginning or very soon thereafter, and he conducts the conferences through to settlement or until deadlock is reached. In the event of deadlock he reports the fact to the Government and is then usually appointed either as a special conciliator or as the chairman of a conciliation commission for the dispute.[38] This practice seems to have its origin in the following provision of the Conciliation and Arbitration Act, 1920 (Section 2):

> If the employer and workers desire that negotiations respecting any agreement shall be conducted before an impartial chairman, and if the conciliator is unable to assist in the negotiations, or it is not considered advisable that he should so act, the Department of Social Affairs may, on the proposal of the parties, appoint a suitable person to conduct the proceedings.

In New Zealand it is the function of a mediator, when he or any employer or union considers that an industrial dispute is likely to arise, to offer his services to the parties to assist in preventing the dispute. It seems that in this case the assistance that the mediator may provide will include his assumption of the chairmanship over the negotiations.

The services of an impartial chairman who is chosen for his knowledge and experience of labour relations would undoubtedly be of great assistance to parties who have had little or no previous experience of collective bargaining. In Sweden, however, even employers' and workers' organisations which have relatively long experience of collective bargaining have found it useful to have an impartial chairman in their negotiations. It appears that in some industries recourse to this practice is had whenever the negotiations in any particular year promise to be difficult. More generally, the parties consider it an advantage to have a qualified impartial chairman who is specially appointed to serve their interest.[39]

The practice in Belgium represents a rather special case of the provision by a government of impartial chairmen in bilateral negotiations. As indicated earlier, the legislation provides for the establishment of joint committees in which industry-wide negotiations are being conducted. The Government provides not only the chairmen but also the secretaries of the joint committees. Very often government conciliators are appointed as chairmen.

In Austria the Collective Labour Relations Act, 1973, makes it a duty of a conciliation office (central or provincial) to participate in the negotiations relating to the conclusion or amendment of collective agreements within its area, if either of the parties so request (Section 153).[40] This function is different from assistance in the settlement of disputes by conciliation.

Assistance in the establishment and operation of joint machinery

In a number of countries where it is the legislative or government policy to promote collective bargaining, the adjustment of grievances, the voluntary settlement of disputes and workers' participation in decision-making, one of the ways of advancing and implementing the policy is for the labour relations service to advise and assist interested parties in establishing and operating joint machinery for one or other of these purposes. Some information concerning administrative action in support of policies to promote agreed conciliation and arbitration machinery was given in Chapter 4 (pp. 73–74).

The work of the former Ministry of Labour in the United Kingdom for the development of Whitley Committee machinery has served as a pattern for similar work by labour or industrial relations departments in a number of the former British territories. In the United Kingdom itself, among the specific matters on which the advice of the Advisory, Conciliation and Arbitration Service may be sought are those relating to the machinery for collective bargaining and for joint consultation, procedures for avoiding and settling disputes and workers' grievances and facilities for trade union officials. In effect, one of the most important areas for the Service's advisory work concerns the development and reform of collective bargaining in connection particularly with procedures for negotiation and for the prevention and settlement of disputes at the factory and workshop levels. This emphasis on the Service's advisory work is based on the recommendations of the Royal Commission on Trade Unions and Employers' Associations regarding the need "to introduce greater order into factory and workshop relations".[41]

In the United States it is the policy of the Federal Mediation and Conciliation Service to promote non-crisis dialogue or bargaining during the period between negotiations of collective agreements, as distinguished from crisis bargaining which takes place under a strike deadline. In the furtherance of such a policy it encourages and assists managements and trade unions in the establishment and operation of at least four types of joint committee:

(1) Pre-negotiation committees meet well in advance of a strike deadline to

discuss, study and make recommendations on one or more issues that are judged to be otherwise certain to become most troublesome in the forthcoming negotiations. The issues selected are those that require more time and study than is typically available in normal negotiations.

(2) Post-negotiation committees are established in situations where it has not been possible to settle all the issues in the negotiation of a collective agreement, where the negotiating committees have been willing to conclude an agreement and to agree to defer one or more issues for resolution by a joint committee. Frequently the negotiating committees have established certain criteria within which the joint committees are to work.

(3) Grievance procedure correction committees are established to try and do whatever may be necessary to improve and revitalise a grievance and arbitration procedure that is not working satisfactorily. Such a programme often includes extensive training programmes for management and union representatives who participate in the procedure.

These three committees are ad hoc committees which are dissolved when they have accomplished the purposes for which they were set up. The mediator's role may include any or all of the following functions: (a) stimulation of the idea; (b) assistance in the formative stages; and (c) active participation in the work of the committee. A mediator may meet the committee to help to get it started, and later only if difficulties arise. Mediators have also participated in a leadership capacity in training programmes.

(4) In contrast with the committees mentioned above are the continuing labour-management committees established at the company or plant level. The membership of a committee often includes higher-level company and union officials who do not participate in bargaining negotiations and routine grievance procedure. The permanent committee is usually a multipurpose committee; while it does not normally deal with collective bargaining issues and grievances, many matters of common concern to management and the workers may be brought within its scope.[42]

The Canada Department of Labour has a programme for the development of constructive labour-management relations which is the responsibility of the Union-Management Services Branch. This unit started as a Labour-Management Co-operation Service, set up during the Second World War for the promotion of joint consultation committees, but was upgraded in 1966 from a division to the status of a branch. It now promotes and assists in the establishment of labour-management committees whose terms of reference are not limited to the traditional area of consultation but also include those increasingly complex issues that are reaching the collective bargaining table, such as cost-of-living clauses, pension plans and provisions for technological change.[43]

The Branch provides assistance to interested unions and management during the period between the negotiation of collective agreements. Most of the assistance is provided through specially trained officers who are engaged full time by the Branch (who do not function as conciliation officers or mediators). Their services concentrate on three main types of activity: (a) assisting in the establishment of a committee so that its structure and operation will best meet the particular needs of the parties; *(b)* providing advice and information on issues that the parties discuss in consultation; *(c)* finding ways of upgrading the performance of a committee once it is established.

Before actually becoming involved in the establishment of a labour-management committee, the field officers carry out investigation and fact-finding with the union and the management concerned, in order to be sure that there is a realistic practical basis for setting up a committee, especially from the point of view of the parties' attitudes and their understanding of the problems.

Advice and consultation

Another form of preventive mediation activity is the provision of advice on labour relations questions other than those relating to joint machinery. For example, in the United Kingdom, under the Employment Protection Act, 1975, the advisory work of the Advisory, Conciliation and Arbitration Service extends to questions concerning communication between employers and workers, procedures relating to termination of employment, disciplinary matters, manpower planning, labour turnover and absenteeism, personnel procedures, vocational training of workers and payments systems, including joint evaluation and equal pay. As a result of new employment legislation and developments concerning collective bargaining at the factory and workshop levels, there has been a considerable expansion in recent years of the advisory work of the Service as regards these questions, including those relating to contracts of employment and to the individual rights of workers.

In the United States the preventive mediation programme of the Federal Mediation and Conciliation Service includes advisory services performed during the life of a collective agreement. Mediators who, in the exercise of their normal conciliation function in connection with collective bargaining and disputes settlement, become aware of problems inherent in a particular labour-management relationship may provide further advice to the parties after the conclusion of the agreement itself with a view to assisting them in improving the industrial relations climate, communications, procedures for dealing with problems that arise and bargaining structures and techniques.[44]

In Canada a preventive mediation service was established in the Department of Labour in the early 1970s, comprising a team of industry specialists. Their function is to consult with management and union officials in a particular industry during the life of a collective agreement in order to clarify problems and develop understanding and co-operation that will make for less contentious bargaining when the existing collective agreement comes up for renewal.[45]

In Australia an interesting development was noted by the President of the Australian Conciliation and Arbitration Commission in his eighteenth annual report:

> It has been the experience of at least some members of the Commission that parties are increasingly seeking to use the Commission in a role which may not strictly speaking flow from the provisions of the Act. Members of the Commission are being used as a means of communicating between the parties leading to an exchange of ideas. On occasions it goes beyond communication to the seeking of advice on matters which may not be before the Commission or which may not be industrial matters in the statutory sense.

. . . It is difficult to put the tag of conciliation or arbitration on these activities, but they seem to indicate a desire of at least some of the parties to use the Commission in an extended way, and to seek its help in matters which may in a strict sense not fall within its powers. . . . This development is I think to be welcomed, indicating. as it does an acceptance by the parties that the Commission can help them even though it may have to go outside its expressed statutory function. In the broader sense of course all this is covered by the first chief object of the Act, namely to promote good will in industry.[46]

Inquiries

Another form of preventive mediation is the making of inquiries into labour relations questions in a situation involving particular parties. This type of inquiry is not undertaken in connection with an actual dispute with a view to its settlement and is therefore to be distinguished from fact-finding as a method of settling disputes, discussed earlier.

In Belgium it is a function of the Collective Labour Relations Service to report to the Minister on labour relations within a branch of activity, an industrial sector or a specific enterprise.

In connection with the promotion of industrial peace in Canada, the Minister of Labour, upon application or on his own initiative, may make any inquiries that he considers advisable regarding matters that may affect industrial relations.

In the United Kingdom the Advisory, Conciliation and Arbitration Service may, if it thinks fit, inquire into any question relating to industrial relations in any particular industry or undertaking or part of an undertaking. Such an inquiry must have the voluntary co-operation of all the parties concerned. It can take a variety of forms, ranging from an extensive study of the way in which a whole industrial relations system is working in a particular industry, company or plant to a more limited study of any particular problem area, such as the operation of negotiating or disputes procedure or the working of the payments system. An inquiry involves the thorough and systematic collection of information and a careful consideration of the views of those concerned, followed by a detailed analysis and evaluation. On the basis of a draft report, the parties are then engaged in discussion in an endeavour to reach agreement on appropriate measures.[47]

The process of inquiry may be considered a clinical approach to labour relations. Its purpose is to find out what is wrong—the causes of malaise and bad relations—in a particular situation. The process may be limited to bringing to light the malady which afflicts the system, in which case it will be for the parties concerned to work out between themselves how to remedy the situation; or the process may include specific recommendations on how the existing difficulties may be removed, in which case it is again for the parties to discuss the recommendations between themselves and come to a joint decision. In the discussions between the parties the person making the inquiry can serve as an adviser or consultant.

Notes

¹ For the text of the agreement, see ILO: *Basic agreements and joint statements* . . ., op. cit., pp. 39–41.

² Ministry of Labour and Social Insurance, Industrial Relations Section: *Industrial Relations Code*, Labour publications series, No. 58 (Nicosia, 1977). Similar provisions were contained in the Basic Agreement of 1962, superseded by the Code.

³ Marsh and McCarthy, op. cit., p. 104.

⁴ ILO: *Legislative Series (LS)*, 1921 (Part II)—Den. 2.

⁵ ibid., 1958—Den. 1.

⁶ In Switzerland, for example, the conciliation board "shall endeavour to attain agreement between the parties".

In the United Kingdom the Advisory, Conciliation and Arbitration Service may offer to the parties to the dispute "its assistance with a view to bringing about a settlement".

In the United States it is the duty of the Federal Mediation and Conciliation Service to use "its best efforts, by mediation and conciliation, to bring the parties to agreement".

In Trinidad and Tobago the Minister of Labour "shall take steps to secure the settlement of the dispute by conciliation".

In Venezuela the labour inspector invites the parties to discuss the dispute "with a view to conciliation".

⁷ The collection by an individual conciliator of information without a specific reference to an existing dispute and with a view to possible use in future disputes may be seen from two angles. From one angle it is a part of his personal effort to improve his technical qualifications and professional competence. This is true especially with regard to developments which have a long-term significance. From another angle it is a part of his general preparation or readiness for dealing with any kind of dispute in which he may be involved. See ILO: *Conciliation in industrial disputes*, op. cit., pp. 28–30 and 31–35.

⁸ As regards mediators in France and mediation boards in Mauritania and Zaire, confidential information includes documents submitted to them and facts which come to their knowledge in the performance of their functions. In Norway it extends to all matters discussed in conciliation proceedings.

In Denmark no statement may be issued nor witnesses produced to give evidence with respect to information given and proposals made by the parties in conciliation proceedings unless both parties agree.

In Indonesia a conciliator or a dispute settlement committee which becomes aware of confidential information is obliged to keep secrecy unless the performance of his or its duties requires otherwise.

In Israel facts which come to the knowledge of the conciliator in the course of conciliation and which are not generally known are to be treated by him as confidential except in so far as required for carrying out his functions.

In India any information obtained in the course of an investigation which is not available otherwise than through evidence given before a conciliation officer or a conciliation board must be treated as confidential information if the person or union giving such information has made a request to that effect; and such information may not be disclosed except with the consent of the person or union concerned and may not be included in any report.

In Finland and Norway either party supplying information to the conciliator may make it a condition that it is not to be revealed without its consent to the other party.

In New Zealand, when a person gives evidence before a conciliator sitting alone, the latter may not disclose the particulars of such evidence to the assessors but may inform them whether or not any particular claim or allegation is supported by the evidence.

In the Philippines any statements made at conciliation proceedings must be treated as privileged communications and may not be used as evidence in proceedings before the National Labour Relations Commission (an appellate body in compulsory arbitration). Conciliators and similar officials may not testify in any court or body regarding any matters taken up at conciliation proceedings before them.

Finally, in Sweden a person who is or has been a conciliator may not without authority disclose or make use of information he has acquired through his work.

⁹ Ministry of Labour: *Japan Labor Code 1952* (Tokyo, 1953), p. 88.

¹⁰ Federal Mediation and Conciliation Service Regulations (29 CFR, Ch. XII, Part 1401), Sections 1401.2 and 1401.3, in Bureau of National Affairs: *Collective bargaining negotiations and contracts* (Washington, DC), p. 10:932.

¹¹ ibid., p. 10:902.

[12] See, with regard to the various phases of the conciliation process, ILO: *Conciliation in industrial disputes*, op. cit., Ch. 8.

[13] Jacobsen: "Denmark", p. 296, in Blanpain: *International encyclopaedia for labour law and industrial relations*, op. cit.

[14] Act No. 50–205 of 11 Feb. 1950 respecting collective agreements and proceedings for the settlement of collective labour disputes, as amended on 13 July 1971 (ILO: *LS*, 1950—Fr. 6A; 1971—Fr. 3).

[15] Labour Code, Section 182 (ibid., 1964—IC 1).

[16] Industrial Disputes Act, 1950, as amended on 17 Feb. 1956 (ibid., 1950—Cey. 1; 1956—Cey. 1).

[17] Amendments to Article 38 of the Labour Code, dated 11 July 1974 (ibid., 1974—Mau. 1).

[18] Labour Code, Article 221 (ibid., 1967—Congo (Kin.) 1).

[19] To guide the joint committees, the Royal Order of 27 July 1950 laid down a list of vital needs to be protected. The list is divided into main sectors, including industrial-economic (such as flour mills, bakeries, yeast factories, distribution of motor fuel); communications (shipping, road transport, air transport, telephone, radio and postal services); and public health (hospitals, clinics, sanatoria, waste and garbage disposal).

[20] OECD, Manpower and Social Affairs Directorate, Industrial Relations Division: *Emergency disputes*, report by K. H. Baker (Paris, doc. MS/IR/73.56, 14 Dec. 1973; mimeographed), pp. 15–17.

[21] Simkin, op. cit., pp. 129–130.

[22] Act respecting co-determination at work, 1976 (ILO: *LS*, 1976—Swe. 1), Section 52.

[23] In the United Kingdom a private person who is appointed to conciliate in a dispute is known as a mediator.

[24] Webb and Webb, op. cit., p. 242.

[25] Simkin, op. cit., pp. 130–131.

[26] *International Herald Tribune* (Paris), 17, 18 and 19 Feb. 1978.

[27] *Financial Times* (London), 15, 16, 17 and 18 Mar. 1978.

[28] Advisory Committee on Labour-Management Policy: *Free and responsible bargaining and industrial peace*, Report to the President (Washington, US Government Printing Office, 1962), p. 4. Quoted in Simkin, op. cit., p. 243.

[29] Thomas Claro: "The system of settling industrial disputes in the United Kingdom", in ILO: *Conciliation and arbitration of industrial disputes in English-speaking countries of Africa*, Labour-management relations series, No. 37 (Geneva, 1970), pp. 41–48; Sharp, op. cit., pp. 360–364. Notwithstanding the transfer of conciliation to the Advisory, Conciliation and Arbitration Service, the Secretary of State for Employment continues to be responsible for the appointment of courts of inquiry under the Industrial Courts Act, 1919.

[30] Public Law 93–360, 93rd Congress, S. 3203, dated 26 July 1974.

[31] ILO: *LS*, 1920—Swe. 6.

[32] ibid., 1976—Swe. 1.

[33] ibid., 1975—UK 2.

[34] ibid., 1947—USA 2.

[35] Central Office of Information: *Manpower and employment in Britain: Industrial relations*, Central Office of Information reference pamphlet 148 (London, HMSO, 1977), p. 22.

[36] "Second Report by the National Labor-Management Panel to the Director of the Federal Mediation and Conciliation Service", in Federal Mediation and Conciliation Service: *Eighteenth annual report: Fiscal year 1965* (Washington, DC, 1965), Appendix D, pp. 83–84. Reprinted in Simkin, op. cit., pp. 393–397.

[37] Federal Mediation and Conciliation Service: *Twenty-seventh annual report: Fiscal year 1974*, op. cit., p. 41.

[38] Howard E. Durham: "The place of mediation in the Swedish collective bargaining system", in *Labor Law Journal* (Chicago), Aug. 1955, pp. 540–541.

[39] ibid.

[40] ILO: *LS*, 1973—Aus. 2.

[41] op. cit., para. 162.

[42] Simkin, op. cit., pp. 324–327.

[43] Canada Department of Labour: *The Labour Gazette*, Anniversary issue 1975, pp. 613–615.

[44] Federal Mediation and Conciliation Service: *Twenty-fourth annual report: Fiscal year 1971* (Washington, DC, 1974), pp. 35–37.

[45] Canada Department of Labour: *The Labour Gazette*, Anniversary issue 1975, p. 612.

[46] *Eighteenth annual report of the President of the Australian Conciliation and Arbitration Commission: Year ended 13 August 1974* (Canberra, Australian Government Publishing Service, 1974), p. 8.

[47] Central Office of Information, op. cit., p. 22.

ARBITRATION UNDER GOVERNMENTAL AUSPICES

7

In conciliation and mediation the responsibility for settling disputes rests with the parties themselves. In arbitration the centre of gravity shifts from the parties to the third party who is called in as arbitrator.

The word "arbitration" is derived from the Latin *arbitrari*, meaning "to give judgement" or "to make a decision". It will be seen that this method of settling disputes is similar to adjudication or judicial settlement. However, whereas in the latter method the judge is a state-appointed public official, in the original conception of arbitration the arbitrator was selected by the parties to the dispute. This is still largely the case in commercial and international arbitration, but it has become common practice in labour arbitration for the arbitrator to be selected by a public authority or to be a public official.

Probably with the benefit of experience in commercial and international arbitration, voluntary arbitration found early acceptance as a method of settling labour disputes; it has been given a place in one form or another in most systems of disputes settlement under government auspices. Compulsory arbitration in the settlement of labour disputes was limited to a very few countries until the Second World War, but has become more widely applied during the past 30 years, as it has been adopted in many developing countries.

In the following discussion systems of voluntary arbitration and systems of compulsory arbitration are first dealt with separately. The latter part of the chapter, concerning arbitration proceedings and awards, relates to both voluntary and compulsory arbitration.

OFFICIAL SYSTEMS OF VOLUNTARY ARBITRATION

Agreed procedures for the prevention and settlement of labour disputes, which were considered in Chapter 4, very often include arbitration. In official systems of voluntary arbitration the process of arbitration is carried out through the machinery or facilities provided by the government or in accordance with the rules and procedures prescribed in the legislation.

Official systems of voluntary arbitration frequently deal with situations in which the parties agree to submit disputes to arbitration on an ad hoc basis. In certain countries they also include situations in which the parties agree to submit future disputes to arbitration, through the machinery or facilities made available by the government or through ad hoc machinery.

Most of the official systems of voluntary arbitration in labour disputes are concerned with collective economic or interests disputes. In countries in which the legislation does not distinguish between the various types of dispute, voluntary arbitration would apply to all disputes which come within the legal definition of "dispute", including interests and rights disputes.

As indicated in Chapter 1, voluntary arbitration can take three main forms: the voluntary submission of a dispute to arbitration, i.e. with the agreement of both parties, in which the award is subject to their acceptance; the compulsory submission of a dispute to arbitration, i.e. at the instance of only one party or by the decision of the competent authority, in which the award is subject to the acceptance of both parties; or the voluntary submission of a dispute to arbitration, in which the award is legally binding.

Voluntary arbitration with advisory award

In the first and second forms of voluntary arbitration noted above, the award does not bind the parties unless it is accepted by both of them. The award therefore has only the effect of a recommendation. For this reason these forms of arbitration may be described as "advisory arbitration".

The system in the United Kingdom is probably the oldest example of advisory arbitration in which the dispute is submitted to arbitration on a voluntary basis; given a more definite form in the Industrial Courts Act, 1919, it is now governed by the Employment Protection Act, 1975.[1] Arbitration is set in motion by the competent authority, which, however, cannot act without the consent of all the parties to the dispute, although it is sufficient for one or more of them to make the request for arbitration.

Voluntary advisory arbitration has been the traditional system of labour arbitration in the United Kingdom. Except during wartime, Parliament has not intervened to make the decisions of arbitration bodies legally enforceable or subject to appeal. However, as such decisions result from a joint desire of the parties for settlement by arbitration, the question of the enforcement of arbitration awards does not arise in practice.[2]

Voluntary advisory arbitration would be of interest in countries where no legislation has been enacted providing for voluntary arbitration or making arbitration awards legally binding. The absence of such legislation would not normally prevent interested parties from agreeing to submit disputes to arbitration, although they could not enforce awards before the courts. The legal situation in such cases would be similar to that in the United Kingdom.

Examples of advisory arbitration in which the dispute is submitted to arbitration on a compulsory basis are found in Bolivia and Nigeria. Under the Bolivian Labour Code a dispute which has not been settled by conciliation has to be submitted to arbitration; if the dispute does not involve an essential service, the award is binding on the parties only if they agree thereto (but is legally binding in essential services disputes). In Nigeria, under the Trades Dispute Decree, 1976, a dispute has to be submitted to arbitration if conciliation fails; if no objection to the award of the arbitration tribunal is received from either party within a prescribed period, it will be confirmed by the Commissioner of Labour and is then binding on the parties.[3]

It will be noted that advisory arbitration on a compulsory basis bears some resemblance to compulsory conciliation where the conciliation body is given powers of investigation and has to make a recommendation for settlement, as well as to the procedure of fact-finding with recommendation. The similarity is close enough that compulsory advisory arbitration may be selected in lieu of compulsory conciliation or fact-finding, to perform a role substantially similar to that of either of these procedures. The role, for example, of advisory arbitration in Nigeria appears hardly distinguishable from that of the mediation procedure in France or the Ivory Coast.

Nevertheless, compulsory advisory arbitration differs sufficiently from compulsory conciliation and fact-finding for it to be included with these two procedures in a system giving the competent authority the choice as to which procedure should be applied in a particular case. The competent authority will then be able to decide that in the particular circumstances of the case it would, for example, be desirable to apply advisory arbitration, while in a case involving a different set of circumstances it may conclude that compulsory conciliation or fact-finding would be more appropriate. Thus, compulsory conciliation will usually be selected where the element of give-and-take or compromise is important; but fact-finding may be preferred where highly technical issues are involved or where an objective assessment of the facts will assist the parties in reaching agreement; while compulsory advisory arbitration may be considered useful where it is difficult for the parties to retreat from their positions and an independent award may be acceptable to them as a face-saving settlement.

Voluntary arbitration with binding award

The most widely used form of voluntary arbitration is that in which the submission to arbitration is voluntary but the arbitration award is legally binding on the parties. As regards the timing of the application of the procedure, official systems using this form of voluntary arbitration fall into two main patterns.

Under one pattern, a dispute may be referred to voluntary arbitration at any time after it has arisen or been apprehended. It is therefore possible for the parties to proceed directly to arbitration without prior resort to conciliation. While, in principle, the legislation gives this choice to the parties (particularly if they wish to settle a dispute as quickly as possible), they may also agree to submit the dispute to arbitration if a settlement has not been reached through the state conciliation machinery. This pattern is provided for in the legislation of Colombia, Egypt, El Salvador, Guatemala, Honduras, India, Ireland, Israel, Japan, Kenya, Luxembourg, Mauritius, the Philippines, Singapore, Sri Lanka, the Syrian Arab Republic, Tanzania, Uganda, the United States (under the Railway Labour Act, 1926) and Zambia.

In Mauritius a dispute may be referred to arbitration after it has arisen, but the arbitration tribunal cannot take action on it if conciliation proceedings are pending before the Industrial Relations Commission.

In India the parties may submit a dispute to arbitration at any time before it has been referred to compulsory arbitration. In the Philippines a dispute may be referred to voluntary arbitration even after it has been certified for compulsory arbitration but before the submission of the case for decision.[4]

In other countries following this pattern, a dispute may be referred to arbitration after it has been reported to or apprehended by the competent authority. In Kenya and Sri Lanka the submission of a dispute to voluntary arbitration is one of the steps that can be considered in regard to the dispute. In Egypt, the Syrian Arab Republic, Tanzania and Zambia, as regards disputes involving 50 or more workers, the parties may request the competent authority to submit the dispute to arbitration instead of referring it to a conciliator or a conciliation board.

Under the second pattern the legislation envisages the submission of disputes to the official machinery for voluntary arbitration after the failure of conciliation. Among the countries in which this pattern is followed are Argentina, Costa Rica, Indonesia, the Ivory Coast, Jamaica, Malaysia, Norway, Pakistan, Panama, the Sudan, Sweden, Switzerland, Thailand, Trinidad and Tobago, Tunisia and Venezuela. In France, in cases where a collective agreement does not provide for a contractual arbitration procedure, the parties may agree to submit to arbitration issues which remain unsettled after conciliation.

The legislation may provide that the conciliator or conciliation board should propose or recommend to the parties or try to persuade them to submit the dispute to arbitration (for example in Argentina, Indonesia, Pakistan, Sweden and Venezuela). In the United States also, under the Railway Labour Act, 1926, as amended, when the National Mediation Board intervenes in a dispute and fails to bring about a settlement, it must endeavour to persuade the parties to submit the controversy to arbitration.

As regards the manner in which a dispute is submitted to arbitration, the parties themselves may directly make a joint request or application to the arbitration authority (e.g. in Kenya and Singapore). In Japan a labour relations commission may arbitrate in a dispute at the request of only one party in a case where the collective agreement provides that application for arbitration by the commission must be made.

Under another pattern, it is the administrative or conciliation authority concerned which refers a dispute to the arbitration body on the basis of the joint consent or request of the parties (e.g. in Sierra Leone and Sri Lanka). These cases generally involve arbitration machinery set up by the government, and the issue or issues for decision are those specified by the parties in their request or application, or by the competent authority in making the reference to arbitration or in the report or record of non-conciliation.

In other cases, particularly where the parties themselves appoint the arbitrators or arbitration board, a dispute is submitted to arbitration on the basis of an agreement between the parties (e.g. in Argentina, India, Indonesia, Luxembourg, the Philippines and the United States). In Luxembourg the arbitration is null and void unless the name and status of the arbitrator, the issue for arbitration and the procedure to be followed are recorded in writing. In India the form of the arbitration agreement must be prescribed by regulations. Both the Indonesian legislation and the United States Railway Labour Act, 1926, specify certain points to be provided for in the arbitration agreement, including the issues to be submitted for decision.

Arbitration machinery

As in conciliation, voluntary arbitration may be performed by a body acting on its own authority. This is usually the situation with regard to permanent arbitration bodies which may take cognisance of disputes on direct submission by the parties. Voluntary arbitration may also be provided by the government under the responsibility of an administrative authority which is given a number of relevant functions and powers, among them receiving and considering reports of disputes or requests for arbitration, appointing or arranging the appointment of arbitrators and arbitration boards and making formal references of disputes to the arbitration body. The exercise of such powers and functions may require some kind of administrative organisation, which would be generally the same organisation as that responsible for conciliation—for example, the Bureau of Labour Relations in the Philippines, the Advisory, Conciliation and Arbitration Service in the United Kingdom and the National Mediation Board under the United States Railway Labour Act, 1926, as amended.

In general, the main function of such organisations is to implement the legislative provisions concerning voluntary arbitration. In the United Kingdom the Advisory, Conciliation and Arbitration Service provides technical and secretarial services to the arbitration bodies; its work in the promotion of agreed procedures for settling disputes includes voluntary arbitration. In the Philippines the Bureau of Labour Relations also promotes voluntary arbitration in interests disputes; this is carried out in close connection with its work concerning grievance arbitration.[5]

As a rule, the machinery for voluntary arbitration provided by the government is resorted to where the parties themselves have not set up their own machinery or where, for one reason or another, the machinery envisaged in the collective agreement has not been set up or has been unable to function. It is not unusual for matters concerning voluntary arbitration to be left to the discretion and agreement of the parties concerned, although the legislation may provide for some formality or some form of intervention by the competent authority in regard to the arbitration agreement, the appointment of arbitrators, the arbitration procedure and the arbitration award.

Various types of arbitration machinery have been devised. In Austria and Switzerland the conciliation board may, by agreement of the parties, be empowered to issue an arbitration award. In Ireland, when the parties agree to voluntary arbitration the Labour Court may appoint one or more arbitrators or may itself arbitrate upon the dispute. In most other countries where recourse is had to voluntary arbitration, it is carried out by persons appointed as arbitrators or constituted as arbitration tribunals. National practices in this regard fall into three main patterns: *(a)* arbitration by ad hoc bodies only (the most common pattern); *(b)* arbitration by permanent bodies only (e.g. in Egypt, Jamaica, Kenya, Lebanon, Malaysia, Mauritius, Nigeria, Norway, Sierra Leone, Singapore, the Sudan, the Syrian Arab Republic and Trinidad and Tobago); and *(c)* arbitration by either ad hoc or permanent bodies (e.g. in Sri Lanka, Uganda and the United Kingdom).

In a number of countries the same arbitration machinery, or the same type of machinery, is set up both for voluntary arbitration and for compulsory arbitration (e.g. in Bolivia, Colombia, Egypt, Ghana, Jamaica, Kenya, Lebanon, Malaysia, Mauritius, Panama, Singapore, the Sudan, the Syrian Arab Republic, Trinidad and Tobago, Uganda and Venezuela). This form of machinery will be further discussed below, in connection with compulsory arbitration.

So far as ad hoc bodies are concerned, the legislation in many countries gives the parties the choice of having either single arbitrators or a number of arbitrators acting individually or constituted as an arbitration board. In Sri Lanka and the United Kingdom a dispute may be referred to a single arbitrator; the prevalent practice in the Philippines is also for the appointment of single arbitrators. In Japan and Venezuela, on the other hand, provision is made for three arbitrators; and under the United States Railway Labour Act, 1926, for from three to six arbitrators. In most cases arbitration boards include members representing employers and workers. In the Ivory Coast and Japan they consist of impartial third parties only.

Arbitrators may be appointed from lists or panels of arbitrators, the establishment of which is governed in many countries by specific legislative provisions. In the Ivory Coast, Pakistan, the Philippines and the United Kingdom there is only one list of impartial arbitrators; in Costa Rica, Israel and Venezuela there are two separate lists of employers' and workers' arbitrators; Israel has a third list of chairmen of arbitration boards. A variation of this method is found in Japan, where the members of an arbitration committee are selected from the members of the labour relations commission itself and from the panel of special adjustment committeemen attached to it, who represent the public interest. Under another system the arbitrators are appointed on the basis of free selection, without regard to any previously established list or panel of arbitrators (e.g. in Argentina, El Salvador, France, India, Tunisia and the United States); but even where such a list or panel exists, the parties may have the freedom to select any person not included in it (e.g. in Pakistan and the Philippines).

In a number of countries the parties themselves select the arbitrator or arbitrators, who may be named or whose appointment may be provided for in the collective or arbitration agreement, or who may be jointly nominated on an ad hoc basis (e.g. in Argentina, El Salvador, France, India, Luxembourg, Pakistan, the Philippines and Thailand). In some other countries each party appoints an arbitrator; a third arbitrator is then appointed by the two arbitrators (e.g. in Tunisia and the United States). In Japan the members of an arbitration committee are designated by the chairman of the labour relations commission in agreement with the parties concerned.

When the appointment depends on the agreement of the two parties or of the arbitrators appointed by them, it is usually provided that in the event of disagreement the appointment is to be made by the competent authority. In the Philippines, if the parties cannot agree on appointing an arbitrator or if they so prefer, they may request the assistance of the Bureau of Labour Relations in his selection; regulations issued by the Bureau lay down the selection procedure to be followed in reply to such a request.[6]

In another group of countries, including Sri Lanka and the United Kingdom, the arbitrator or arbitrators are appointed by the competent authority. In Israel the employers' and workers' members of an arbitration board are appointed in consultation respectively with the parties represented by them, while in Costa Rica they are selected from the lists of employers' and workers' arbitrators according to an order of priority established in the legislation.

In cases where the parties' arbitrators or the competent authority appoint a third arbitrator, the latter will be a neutral person and will act as chairman of the arbitration board. In Costa Rica the chairmanship of the board is assumed by the competent labour judge, and in Israel the chairman is appointed from the panel of chairmen of arbitration boards. In Japan the three arbitrators elect one of themselves as chairman.

As regards permanent bodies, the Trade Disputes Decree, 1976, of Nigeria established an Industrial Arbitration Panel which consists of a chairman, a vice-chairman and not fewer than ten other members, all of whom are appointed by the Commissioner of Labour. Of the ten members, two are nominated by representative employers' organisations and two by representative workers' organisations. For dealing with a dispute which has been referred to the Panel, the chairman must constitute an arbitration tribunal. This may consist of a single arbitrator selected from the Panel, either acting alone or assisted by an equal number of employers' and workers' assessors. The arbitration tribunal may also consist of an equal number of arbitrators representing the two sides, nominated by the employers and workers concerned from among the members of the Panel, and presided over by the chairman or vice-chairman of the Panel.

In Norway voluntary arbitration is carried out by the National Wages Committee, which was set up by the Act respecting wages committees in labour disputes, 1952, and consists of a chairman and six members.[7] The chairman and four members are appointed by the Government for three years at a time, while the other two members represent employers' and workers' interests respectively. When the Committee is dealing with a particular dispute, each of the parties involved designates an additional member. However, the chairman may, with the consent of the parties, decide to refer a dispute to a committee of three members only. Smaller tripartite wages committees are also established in the different conciliation districts of the country. With the parties' agreement, the chairman may refer a dispute to such a committee.

In the United Kingdom a standing Industrial Court was established by the Industrial Courts Act, 1919.[8] Renamed the Industrial Arbitration Board by the Industrial Relations Act, 1971, it became known as the Central Arbitration Committee under the Employment Protection Act, 1975. Functioning as an autonomous unit of the Advisory, Conciliation and Arbitration Service, it consists of a chairman, a number of deputy chairmen and several other members. They are all appointed by the Secretary of State for Employment, the chairman after consultation with the Service and the other members from persons nominated by it. All of them are nominated as persons experienced in industrial relations, some with experience as representatives of employers and workers respectively. When dealing with cases, the Committee may sit in two or more divisions, each consisting of such members as the chairman may direct, under the chairmanship of the chairman or a deputy chairman of the Committee.

Promotion of voluntary arbitration

Paragraph 6 of the ILO Voluntary Conciliation and Arbitration Recommendation, 1951 (No. 92), states: "If a dispute has been submitted to arbitration for final settlement with the consent of all parties concerned, the latter should be encouraged to abstain from strikes and lockouts while the arbitration is in progress and to accept the arbitration award."

The legislation in some countries provides that where there is a work stoppage at the time a dispute is submitted to voluntary arbitration, its continuance may be prohibited or a resumption of work on production may be ordered by the competent authority (e.g. in El Salvador and India) or that the arbitration proceedings shall be suspended until the workers return to work (e.g. in Peru). Very often, however, when parties agree on arbitration they also undertake (tacitly or expressly, and of their own volition) not to engage in a strike or lockout in furtherance of the dispute. In general, voluntary arbitration is a deliberate choice by the parties concerned for the peaceful settlement of a dispute; and it needs little encouragement or persuasion by third parties to obtain their agreement to abstain from industrial action.

The governments in many countries thus see in voluntary arbitration a method of settling labour disputes which operates effectively as a substitute for the strike or lockout. It is a method of settlement which contributes in the fullest measure—whenever it is agreed to by the parties concerned—to the policy of industrial peace. Voluntary arbitration has therefore been encouraged and promoted as a matter of public policy in a good number of countries, mainly by giving it a statutory basis, by making arbitration awards legally binding on the parties, and by providing machinery and facilities for arbitration.

Different countries have had varying degrees of success in the implementation of this policy. The extent to which voluntary arbitration is applied in practice appears to vary greatly from country to country. It appears that in not a few countries legislative provisions concerning voluntary arbitration have had very little or no practical application. The question of bridging the gap between policy and practice appears to be a real problem in some countries.

While this problem needs to be studied in the light of national conditions, it may be pointed out that, even with the most favourable legislative framework for voluntary arbitration, it cannot be assumed that employers and trade unions would always be willing to submit their disputes to this method of settlement. Nor can it be assumed, even when full facilities for voluntary arbitration have been made available, that the parties to existing or future disputes would be willing to make use of them or take the initiative to do so. Experience appears to show that in the large majority of cases voluntary arbitration is not likely to be agreed upon by the parties without some effort at persuasion by a third party.

This is recognised in the legislation in some countries, which directs conciliators to try to induce or persuade the parties to agree to arbitration. (It is possible that this work of persuasion is being done by conciliators in other countries where the legislation does not contain a similar directive.) Getting the parties to agree on submission to arbitration as a means of settling a dispute may call for powers of persuasion on the part of conciliators in the same way as when they try to persuade the parties to accept the terms of settlement proposed by them. Perhaps the most obvious and strongest argument that a conciliator may present to the parties in trying to persuade them to agree to arbitration is that they will thereby avoid having to resort to a strike or lockout, either of which could be very costly and damaging for both of them as well as prejudicial to the community, and the outcome of which is by no means certain.

There are grounds for supposing that this work of persuasion can be carried out more consistently and more effectively if conciliators perform their mission under an administrative policy aimed at the active promotion of voluntary arbitration. Such a policy can provide conciliators with arguments as well as with material for their task of persuasion, and may also contain elements intended to exert a direct influence on employers and trade unions in considering this method of settlement. If it is desired to achieve satisfactory progress in the development of voluntary arbitration, an active policy for its promotion may be considered essential.

The failure of conciliation provides an excellent occasion for persuading the parties to accept voluntary arbitration as a means of settling a dispute. Since the parties have already embarked on a procedure for the peaceful settlement of the dispute, they should be encouraged to pursue this initiative and apply other procedures to the same end. However, the promotion of voluntary arbitration need not be limited to situations in which disputes have arisen; it may also be followed with respect to parties in collective bargaining relations who are not actually in dispute. Such parties may be persuaded that it is in their interest to submit future disputes to arbitration, possibly through the machinery provided by the government or with the assistance of the administrative service concerned, or through private machinery set up and operated by themselves.

COMPULSORY ARBITRATION

Compulsory arbitration, as understood here, is the submission of a dispute to arbitration without the agreement or consent of all the parties involved in it, and with a legally binding award. The following discussion is concerned mainly with systems of compulsory arbitration which operate on a more or less permanent basis.

It may be noted that in some countries where, normally, only voluntary methods of settlement are employed, compulsory arbitration has occasionally been decreed by the legislature as an exceptional measure for the settlement of an important dispute. The legislature may provide for the submission of the dispute to an arbitration tribunal, or it may itself assume the role of arbitrator and enact a law establishing the terms upon which the dispute is to be settled—as, for example, in Canada, Denmark, Norway and the United States.

Public policy and compulsory arbitration

The two questions of compulsory arbitration in interests disputes and of legislative restrictions on the right to strike in this category of dispute are probably the most controversial issues facing those responsible for public policy as regards the extent of state intervention in the settlement of labour disputes. Compulsory arbitration is a subject of controversy both as a method of settling disputes and as a means of preventing strikes.

The introduction of some form of compulsory arbitration as a permanent feature of the system of settling disputes, particularly in disputes involving public utilities and in the public service, has for many years been a lively issue in Canada and the United States. It also appears to be a latent issue in certain other countries where only voluntary settlement procedures are recognised—an issue that comes to the surface whenever a major strike occurs that causes considerable hardship to the public or serious economic difficulties. Even in countries where a system of compulsory arbitration is already in force, its use is by no means a foregone conclusion; the question often arises whether or not the existing system should be modified, with a view either to enlarging or limiting its scope or simply to improving its operation and rendering it more effective.

It is useful to place this issue in its historical perspective, for the terms in which it is now considered differ from those in which it first arose as a problem facing public policy. It can be said that the earlier legislative attempts to introduce compulsory arbitration were made without regard to collective bargaining. This appears to have been the case with respect to the Arbitration Act, 1824, in the United Kingdom,[9] to the original Industrial Conciliation and Arbitration Act, 1894, in New Zealand,[10] and to the original Commonwealth Conciliation and Arbitration Act, 1904, in Australia,[11] as well as to the laws enacted later on in a number of developing countries, such as the Court of Industrial Relations Act, 1936, in the Philippines[12] and the Industrial Disputes Act, 1947, in India.[13]

In these instances, the purpose of the government in providing for compulsory arbitration was principally to prevent strikes and lockouts. The laws in Australia, New Zealand and the Philippines were all enacted against a background of disastrous strikes or great industrial unrest. In the case of the 1904 Australian legislation, the first of the stated chief objects of the Act was "to prevent strikes and lockouts in relation to industrial disputes" (this object was deleted in a later amendment to the Act). Compulsory arbitration was introduced in India during the Second World War and was subsequently made a permanent feature of the system of disputes settlement.

In practical terms, in this earlier approach to the settlement of labour disputes, the issue facing public policy was considered to be that of compulsory arbitration versus strikes. At that time the resort to strikes was largely deemed to mean the use of force, and the dispute was always decided according to the terms imposed by the stronger, victorious party. In contrast with this method of settling disputes, compulsory arbitration was advanced as a peaceful, preferable and more rational and equitable method of settlement.

Even today, there seem to be proponents of compulsory arbitration who conceive of the issue solely or very largely in these terms, and who would support their view by expressing the issue as one between compulsory arbitration and the "law of the jungle". In the main, however, the question of compulsory arbitration is now considered mainly in relation to collective bargaining, where the right to strike is held to be an essential element of the right to bargain collectively. The emergence of collective bargaining as a distinct institution in the field of labour relations has substantially changed the contours of the problem of compulsory arbitration.

When collective bargaining is taken into account, compulsory arbitration ceases to be just a question of preventing strikes and lockouts. In collective bargaining the parties are making an agreement which is to be the law regulating their mutual relationship, and they alone determine the terms of the agreement. In compulsory arbitration the State replaces this contractual freedom of the parties with the power of a third party to determine the terms of their relationship. Besides this immediate effect on the parties' contractual freedom, it is also commonly assumed that, where compulsory arbitration is applicable, it will tend to discourage collective bargaining and to become the dominant method of regulating the relations between employers and workers.

It is not intended to examine in detail here the pros and cons of compulsory arbitration and collective bargaining. It is undeniable that, as a matter of principle, it is in the highest public interest that employers and employees should be able to negotiate collective agreements and that collective bargaining should accordingly be promoted. The question, however, is whether there may be circumstances in which other considerations of public interest might justify the imposition of compulsory arbitration.[14]

Views differ about which considerations of public interest will be sufficient to provide justification for including compulsory arbitration in the national system of disputes settlement. While it can be debated in the abstract, the issue can perhaps be most fruitfully weighed in connection with a concrete proposal for applying compulsory arbitration, since the considerations to be taken into account will differ according to the specific nature of each proposal. In particular, a proposal for a system of compulsory arbitration which is more or less of a general character will involve considerations different from those which will be advanced in connection with a proposal for compulsory arbitration which is limited to a specified category of disputes or cases.

In developing countries which have introduced a more or less general system of compulsory arbitration, one of the reasons often advanced to justify the taking of that measure is the weakness of the trade unions. In Sri Lanka "most of the unions themselves are as institutions not sufficiently equipped or developed like those of the Western industrial States, to make a significant contribution to the collective bargaining process."[15] Similarly, in India "the parties, particularly unions, are still unprepared and incapable, because of organisational and other weaknesses, to shoulder full responsibilities of collective bargaining".[16] It is stated that in this situation compulsory arbitration has helped not only "to avert many work stoppages by providing an acceptable alternative to direct action" but also "to protect and promote the interests of the weaker sections of the working class, who were not well organised or were unable to bargain on an equal footing with the employer".[17] It is also argued that compulsory arbitration of more or less general application is justified in these countries by the need for industrial peace on behalf of development programmes—that strikes are a luxury which developing countries cannot afford, that they can jeopardise the achievement of planned levels of economic growth and that they can create a climate of labour relations unfavourable to investment in industry.

In a general system of compulsory arbitration any dispute can be submitted to this procedure of settlement, irrespective of its magnitude or the probable consequences of a strike it may give rise to. The general inhibition against strikes will apply even in small and medium-sized manufacturing and service establishments where a work stoppage can have no direct, significant consequence on the public at large.

In certain other developing countries the abridgement of the parties' contractual freedom and its consequences for the growth of collective bargaining are considered too high a price to pay for compulsory arbitration. However, as noted earlier, a number of these countries have accepted a limited application of compulsory arbitration for settling disputes in so-called essential services. In these cases the interest of the public in being protected from hardship caused by work stoppages which curtail the supply of essential goods and services is considered to be of over-riding importance and to provide sufficient warrant for compulsory arbitration. On the other hand, while the question of applying compulsory arbitration in essential services, especially the railways, has been debated for many years in Canada[18] and in the United States,[19] in both countries the primacy of the public interest in collective bargaining in the private sector generally continues to be maintained, unimpaired by any permanent scheme of compulsory arbitration.[20]

Certainly, whenever governments seek to introduce compulsory arbitration, whether as a generally applicable system of disputes settlement or as a procedure of more limited scope, they justify this by a reference to certain considerations of public interest which they consider to be paramount and to over-ride the public interest in the development and growth of collective bargaining. As a practical proposition, however, the issue between compulsory arbitration and collective bargaining is for the government not only a matter of arguments for and against: it is also very much a question of the convictions held by independent employers' associations and trade unions which have reached a certain level of strength. Any scheme of compulsory arbitration is almost certain to encounter serious difficulties if on either or both sides there is strong and adamant objection to it.

International labour standards and compulsory arbitration

Certain international labour standards adopted by the International Labour Conference have a bearing on the acceptability of compulsory arbitration. They do so through their relationship to the right to strike, which is most often prohibited in the spheres covered by systems of compulsory arbitration, as well as through their relationship to collective bargaining, which may also be affected by compulsory arbitration, as indicated above.

The principles concerning the right to strike upheld by ILO supervisory bodies have been derived from the Freedom of Association and Protection of the Right to Organise Convention, 1948 (No. 87), which lays down a number of guarantees of trade union rights. These bodies (Committee of Experts on the Application of Conventions and Recommendations, Committee on Freedom of Association, Fact-finding and Conciliation Commission on Freedom of Association and Commissions of Inquiry) have held these guarantees to cover the right to strike, although permitting restrictions to be placed on that right within certain limits. Systems of compulsory arbitration entailing strike prohibitions which do not fall within the limits deemed to be acceptable are held to be incompatible with the guarantees of Convention No. 87.

The ILO supervisory bodies have considered that general systems of compulsory arbitration under which all disputes may be submitted to compulsory arbitration and strikes prohibited are incompatible with the above-mentioned guarantees. On the other hand, they have accepted that the systems of compulsory arbitration involving a prohibition of the right to strike could be compatible with those guarantees in certain cases, in particular in the civil service, in essential services (in the strict sense of the term) and in key sectors of a country's economy where—and to the extent that—a work stoppage may cause serious hardship to the community.[21]

In all such cases in which strikes are prohibited for certain workers, the ILO supervisory bodies have considered that sufficient guarantees should be afforded to them in order to safeguard their interests, and have in particular placed emphasis on the need for the conciliation and arbitration procedures applicable to them to be adequate, impartial and speedy, for the parties concerned to be able to participate at all stages, and for the awards to be binding on both parties and to be fully and promptly implemented.[22]

The other international labour standards relevant to compulsory arbitration are those regarding collective bargaining. These are found in the Right to Organise and Collective Bargaining Convention, 1949 (No. 98), Article 4 of which provides for the promotion of collective bargaining (this Convention does not deal with the position of public servants engaged in the administration of the State). While certain types of compulsory arbitration may operate to support collective bargaining, other types may undermine collective bargaining as a method of joint determination of terms and conditions of employment. Systems of compulsory arbitration which undermine collective bargaining might be considered to be contrary to the obligations laid down by Convention No. 98. Finally, it should be noted that an item on the promotion of collective bargaining is on the agenda of the 1980 and 1981 sessions of the International Labour Conference and that one or several instruments aimed at giving further substance to the general principle laid down in Article 4 of Convention No. 98 will probably be adopted.[23]

Systems of compulsory arbitration

One way of looking at compulsory arbitration is to see it as a substitute for collective bargaining when this results in deadlock. Systems of compulsory arbitration may therefore be classified by reference to the systems of collective bargaining which they replace. From this point of view, the countries which apply compulsory arbitration may be considered to fall into three main groups.

In one group of countries the disputes submitted for arbitration are mainly industry-wide or occupation-wide in scope, either on a national basis (e.g. in Australia) or on a district/regional basis (e.g. in New Zealand). In a second group of countries the disputes arise mainly from deadlocks in bargaining at the level of the plant or undertaking. In a third group of countries compulsory arbitration covers both types of dispute.

The type of dispute normally submitted to arbitration has important implications for the planning and development of the arbitration system. Industry-wide or occupation-wide disputes tend to be more important, as regards the number of undertakings and workers involved, than plant-level or undertaking-level disputes. On the other hand, the latter are obviously far more numerous than industry-wide or occupation-wide disputes. The issues involved in the two types of dispute are also often of a different character.

Systems of compulsory arbitration may also be classified according to the extent of state intervention. From this point of view, and as indicated earlier, the systems may be grouped into two main types: those in which compulsory arbitration is of more or less limited application, and those in which compulsory arbitration is of more or less general application.

Systems of limited application

Compulsory arbitration of limited application may be designed according to different principles. In one group of countries (e.g. Costa Rica, Honduras, Kenya and Sierra Leone) compulsory arbitration is applied to disputes involving essential services. Under this system the industries or undertakings which fall within the category of essential services are specified in the legislation, in a schedule appended to it or in supplementary regulations. A dispute cannot be referred to compulsory arbitration unless it involves an essential service.

The industries or undertakings most often listed as essential services include public transportation, telecommunication, gas, electricity and water supply and hospital, health and sanitary services. In some countries certain types of mining and the manufacture or distribution of certain products are also considered, in view of their importance to the national economy, as essential services. The list varies from country to country, and power may be given to the minister of labour or other competent authority to make such addition to the list as he deems necessary, as well as to delete therefrom.

In the United States compulsory arbitration has been adopted in a number of states with respect to labour disputes involving privately owned companies in essential services. Among the state laws note may be taken of the so-called Slichter Law in Massachusetts, which gives the chief executive of the state a choice of procedures, in cases where a vital public service is interrupted as a result of a dispute; this choice includes compulsory arbitration.

In Japan, while only voluntary procedures are available in the private sector, compulsory arbitration may be resorted to in disputes affecting public corporations and national enterprises, not all of which have the characteristics of essential services.

In a second group of countries compulsory arbitration is applied to what may be broadly described as public interest disputes (e.g. in Argentina, Senegal, Trinidad and Tobago and Venezuela). Under this system the competent authority (usually the minister of labour) is empowered to refer a dispute to arbitration if he considers that a strike or lockout will adversely affect the public interest. The discretion given to the competent authority may be circumscribed within broader or narrower limits according to the specific language used in the legislation to define the nature of the public interest involved. A dispute, for example, may be referred to arbitration in Argentina if it will hold back or slow down the country's economic recovery, and in Senegal, Trinidad and Tobago and Tunisia if it will threaten the general or national interest. In practice, the language of the statute can be loosely or strictly interpreted, and much depends on the attitude of the public authority concerned in the exercise of the discretionary power invested in him. If he follows the path of strict interpretation, few disputes will be referred to compulsory arbitration; but if he takes a broader view of his powers, compulsory arbitration will be applied more frequently.

In a third group of countries compulsory arbitration is applied on a basis which permits strikes or both strikes and lockouts under certain conditions. In Mexico, for example, the workers have the choice either of going on strike or of accepting arbitration for the settlement of a dispute. If they decide on arbitration, this becomes compulsory for the other party—but they thereby also forgo their right subsequently to opt for a strike. While, in principle, arbitration may be initiated by the employers, it will not in any way prevent the workers from exercising the right to strike. More or less the same principle is followed in Panama, where the workers involved in a dispute may apply for arbitration at any time before or during a strike.

A similar system was established by the French Labour Code (Overseas Territories),[24] the essential elements of which are still in force in several French-speaking African countries. Under this system an unsettled dispute must be submitted to arbitration and the arbitration award is binding unless timely objection to it is made by either party; where such objection is made, a strike declared after notification of the objection would not be illegal. This system has been followed, with certain modifications, in the Labour Codes of Benin,[25] the United Republic of Cameroon,[26] Madagascar[27] and Mali.[28] A substantially similar system has been provided for in the Labour Code of Zaire.[29]

In a number of countries compulsory arbitration is designed on the basis of at least two of the principles noted above. It applies to essential services disputes in Colombia, Guatemala, Jamaica, Lebanon, Thailand and Trinidad and Tobago; and additionally to public interest disputes in Jamaica, Thailand and Trinidad and Tobago. It also applies to non-essential services disputes in Colombia at the option of the workers; in Guatemala to cases where a lawful strike or lockout has not been declared; and in Lebanon after a stoppage of work has lasted for more than 15 days. In Pakistan a strike or lockout may be declared after the failure of conciliation, but may be prohibited by the Government if the dispute relates to an essential service; in other cases it may also be prohibited if it has lasted for more than 30 days or even before the expiration of this period if it affects the public interest; where the Government prohibits a strike or lockout, the dispute is forthwith to be referred to arbitration.

Systems of general application

In compulsory arbitration systems of general application, any dispute can be referred to arbitration without the consent or agreement of both parties, irrespective of whether or not it relates to an essential service or seriously affects the public interest or whether it is a major dispute or one of relatively minor importance. There are two main ways by which compulsory arbitration acquires a general character; first, the legislation may provide for the automatic reference of a dispute to arbitration after the failure of conciliation or some other method of voluntary settlement which has been provided for; second, arbitration can be applied for the settlement of any dispute at the instance of the competent authority or on the application of only one party on either side of the dispute.

Among the countries in which a dispute is automatically referred to arbitration in the absence of a voluntary settlement are Australia,[30] Bolivia, Brazil, the United Republic of Cameroon, Ecuador, Egypt, Gabon, Greece, Haiti, Jordan, the Libyan Arab Jamahiriya, Madagascar, Mali, New Zealand,[30] Nigeria, Paraguay, the Philippines, the Syrian Arab Republic and Zambia. Under this system the procedure of conciliation is usually compulsory or may be initiated ex officio by the competent authority.

In Bolivia and Nigeria compulsory arbitration is related to the system of advisory arbitration. In Bolivia the award in essential services disputes is always legally binding; but in non-essential services disputes an award which has not been accepted by both parties can be made legally binding by order of the President. In Nigeria, if objection is made to an award of an arbitration tribunal, the dispute has to be referred to the National Industrial Court for a binding decision; a dispute has also to be referred to the Court if it involves an essential service or if the Commissioner of Labour considers that reference to an arbitration tribunal would be inappropriate.

In some countries (e.g. Australia, Brazil and Ecuador) where the machinery concerned has been established both for conciliation and for arbitration, an attempt is first made to settle the dispute by conciliation; if this fails, the dispute will be dealt with through arbitration. In most of the other countries listed conciliation and arbitration are performed by different authorities; on the failure of conciliation the dispute is submitted to the arbitration machinery by the conciliation or administrative authority concerned.

A dispute can be submitted to compulsory arbitration by decision of the competent authority in Ghana, India, Malaysia, Mauritius, Singapore, Sri Lanka and Tanzania. The power given to the competent authority to refer disputes to arbitration is discretionary and every dispute is potentially liable to be so referred. However, the discretionary power given to the competent authority also means that he may decide against referring a dispute to arbitration. In most countries the competent authority is the minister of labour, and different ministers of labour may use their powers in different ways. In Turkey either of the parties to a dispute which is not settled by conciliation may apply directly to the competent arbitration authority for the settlement of the dispute.

Arbitration machinery

As in voluntary arbitration, the machinery for compulsory arbitration may be ad hoc or permanent. While in voluntary arbitration ad hoc machinery is more widely used, in compulsory arbitration it is the permanent type of machinery which prevails.

Ad hoc machinery is used in Bolivia, Colombia, Costa Rica, the Dominican

Republic, Ecuador, Ghana, Guatemala, the Ivory Coast, Panama, Senegal, Tunisia and Venezuela. In Senegal and Tunisia compulsory arbitration is performed by single arbitrators, while in the Ivory Coast it is carried out by a board consisting of independent members only. In Ghana an arbitration tribunal may consist of a single member or of an independent person assisted by the parties' assessors, or of two members appointed respectively by the parties and a government-appointed chairman.

In most other countries the ad hoc machinery includes employers' and workers' representatives who may be appointed by the parties to the dispute on the basis of free selection (e.g. in Bolivia and the Dominican Republic) or may be selected from previously established lists or panels of employers' and workers' arbitrators. In the latter case the appointments may be made by the parties to the dispute (e.g. in Colombia and Panama), by the competent labour judge (e.g. in Costa Rica and Guatemala) or by the conciliation board concerned (e.g. in Venezuela).

The chairmanship of the board is assumed ex officio by the competent labour official or labour inspector in Bolivia and Venezuela, and by the labour judge concerned in Costa Rica and Guatemala. The chairman is appointed by the Minister of Labour in Colombia but is selected from a list of independent arbitrators nominated by the Government.

With regard to permanent machinery, compulsory arbitration may be entrusted to officials or bodies which function at the regional level (e.g. in the United Republic of Cameroon, Egypt, Greece, India, Indonesia, the Libyan Arab Jamahiriya, Madagascar, Mauritania, the Syrian Arab Republic and Turkey) or to organs which exercise nation-wide jurisdiction (e.g. in Australia, Kenya, Lebanon, Malaysia, Mauritius, New Zealand, Sierra Leone, Singapore, Sri Lanka, Tanzania, Trinidad and Tobago, Uganda and Zambia). While the regional arbitration machinery is invariably concerned only with the settlement of disputes, in some countries the national organ for compulsory arbitration may be given other functions besides disputes settlement, including in particular the registration, certification or approval of collective agreements.

Like ad hoc machinery, the permanent machinery for compulsory arbitration may consist of independent persons only or may include employers' and workers' representatives designated either as members or as assessors. Most countries use only one of these two types of machinery but in some countries both types are employed (e.g. in Pakistan and the Philippines).

The Australian Conciliation and Arbitration Commission consists of independent members only, appointed either as presidential members (president and deputy presidents) or as commissioners. As indicated earlier, the members of the Commission individually act as conciliators and arbitrators, but in a particular case a party may object to a commissioner who has attempted conciliation continuing as arbitrator. While most of the cases are handled individually by the members of the Commission, certain types of important disputes can be dealt with only by a Full Bench, which includes at least two presidential members and one or more additional members.

In India the labour courts and industrial tribunals established by the central and state governments and granted arbitration functions are single-member tribunals. In Sri Lanka a minor dispute may also be referred to a single-member labour tribunal, but a major dispute has to be submitted to an industrial court. The latter body is constituted from a permanent panel of not fewer than five independent persons, one of whom is appointed as chairman. For the purpose of dealing with a dispute the chairman of the panel constitutes an industrial court which may consist of one member or of three members.

When the Industrial Court in Kenya was first set up in 1964 it included employers' and workers' members. As reconstituted in 1971, it now consists of a judge and four other independent members.[31] The industrial courts in Nigeria and in Trinidad and Tobago are also collegiate bodies consisting of independent members only.

In Pakistan the labour courts operating at the provincial level are single-member tribunals, but the National Industrial Relations Commission, which is competent to hear disputes of national importance, is a collegiate body. In the Philippines compulsory arbitration is in most cases exercised in the first instance by regional arbitrators; appeals may be made against their awards to the National Labour Relations Commission, which includes employers' and workers' members; the Commission's function largely consists in exercising this appellate jurisdiction but it takes original action in major disputes certified by the President.

In Egypt and the Syrian Arab Republic the meetings of a regional arbitration board are to be attended by an employers' representative and a workers' representative who have no voting rights. The National Industrial Relations Commission in Pakistan includes an employers' member and a workers' member whose function is to advise the chairman. The Industrial Court in Sierra Leone, the Permanent Labour Tribunal in Tanzania, and the Industrial Relations Court in Zambia include employers' and workers' assessors whose role is also essentially advisory.

In a good number of countries the employers' and workers' representatives participate fully in the deliberations and decision-making processes of the arbitration machinery (e.g. in Benin, the United Republic of Cameroon, Greece, Indonesia, Jamaica, Jordan, Lebanon, the Libyan Arab Jamahiriya, Madagascar, Malaysia, Mauritania, Mauritius, Mexico, New Zealand, Singapore, the Sudan, Thailand and Turkey). The number of employers' and workers' representatives ranges from one from each side (e.g. in the United Republic of Cameroon, Greece, the Libyan Arab Jamahiriya, Madagascar, Mauritania, Mauritius, New Zealand and Uganda) to two or three or more (e.g. in Benin, Indonesia, Lebanon, the Philippines, Thailand and Turkey).

The advantages of tripartite machinery in arbitration are the same as in conciliation: the parties may show greater confidence in it, and it enlists the practical knowledge and experience of the employers and workers themselves. However, in Latin America the acceptance of the tripartite principle by the bodies responsible for settling rights or legal disputes is not unanimous. Some authors consider that the administration of justice in these cases should be entrusted only to persons with special legal training. The opponents of tripartism in this context also invoke practical difficulties, in particular the inadequate training of lay judges.[32]

The employers' and workers' representatives may be appointed on the basis of free selection, either by the parties to the dispute (e.g. in Turkey and in

Jamaica with respect to interests disputes in non-essential services), by designated employers' and workers' organisations (e.g. in Sierra Leone and Tanzania) or by the competent authority (usually the minister of labour). In the last-mentioned case the appointment may be made on nomination by each of the parties to the dispute (e.g. in the Sudan) or after consultation with, or from nominations of, representative employers' and workers' organisations (e.g. in Mauritania, Mauritius, New Zealand and the Philippines).

Second, the appointment may be made from lists or panels of employers' and workers' arbitrators or assessors. Under the more common practice, persons are included in a list or panel on the proposal of employers' and workers' organisations respectively. In the United Republic of Cameroon, Greece and Lebanon the employers' and workers' representatives chosen from the panels are appointed for fixed terms and become permanent members of the arbitration board. Under another pattern (e.g. in Benin, Malaysia, Singapore, Tanzania and Zambia) the employers' and workers' panels are set up within the arbitration machinery, and the members are selected from the panels in connection with a particular dispute only. This is also the position in Jamaica when the Industrial Disputes Tribunal is dealing with essential services disputes.

When the permanent machinery is constituted on a tripartite basis, it may have only one independent member, in the person of the president or chairman of the tribunal (e.g. in Benin, Jamaica, Mauritius, Singapore and Tanzania), or it may include a further one to four or more independent members. There is usually provision for a vice-president, whose role is limited to assuming the duties of the president in the latter's absence, or for a number of deputy presidents or chairmen who may be designated as panel or division chairmen. In most countries the independent members come from government circles, including members of the judiciary, labour inspectors, other labour officials and law officers and representatives of certain ministries. In Malaysia the Industrial Court includes a panel of independent persons (in addition to the chairman and the employers' and workers' panels), while in New Zealand the three independent members of the Industrial Commission may be persons not connected with the Government.

Unlike ad hoc machinery, which deals only with the dispute for which it has been set up, permanent machinery may have a number of pending cases at the same time; the latter thus runs the risk of accumulating cases on its calendar and of incurring delays in the processing of each case. The risk is much greater if the machinery can hear only one dispute at a time, as in the case of a single-member tribunal or of a collegiate body in which the chairman presides over every case. However, certain types of arrangement make it possible to minimise that risk by enabling the arbitration body to hear a number of cases simultaneously.

This is the case, for example, with respect to the Australian Conciliation and Arbitration Commission, where cases are normally dealt with individually by the members of the Commission (except in cases reserved for a Full Bench). The legislation has not fixed the number of members of the Commission, and the competent authority may appoint such a number of deputy presidents and commissioners as the case-load of the Commission demands.[33] A similar arrangement is followed in Trinidad and Tobago, where the President of the Industrial Court may assign cases to individual members of the Court. It may be noted that this type of arrangement relates to arbitration machinery consisting of independent members only.

Under a second type of arrangement, as in the case of the industrial courts in Malaysia, Singapore and Sri Lanka, members are appointed from the panels for the purpose of considering a dispute, and different sets of members may be appointed for different disputes. Under a third type of arrangement the arbitration machinery is empowered to sit in two or more benches or divisions, with each bench or division being responsible for a certain category of dispute. These two types of arrangement may be employed both in cases where the machinery consists of independent members only, or in cases where it includes employers' and workers' representatives.

The extent to which these arrangements can work satisfactorily depends on certain factors, including the number of cases referred to the arbitration machinery and the average time it takes to process each case. It is especially important that the machinery's capacity to dispose of cases should have a reasonable relationship to the number of cases placed on its calendar. It appears that in Malaysia the Department of Industrial Relations of the Ministry of Labour and Manpower, and more particularly its staff of 43 conciliation officers, has been effective in reducing the number of disputes that may be referred to compulsory arbitration; in 1976, for example, 90 per cent of the disputes submitted to the Ministry were settled through conciliation. With a view also to reducing the case-load of the Industrial Court, as well as to promoting collective bargaining, it appears that the Malaysian Minister of Labour and Manpower has refrained from using too frequently his discretionary power to refer collective bargaining disputes to the Court.

Qualifications and official status of arbitrators

Although the question of compulsory arbitration is controversial, once a policy decision is taken in favour of this method of settling labour disputes it becomes of paramount importance to ensure that it will work satisfactorily in practice. Basic to this issue is the question of the qualifications and official status of the arbitrators, especially the independent members of the arbitration machinery. In more practical terms, this issue centres on the person of the president or chairman of the arbitration tribunal. Because of his office, he occupies a central position in the system of compulsory arbitration.

The office of president/chairman of a permanent tribunal which exercises compulsory arbitration in interests disputes is one of awesome responsibility. Arbitral discretion is often compared to judicial discretion, and both need to be exercised in absolute independence of any external influences. However, the discretion of an arbitrator in interests disputes differs from that of a judge of a court of law in one fundamental respect. The latter has to exercise his discretion within the four corners of the law or legal instrument which he is called upon to interpret and apply. There is no such limitation on the discretion of a compulsory arbitrator in interests disputes, for his function is rather to decide what should be the law between the parties. In effect, when a parliament provides for compulsory arbitration, it delegates to the arbitration authority the power to make the law for the parties concerned.

The importance of the office of president of an industrial court or chairman of an arbitration board, council or commission is generally well recognised in national practices. In a good number of countries the legislation prescribes relatively high qualifications for appointment to the office and accords to the holder of the office a relatively high official status, with commensurate pay and conditions of service. In order to be eligible for appointment as president or chairman, a person must be or must have been a judge of the High Court or the Supreme Court, or must be qualified for appointment as such a judge or possess legal qualifications and experience (e.g. in Australia, India, Mauritius, Nigeria, Sri Lanka, Trinidad and Tobago and Zambia). In various countries the chairmen of arbitration boards are serving judges of courts of superior jurisdiction or of labour courts (e.g. in the United Republic of Cameroon, Costa Rica, Egypt, Greece, Lebanon, Madagascar and Turkey), while in Brazil, Guatemala and Mexico the conciliation and arbitration boards form part of the labour court system and the chairmen of the boards have the qualifications and official status of members of the judiciary.

In Singapore the president of the Industrial Arbitration Court has the same rights, privileges and immunities as a judge of the Supreme Court, but the legislation does not expressly provide that he should be a person possessing legal or judicial qualifications. In this connection, there appears to have been increasing recognition in recent years of other qualifications than judicial experience or legal training. A person may now be appointed a deputy president of the Australian Conciliation and Arbitration Commission if he has had experience at a high level in industry, commerce, industrial relations or government service.[34] In Jamaica the president and deputy president of the Industrial Disputes Tribunal must be persons with sufficient knowledge of or experience in labour relations; and in New Zealand the independent members of the Industrial Commission are appointed "by reason of their having appropriate qualifications and experience". In Trinidad and Tobago among the persons who may be appointed as members of the Industrial Court (other than the president and the vice-president) are those experienced in industrial relations or qualified as economists or accountants.

Because of their high qualifications and high official status, the presidents or chairmen and other independent members of compulsory arbitration tribunals frequently enjoy high moral authority, which contributes in no small measure to the acceptability of arbitration awards on the part of employers and trade unions. This is desirable for the satisfactory operation of the system of compulsory arbitration.

The fact, however, that arbitrators possess top qualifications and enjoy an official status of a relatively high order can have a negative effect on conciliation. This may happen if the qualifications of conciliators, their official status and their moral authority are much lower than those of arbitrators. Where the parties to a dispute are to appear before a conciliator whom they regard as a relatively minor official, compared with the president of the industrial court, it is possible that they will have no real interest in the conciliation proceedings and will want to have them terminated as soon as possible so that the case can go to arbitration.

If this should be the case, the remedy is surely not to lower the qualifications and official status of arbitrators but to improve the functioning of the conciliation procedure by raising the qualifications and official status of conciliators. While the function of the arbitrator—that of making a decision on the issues in dispute—involves a higher degree of responsibility, the function of the conciliator—that of persuading the parties to reach agreement—is often a more difficult task. If conciliation is to play a more effective role in the national system of prevention and settlement of labour disputes, therefore, there should be an appropriate balance between the qualifications and official status of conciliators and of arbitrators.

ARBITRATION PROCEEDINGS AND AWARDS

The difference noted above between the functions of a conciliator and those of an arbitrator is reflected in the character of the proceedings. While conciliation is basically a dialogue between the parties to the dispute under the guidance of the conciliator, in arbitration each party addresses himself mainly to the arbitrator so as to influence the latter's thinking in arriving at his decision. In this respect the conduct of arbitration proceedings is essentially similar to that of judicial proceedings: in both cases it is required that each of the parties should have his "day in court"—the opportunity to state his case, to submit evidence and arguments and to make other submissions before judgement is pronounced.

Rules of procedure

In most countries certain rules of procedure are prescribed in the legislation or regulations issued thereunder to govern the conduct of arbitration proceedings. While the rules are specially designed for the machinery set up by the government for voluntary or compulsory arbitration, they may also supplement the rules of procedure laid down in collective agreements. In certain countries the statutory rules of procedure are limited to a few essential points, with the arbitration authority being empowered to prescribe its own procedure—subject, however, to legislative provisions (e.g. in Australia, Israel, the Philippines, Singapore, Trinidad and Tobago, the United Kingdom and Zambia).

The object of these provisions appears to be mainly to ensure that cases are dealt with speedily and to simplify the conduct of the proceedings, especially by avoiding the formalities, technicalities and legalism of judicial proceedings. In Panama the Arbitration Board is required to "eschew formalistic ceremony, simplifying procedure while safeguarding the equality of the parties and guaranteeing their right of defence".[35] In some countries the arbitration body is not bound to act in a formal manner or by the rules of evidence but may inform itself in such a manner as it thinks fit or deems most conducive to the clarification of the matter at issue (e.g. in Australia, Israel, Singapore, Trinidad and Tobago and Zambia). Under another type of provision the arbitration body may use every and all reasonable means to ascertain the facts speedily and objectively without regard to the technicalities of law and procedure (e.g. in the Philippines). On the other hand, in the majority of Latin American countries the procedure of arbitration boards is governed by comprehensive provisions which deal in detail with the various stages of the procedure and which leave little or no room for the application of the rules of ordinary court procedure.

Another factor which contributes to a greater degree of informality in arbitration proceedings than in ordinary judicial proceedings is the representation of the parties. In general, trade unions, undertakings and employers' associations may be represented in arbitration proceedings by their officers or other authorised agents who may be laymen and not lawyers. The appearance of legal practitioners in a professional capacity (and not as officials or paid employees of the organisation concerned) is, however, permitted in most countries. A legal practitioner may not appear in New Zealand except with the consent of all parties, nor in Singapore, on behalf of a party which is not a trade union, except in cases of contempt.

Fact-finding

In arbitration proceedings the parties themselves will seek to submit as much information as possible in support of their respective claims, through oral or documentary evidence and oral or written submissions, upon which the arbitration tribunal will make its findings of fact, as a basis for its decision. There is, however, a danger that the presentation of oral evidence can become an interminable process of examination and cross-examination of witnesses, which leads to protracted proceedings. If an arbitration tribunal is vested with the general power to control its procedure, it may be able to limit the amount of evidence that can be presented in relation to any matter. In Australia and in Trinidad and Tobago the arbitration authority is given specific power to require evidence in writing and to decide upon matters in respect of which it will hear oral evidence or arguments.

Compulsory arbitration bodies are generally vested with powers of investigation to enable them to obtain information in addition to that presented by the parties. Such powers include, among others, the power to compel the attendance of witnesses for the purpose of giving evidence, and the power to compel the production of books and records. While, in practice, these powers are usually invoked at the instance of a party to the dispute, they may be exercised by the arbitration authority on its own initative. However, any evidence has to be presented at a hearing.

Other types of arrangement have been developed in connection with fact-finding in arbitration, sometimes relating to the arbitration function as a whole. The arbitration board may call upon the labour authority for assistance in its investigation (e.g. in Panama), or may request a technical or economic report from the ministry of labour (e.g. in Guatemala). The arbitrator or the arbitration authority may arrange to be assisted by experts (e.g. in Tunisia) or may refer technical matters or accounts to an expert and accept his report as evidence after due hearing (e.g. in the Philippines). The arbitration authority may call in the aid of one or more assessors (e.g. in the United Kingdom) or may appoint a person with especial knowledge of the matter under consideration as an assessor to advise it in the proceedings before it (e.g. in India).

In Australia and Indonesia the legislation permits the use of fact-finding as a subsidiary procedure in arbitration. The Australian Arbitration and

Conciliation Commission may refer an industrial dispute to a local industrial board for investigation and report. This board may be a state industrial authority willing to act or a board set up by the Commission and consisting of employers' and workers' representatives and a chairman appointed by it. In Indonesia, in dealing with a dispute, the central or a regional disputes settlement committee may order an inquiry to be held if it does not have sufficient information to arrive at a decision. For that purpose it must set up a committee of inquiry, determine its membership and duties and fix a period of time for completing its work. On completion of its work the committee of inquiry submits a report on its findings and presents its opinion for the settlement of the dispute.

The fact-finding procedure is the "primary procedure" in arbitration in collective disputes concerning wages in Mexico, and is to be applied in every case. If the parties fail to reach agreement during the conciliation phase of the proceedings, the conciliation and arbitration board must appoint not fewer than three experts to investigate the dispute and submit their opinion concerning the manner in which it may be settled. The parties may submit directly to the experts such observations, reports, studies and other elements as may contribute to ascertaining the facts, but the experts themselves are given powers of investigation. Within a prescribed period following their receipt of the experts' opinion, the parties may lodge objections thereto. If such objections are made, the board will take evidence on new facts or evidence contesting the facts stated in the experts' opinion. On completion of the taking of evidence, the parties are given the opportunity to make written submissions. This concludes the primary procedure.

Decision-making

As a rule, an arbitration body, be it voluntary or compulsory, can decide only on the questions submitted to it. This principle is written into the legislation in many countries, particularly in cases of voluntary arbitration. The questions to be decided are those specified in the arbitration agreement or the parties' application or in the terms of reference issued by the competent authority.

This rule is qualified in some countries. In New Zealand, for example, even if conciliation results in a partial settlement, the whole dispute is submitted to compulsory arbitration. In itself a memorandum of partial settlement does not have any binding force, but the Industrial Commission may incorporate in its award any terms of the memorandum without inquiring into the matters to which they relate.

In France and certain other French-speaking countries the points for decision are those on which no agreement has been reached through the conciliation procedure, as specified in the report of failure of conciliation or in the record of non-conciliation. However, an arbitration board may take a decision on matters which have arisen out of events occurring after the report or record was made and which are a direct consequence of the dispute.

In making an award in a dispute the arbitration authorities in Australia and Malaysia have been given wider discretion; they are not restricted to the specific relief claimed by the parties or to the demands made by them in the course of the dispute, but may include in their award any matter which they think necessary or expedient for the purposes of preventing or settling the dispute and of preventing further industrial disputes.

In deciding on its award an arbitration body is guided by certain criteria. The criteria to be applied in rights or legal disputes do not present any special problem; the decision has to be based on the provision of law, collective agreement or arbitration award or on the works rule, custom or usage over the interpretation and application of which the dispute has arisen.

National practices are less uniform in regard to the criteria for interests disputes, i.e. those involving the establishment of new terms and conditions of employment or the modification of existing terms and conditions of employment. The legislation in a number of countries provides for certain criteria which may reflect the underlying philosophy of the labour relations policy or system of disputes settlement of the country concerned.

In Tanzania the Permanent Labour Tribunal must have regard, in making any award or decision (including a decision to register a collective agreement), to various factors important to economic development, including the need for capital formation, employment maintenance and creation, an appropriate wage structure, the maintenance of the purchasing power of wages, the promotion of the competitive position of local products and the maintenance of a favourable balance of payments and balance of trade.

In Brazil labour courts are required, in considering remuneration questions, to base their decision on the average real wage for the category of worker concerned and to take account of the repercussions of wage readjustments on the community and the national economy, of the adequacy of such readjustments for the basic needs of the wage earner and his family, of the loss of average real purchasing power and of the necessity to correct glaring wage inequalities.

In making an award the arbitration tribunals in Greece must consider and assess the social and economic needs served by the undertakings in question, their financial stability and technical efficiency, the level of salaries and wages in relation to the cost of living, the conditions and nature of the employment and the general interests of the national economy.

The Industrial Court in Malaysia is required to have regard to the public interest, the financial implications and the effect of the award on the economy of the country and on the industry concerned, and also to the probable effect in related and similar industries. In Singapore the Industrial Arbitration Court may have regard not only to the interests of the persons immediately concerned but also to the interests of the community as a whole and in particular the condition of the national economy. In Egypt and the Syrian Arab Republic the arbitration boards are to have regard to the general economic and social conditions of the locality.

By far the most common provisions, however, are those requiring arbitration bodies to act according to justice, equity or fairness, good conscience and the substantial merits of the case. It would appear that these are also the criteria followed by arbitration boards in countries where the legislation is silent on the matter. In the absence of express legislative provisions an arbitration board is at least expected to exercise its discretion in a reasonable manner. Even in interests disputes, arbitral discretion is not a warrant for arbitrary discretion.

175

Under the most common practice the arbitration tribunal will proceed directly to its decision after investigating the dispute or after the parties' final submissions. In Mexico, however, after the primary procedure (or investigation) a report is prepared containing proposals as a basis for the settlement of the dispute. The board then summons the parties to a hearing on the report, which consists only of oral proceedings. On completion of these proceedings the board will then take its decision. A substantially similar procedure is followed in the Dominican Republic.

When the arbitration tribunal consists of more than one member, provision has to be made regarding the manner in which it reaches a decision. Under one system the decision is taken by majority vote. This is usually the case where the board consists of three members (the chairman, an employers' representative and a workers' representative). Under another system the decision is also taken by majority vote, but there is a further provision that, in the absence of a majority, the decision of the board will be the chairman's opinion. This system is usually followed where the board or the permissible quorum for a valid decision consists of members in an even number, including the chairman if his vote is included in the calculation of the majority. Still another system is followed by the Central Arbitration Committee in the United Kingdom: if it cannot reach a unanimous decision on its award, the case is to be decided by the chairman acting with the full powers of an umpire.

Arbitration awards

Expressly or implicitly, the legislation may require the arbitration body to give reasons for its award. The making of reasoned awards is also practised in most countries where the legislation does not impose such a requirement. In the United Kingdom, however, it has been the tradition for arbitrators to give no reasons for their awards. As the Royal Commission on Trade Unions and Employers' Associations observed, "This practice has a great deal to recommend it so long as the only object of arbitration is to resolve disputes. One or both parties to a dispute might cavil at the reasoning when they would be willing to accept the award."[36] Under this practice an arbitrator does not have to spend time and effort explaining the reasons for his award, and can thus give the award in a shorter time than would otherwise be the case. For a permanent body the saving in time can be considerable. Nevertheless, the Royal Commission considered the practice of not giving reasons for awards to be "incompatible with any attempt to develop a rational incomes policy".[37] It recommended that "arbitrators should be encouraged to give reasons whenever they can, especially on major decisions on pay which are likely to be significant for the development of incomes policy".[38]

Whether or not reasons should be given for arbitration awards remains an open question in the United Kingdom. So far as interests disputes are concerned, it may also be an open question in various other countries where the practice of making reasoned awards has generally been taken for granted and where the advantages of not giving reasons for arbitration awards have not been seriously considered.

It may be noted that the existing practice in the United Kingdom appears to be related to the fact that in the British system of labour relations the concept of rights or legal disputes is unknown and that arbitration awards are not legally binding and are not subject to appeal. In effect, apart from disputes arising from legislative enactments which may be brought before industrial tribunals, those labour disputes in the United Kingdom which are referred to conciliation and arbitration are in the nature of interests disputes; they may be settled by negotiation and compromise, and if a dispute is referred to arbitration the arbitrator does not act according to any legally binding rule or established criteria.

The need for reasoned awards in rights disputes is the same as that for reasoned judicial decisions. Both clarify or make more definite the meaning of the text, practice or custom which is being interpreted. Reasoned judicial decisions serve as a precedent and a guide for all the parties concerned, and reasoned awards in rights disputes fulfil the same function. In the case, for example, of a particular provision of a collective agreement, the meaning given to it in an arbitration award not only settles the dispute but also binds the future conduct of the parties; depending on the reasons given in the award, the parties may continue to use the same language of the provision or may decide to modify it in future negotiations.

The situation is different in the case of interests disputes. The need for reasoned awards in this type of dispute would depend on other considerations. Where the awards are legally binding, giving the reasons for the award helps to make it more acceptable to the parties and to provide a more satisfactory basis for settlement. Where the awards are subject to appeal or judicial review, it would become important to give the reasons therefor, so that the appellate authority can judge accordingly. The need for giving reasons would also arise where the legislation lays down criteria for making awards, in order to show that these criteria have been properly taken into account. In these situations the need for reasoned awards may be said to be of a more imperative character when they are given by independent persons.

There may, however, be cases when there is no real need to give reasoned awards. Such cases may occur where an arbitration board includes employers' and workers' members with full voting rights. Where these members reach a unanimous decision, it can be fairly assumed that their decision is the result of a compromise. Underlying such a compromise is the hope that it will be mutually acceptable to the parties, but beyond this hope it may be difficult for them to give reasons for their compromise decision. For these cases it would not be necessary to overturn completely the practice of giving reasoned awards, but it may be advisable to provide for some flexibility which would permit the members of an arbitration board to decide, if they think fit in the circumstances of the case, not to give reasons for their award.

One of the principal concerns of policy-makers in planning the design for compulsory arbitration is to avoid the delays usually associated with judicial procedure, of which one of the main causes is the taking of appeals. That concern has been given expression in a large number of countries in provisions making an arbitration award (so far, at least, as it is a determination on the merits of the dispute) final and unappealable. Such provisions generally relate to awards in interests disputes or on issues which do not involve questions of law.

177

As a rule, awards on the merits in disputes submitted to arbitration by the parties' agreement are also not subject to appeal.

In certain countries, however, in cases of compulsory arbitration, appeals from awards are allowed on the merits in interests disputes or on issues of a non-legal character. This practice is found in particular in systems where arbitration is carried out by regional arbitrators or regional arbitration boards (e.g. in Greece, Indonesia, the Philippines and Turkey) or by individual arbitrators assigned to particular industries (e.g. in Australia).

This possibility of appeal in such cases is in part a response to the problem of consistency in arbitration awards. While each arbitrator tries to be consistent in his awards, he is not bound to follow the awards of other arbitrators at the same level of competence. This can lead to a situation where different arbitrators give significantly varying awards in disputes involving similar issues, thereby bringing discredit on the arbitration system. Where appeals on the merits can be made to a superior body or a central authority, the latter can provide the needed consistency in the principles upon which awards are to be based.

At the federal level in Australia an appeal from the award of an individual member of the Australian Conciliation and Arbitration Commission can be taken to a Full Bench of the Commission, but awards of the Commission are not subject to judicial review on the merits. In Greece, Indonesia, the Philippines and Turkey the appellate authority is a superior arbitration body which includes employers' and workers' members. In France appeals from the arbitration awards may be taken to the Superior Court of Arbitration, consisting of independent members.

Under the practice in some countries the award specifies the parties to be bound by it. This practice is usually found in systems where other parties than the original parties to the dispute, or to the negotiations out of which it arose, may be brought into the proceedings (e.g. in Australia, India, Malaysia, Pakistan and Singapore).

In most countries arbitration awards are made legally binding in their character as such, often by virtue of provisions to that effect and sometimes by being given the effect of a court decision (e.g. in Lebanon, the Libyan Arab Jamahiriya and Mexico). In some countries (e.g. Argentina, Colombia, Israel, Japan and Turkey) it is provided that the award shall have the force and effect of a collective agreement.

Such a provision may be related to a policy of promoting collective bargaining. It is not, however, equivalent to a prescription that the terms of the award should be incorporated in a collective agreement to be concluded by the parties. Nevertheless, there may be nothing in the legislation to prevent the arbitration body from including in its award a recommendation to that effect. This may be especially desirable where there is such a policy to promote collective bargaining or where the parties have already had substantial experience of collective bargaining and had previously been able to conclude collective agreements on their own responsibility.

Notes

[1] ILO: *Legislative Series (LS)*, 1975—UK 2. It should be noted that the practice of voluntary arbitration in the United Kingdom began before the Industrial Courts Act, 1919. The Conciliation Act, 1896, empowered the Board of Trade and later the Ministry of Labour, on application of both parties to a dispute, to appoint an arbitrator.

[2] idem: *Report of the Committee on Freedom of Employers' and Workers' Organisations*, doc. GB. 131/7/8, Appendix II, Monograph relating to the United Kingdom, pp. 1547–1548.

[3] idem: *LS*, 1976—Nig. 1.

[4] See also Department of Labour, Bureau of Labour Relations and Institute of Labour and Manpower Services: *Basic information on voluntary arbitration in the Philippines* (Manila, 1978); and C. T. Villatuya: "National Labour Relations Commission of the Republic of the Philippines", in Alan Gladstone (ed.): *Industrial courts in English-speaking developing countries*, Proceedings of a meeting at the International Institute for Labour Studies (Geneva, International Institute for Labour Studies, 1976), p. 79.

[5] Department of Labour: *Basic information on voluntary arbitration in the Philippines*, op. cit., pp. 15–16.

[6] ibid., pp. 7–8.

[7] ILO: *LS*, 1952—Nor. 3.

[8] ibid., 1920—GB 1.

[9] See Sharp, op. cit., p. 275.

[10] For the text of the Act as revised up to 1925, see ILO: *LS*, 1925—NZ 1.

[11] For the text of the Act as revised up to 1926, see ibid., 1926—Austral. 12.

[12] See idem: *Asian labour laws* (New Delhi, 1951), pp. 1201–1210. The system of compulsory arbitration introduced by this Act was in force from 1936 to 1953.

[13] idem: *LS*, 1947—Ind. 1.

[14] See also idem: *Promotion of collective bargaining*, Report V(1), International Labour Conference, 66th Session, Geneva, 1980, pp. 59–60.

[15] *Report of the Commission on Industrial Disputes, Ceylon, 1966–69* (Colombo, 1970), para. 407.

[16] Ministry of Labour and Employment and Rehabilitation: *Report of the National Commission on Labour* (Delhi, 1969), para. 23.34.

[17] ibid., para. 23.29.

[18] See Privy Council Office: *Canadian industrial relations: The report of the Task Force on Labour Relations* (Ottawa, 1969), paras. 575–595; and John Crispo: "Strikes and their alternatives in essential services", in Canada Department of Labour: *The Labour Gazette*, Sep. 1974, pp. 619–628.

[19] See Herbert R. Northrup: *Compulsory arbitration and government intervention in labor disputes: An analysis of experience* (Washington, DC, Labor Policy Association, 1966); The Brotherhood of Railway Trainmen: *The pros and cons of compulsory arbitration* (Cleveland, Ohio, 1965); and Chamber of Commerce of the United States: *Compulsory arbitration: A brief study* (Washington, DC, n.d. [? 1947]).

[20] In a number of jurisdictions in Canada and the United States provision is made for the voluntary or compulsory arbitration of disputes arising from collective bargaining. In some there is provision for so-called "final-offer arbitration" or "last-offer-by-issue arbitration", which seek to safeguard the collective bargaining process within the context of an arbitration system. Under these systems the arbitrator must choose between the final offers of each side (the over-all offer in the first system, the offer on each issue in the second) and cannot adopt his own solution. The purpose is to induce the parties to bargain as near as possible to what the arbitrator might deem to be a reasonable solution, thus increasing the chance of reaching agreement without recourse to arbitration. See T. P. Gilroy and A. V. Sinicropi: "Impasse resolution in public employment: A current assessment", in *Industrial and Labor Relations Review* (Ithaca, NY), July 1972, pp. 496–511; and A. V. Subbarao: "Final-offer-selection vs last-offer-by-issue systems of arbitration", in *Industrial Relations*, Vol. 33, 1978, No. 1, pp. 38–57.

[21] See ILO: *General survey on the application of the Conventions on Freedom of Association and on the Right to Organise and Collective Bargaining*, Report of the Committee of Experts on the Application of Conventions and Recommendations, Report III (Part 4B), International Labour Conference, 58th Session, 1973, paras. 107–111; and idem: *Freedom of association: Digest of decisions of the Freedom of Association Committee of the Governing Body of the ILO* (Geneva, 2nd ed., 1976), paras. 312–326.

[22] ibid.

[23] See idem: *Promotion of collective bargaining*, Reports V(1) and V(2), International Labour Conference, 66th Session, Geneva, 1980.

[24] idem: *LS*, 1952—Fr. 5; 1955—Fr. 3.

[25] ibid., 1967—Dah. 1; 1974—Dah. 2.

[26] ibid., 1974—Cam. 1.

[27] ibid., 1975—Mad. 1.

[28] ibid., 1962—Mali 1.

[29] ibid., 1967—Congo (Kin.) 1; 1973—Zai. 1 and 2.

[30] In Australia and New Zealand this system of reference to arbitration applies only to trade unions which have registered for this purpose under the relevant legislation. Non-registered trade unions may bargain collectively and strike. The reference to arbitration of disputes in which registered trade unions are a party thus has a voluntary basis.

[31] See S. Cockar: "Kenya Industrial Court", in Gladstone, op. cit., pp. 43–56.

[32] ILO: *Strengthening and furthering of tripartite co-operation*, Report III, Tenth Conference of American States Members of the International Labour Organisation, Mexico, 1974, pp. 14–15.

[33] The membership of the Commission has been increased from time to time and stood at around 35 in 1976. *Twentieth annual report of the President of the Australian Conciliation and Arbitration Commission: Year ended 13 August 1976* (Canberra, Australian Government Publishing Service, 1976), Appendix I.

[34] Conciliation and Arbitration Act, 1972, Section 7.

[35] Labour Code, Section 461 (ILO: *LS*, 1971—Pan. 1).

[36] Royal Commission on Trade Unions and Employers' Associations, op. cit., para. 286.

[37] ibid.

[38] ibid., para. 287.

CONCLUSION

8

   Both industrialised and developing countries have always attached particular significance to the establishment of effective procedures for dealing with
labour disputes. This significance has, however, been felt more deeply in recent
years as a result of a growing concern with the effects of labour disputes on
industrial growth, economic development and over-all socio-political stability.
   Because of the increasing concern with improved settlement procedures, this
study has concentrated on the investigation of factors influencing the development of national systems of conciliation and arbitration. This problem involves
many issues of public policy, which may be considered to fall into two main
groups. First, there are the issues of a more general character, relating to the
development of the national system as a whole. These issues are concerned with
the nature, scope, purposes and underlying principles of governmental intervention in labour disputes. They involve a choice of the settlement procedures
to be included in the system, whether voluntary or characterised by compulsory
features, and also include matters relating to the structure of the system and
general administrative arrangements. The second group of issues relates to the
application of the procedures which are to form part of the system.
   With regard to the general problems of conciliation and arbitration, the
over-all evolution of governmental approaches to the prevention and settlement
of labour disputes should be noted. The approaches now being followed in
industrialised countries in particular are far different from those devised during
the early decades of the Industrial Revolution, which were still prevalent in the
early part of the twentieth century.
   As regards the relations between employers and workers, public policy under
earlier approaches was mainly limited to the settlement of labour disputes, as
reflected in legislation dealing wholly or almost exclusively with settlement
procedures and regulations concerning strikes and lockouts. This policy led in
some countries to an ad hoc approach or a case-by-case system in which concern
with the avoidance or settlement of a strike was the over-riding consideration.
Such a concern is still relevant in some cases, particularly in connection with the
settlement of disputes in essential services. In a number of developing countries
there is also a school of thought according to which the avoidance or restriction
of strikes and other overt manifestations of disputes should still deserve first

priority, at least for the time being, in order to create the best possible conditions for economic development. In more and more countries, however, questions dealing with the prevention of labour disputes are tending to acquire growing importance today, while problems concerning the settlement of these disputes are viewed as a part of the larger problem of labour relations policy, in which the basic concern is with the development of satisfactory relations between employers and workers. The central features of this policy are collective bargaining and joint discussions between employers and workers in resolving their problems.

Under earlier approaches the prevention of disputes actually meant the prevention of strikes and lockouts; these were to be prevented by legislative restrictions and by the use of settlement procedures. Today, in an increasing number of countries, efforts are also taken, mostly through the implementation of sound personnel policies, to prevent disputes from arising; since disputes provide the occasion for strikes and lockouts, there would be fewer of these if there were fewer disputes. At the same time, the whole atmosphere of industrial relations would improve if the number of disputes were reduced or maintained at reasonable levels, and this would have some positive repercussions on productivity. Furthermore, disputes can be prevented from arising by making collective bargaining a more effective process of joint decision-making, so that it will normally lead to agreement without either of the parties resorting to a work stoppage. Settlement procedures, especially conciliation, can be applied to promote collective bargaining in this sense. At another level, preventive mediation has been developed for the avoidance of disputes.

Under earlier approaches, public policy concerning labour disputes almost always took the form of statutory enactments and relied mainly on the exercise of governmental authority or the use of compulsion. Today, in more and more countries, administrative decisions have become an important part of public policy concerning labour disputes and labour relations generally. Labour relations are highly dynamic, and administrative policy-making has given a good measure of flexibility to governmental action in meeting problems. In the main, administrative policies are directed towards the fostering of voluntary action or agreement by the parties concerned. Their main reliance is on promotional work and the provision of information, advice or assistance.

It may be expected that the latter approaches will become more widespread and will significantly influence the future development of national systems of conciliation and arbitration. There is no need to emphasise that this development will be affected, as in the past, by economic and social conditions which differ from country to country, such as the stage and degree of industrial development, the characteristics of the private sector of the economy, the structure, strength and characteristics of the labour movement, the types, scope and activities of employers' associations, the structure and experience of collective bargaining, and experience of collective labour disputes.

Statistical data concerning these factors can easily be obtained in a large number of countries. To this extent they can be measured or quantified and be the subject of objective analysis. In the end, however, the decision on any issue is an exercise of judgement, based on intangible, subjective considerations. These include the values to be served by public policy, the attitudes of state policy-makers and those of employers' and workers' organisations. Tradition and culture play a large part in the shaping of such values, while in many developing countries they have also been affected by past political connections.

The differences from country to country as regards these objective and subjective factors explain the great diversity in national systems of conciliation and arbitration. Such diversity may be found, precisely because of varying subjective considerations, even among countries in which the objective factors do not present great dissimilarities. But it is also important to note that the development of national systems of conciliation and arbitration is a fertile field for experimentation and social invention. There is social invention not only when a country devises something new on the basis of its own experience, but also when it *adopts* something from the experience of another country, by *adapting* it to its conditions and requirements.

It is indeed not unusual for a country, when considering what changes to make in its system of conciliation and arbitration, to search for guidance or possible models in the experiences of other countries. It is, of course, often said that a method which one country has developed and found satisfactory in dealing with a particular problem is not exportable; but the whole experience with that method, including the background of the problem, is something else. While this experience cannot be duplicated elsewhere, it can provide useful information for other countries. It can contribute to a larger understanding of a problem and of the issues to be resolved. It can also add to the number of options to be considered in seeking a solution to an issue. This can be very important.

The experience of one country may thus contain the germ of an idea which may thrive and bear fruit in another, in the form of a more effective system of preventing and settling labour disputes, or a more effective procedure of conciliation or arbitration. This possibility is not limited to cases where a country purposely looks to the experience of other countries in connection with its efforts to improve its system of disputes settlement. It also arises and is multiplied through exchanges of views and experiences at the international or regional level between government, employers' and workers' representatives. There is every reason to suppose that such sharing of experiences will play an increasingly important role in national efforts to improve conciliation and arbitration procedures in labour disputes.